# FREEDOM RUN

## A 100-DAY, 3,452-MILE JOURNEY ACROSS AMERICA
## TO BENEFIT WOUNDED VETERANS

D1372006

# FREEDOM RUN

## A 100-DAY, 3,452-MILE JOURNEY ACROSS AMERICA
## TO BENEFIT WOUNDED VETERANS

by **Jamie Summerlin**

with **Matthew L. Brann**

**Fitness Information Technology**
*A Division of the International Center for Performance Excellence*
262 Coliseum, WVU-CPASS  ▪  P O Box 6116
Morgantown, WV  26506-6116

Library of Congress Card Catalog Number: 2013933329

ISBN: 978-1-935412-50-2

Cover Design: 40 West Studios
Typesetter: 40 West Studios
Proofreader: Rachel Tibbs
Indexer: Rachel Tibbs
Photography: All images courtesy of Tiffany Summerlin Photography
Printed by: Sheridan Books, Inc.

10 9 8 7 6 5 4 3 2 1

Fitness Information Technology
A Division of the International Center for Performance Excellence
West Virginia University
262 Coliseum, WVU-CPASS
PO Box 6116
Morgantown, WV 26506-6116
800.477.4348 (toll free)
304.293.6888 (phone)
304.293.6658 (fax)
Email: fitcustomerservice@mail.wvu.edu
Website: www.fitinfotech.com

# Contents

# Foreword

Throughout the past decade, I have had the opportunity to meet many extraordinary people. Of them all, one individual will always stand out because of his passion–Jamie Summerlin.

Meeting Jamie for the first time was an overwhelming experience. He was so engaging. He was so enthusiastic. He was so crazy. When I heard him talk about his plan to run across the United States in 100 days I wondered, can you even do that? It was absurd, farfetched even. Right? No. Not if you spend more than 30 seconds with him. In just a moment, I realized that Jamie was a man on a mission and I immediately offered my total support.

As a former Army soldier, I knew he would inspire and motivate many others just as he did me. When I learned that Jamie's run was going to benefit wounded veterans in particular, that made his mission even more special to me. Not only did many of my fellow soldiers serving with me in Iraq suffer unimaginable physical and emotional impairments, but to this day I continue to carry the physical scars from my service-related injuries.

As Americans, it is sometimes too easy to forget about our soldiers who continue to fight, protect and serve our country. Jamie gives us a very physical reminder. Through his words and actions, he inspires others to stand up for our veterans and support our troops, those stationed throughout the world who continue to protect us and are still fighting at war.

Throughout his run, Jamie proved that he would not be prevented from achieving his goal. He was inspired. He was committed. He was brave. He was tenacious. No matter how many people told him this was an impossible task, he kept striving forward one step at a time. He ran through rain, snow, heat and wind. No matter the weather, he kept his head high and legs running. He was determined to succeed and to raise awareness and appreciation of our nation's veterans.

I am confident Jamie's courage was undoubtedly a source of inspiration and strength for all veterans and their families he met throughout the country. He will tell you it was just his small sacrifice to honor the commitment of our veterans, many of whom returned broken or did not return at all. But Jamie sacrificed so much to ensure America's veterans were appropriately honored. He made a life-changing decision and, in turn, he changed so many lives.

It is important to note, this is not a story of "you had to be there." Rather, this is a story of "what will you do?" This is a story about the very best we as Americans can offer. I hope everyone who reads *Freedom Run* appreciates Jamie's vision and what he has done for America's veterans.

I am confident that once you finish reading his story you, too, will be inspired and realize that for Jamie Summerlin and so many of us, his amazing journey was only the beginning of the mission to honor our deserving veterans.

–Jessica Lynch
former Army PFC and Prisoner of War

# Acknowledgments

At the exact moment I knew I had life figured out, life decided to go in a different direction. Comfort became uncomfortable, uncomfortable became the norm. A life that was focused on personal goals and achievements became unrewarding, leaving me with a void that could not be filled. With the assistance of my wife, Tiffany, I began to understand that life was not about me and my self-gratification, but accepting the idea that those accomplishments could be used to inspire and encourage so many others. I will forever be grateful for her patience and support, as what we accomplished during this journey could not have been successful without her by my side. Understanding that, just as in the military, we work best when we work as a team, and when we do, there is no dream too big, no goal that's insurmountable. Close friends and family that I leaned on, your love, support and encouragement carried me through the good times and bad. I am thankful to the brave men and women who slip on their boots and uniforms every day, always at the ready, willing to pay the ultimate price to secure our freedom when danger knocks at the door. I want to thank Matthew Brann for helping me put our journey to paper, thankful that we can share the stories of not only the heroes who wear the uniform, but the people in the towns and cities who share the same pride in our military and country as we do. To the thousands of people along the way who encouraged me in spirit and deed, this endeavor could not have been the success it was without your support. Lastly, I am so thankful for my children, Nicholas and Shayna, as they continue to amaze me with their desire to love others and the way they challenge me to be a better father every day.

– JS

I owe Jamie Summerlin an immense amount of gratitude for allowing me to be a part of this inspiring project. Sitting down and listening to him talk about his idea for this journey during the early stages of its inception, I knew this was something big that I wanted to be a part of in a small way. I am also appreciative of Fitness Information Technology at West Virginia University for providing me with the training and experience that assisted me in helping to write and publish this book. While working on this project, I have become more appreciative of the dedicated military men and women who volunteer to serve and protect our country, and their families who also sacrifice. Finally, I want to thank my children, Maverick and Makaleigh, for the inspiration they provide, and my wife, Maria, for her encouragement and for being a wonderful example, much like Jamie, of how persistence and hard work enable you to achieve your dreams.

– MLB

# Prologue

Sitting across the dining room table from my wife on a beautiful late morning in July 2010, I knew I had a tough sales pitch to make. What I was about to propose to Tiffany would alter our family's lifestyle in every imaginable way. We were living the proverbial American dream: We had a great marriage, a son and daughter, cats and a dog, a nice house and two good jobs. We were living a *comfortable* life. That Saturday morning, as I chugged a glass of Gatorade, I approached Tiffany about getting out of our comfort zone and supporting me in a run across America.

The idea came to me during a six-hour training run earlier that morning when I was preparing for a 50-mile sunset to sunrise race. Accompanied only by my thoughts during that long run, I began to think about my new passion for long-distance running and my rapid progression, without sustaining injuries, in the sport.

*"There's got to be more to life than this,"* I thought. *"There's got to be a reason why I'm able to increase my mileage so dramatically yet still run injury free when nobody says it's possible. Maybe running is what I can use to accomplish something more meaningful. Maybe that is my calling in life."*

It's only natural that I wanted to tie one of my passions to another—the United States military. My wife and I are both Marine Corps veterans, so our military men and women have always held a special place in our hearts. But as I approached my late 30s and was contemplating the true impact and purpose of my life, I realized that there was so much more I could—and should—be doing to have a greater effect on others.

During that talk with Tiffany at our dining room table, I explained to her my thoughts about where we were in life and how I had a strong desire to do more than just go through the motions. What I was asking our family to do would be a major sacrifice, but I knew it was worthwhile because I hoped to increase awareness and assistance for those who were making the ultimate sacrifice for our country.

"Tiff, you know how I've been reading David Horton's book on running the Appalachian Trail?"

"Yes," she said.

"I've been thinking a lot about that lately. On my run this morning, it hit me. I think I *need* to run across America. I know it may sound a little crazy, but it's something I want to do to make an impact for others."

Without hesitation, Tiffany said, "Let's do it!" but I could see a bit of skepticism on her face.

During that and subsequent talks, we reflected on our time in the military, and how we noticed that people were becoming numb to the conflicts we had been fighting the past decade. Lives were continuing to be lost and men and women were coming home injured. Yet the sacrifices that our military men and women and their families were making had begun to fade from America's consciousness. The stories of the ongoing wars had gone from front-page news to briefs and blurbs buried deep within the daily newspapers. I hoped in some small way to shine a light back on the amazing heroes who were serving and had served our country.

We also saw in our own dealings with government agencies that had been set up to provide assistance to veterans that some needs were not being met. Yet we had also witnessed first-hand how some great private and not-for-profit organizations were making an impact in our military veterans' lives. It was my desire to assist those deserving organizations by raising funds that could help them carry out their mission.

Considering the challenges our men and women were facing as they returned home from overseas—sometimes with injuries that would change their lives forever—I wanted to dream of something big. I envisioned tackling a challenge that few had ever attempted, and even fewer had accomplished. I wanted to do something that wasn't just a one-night wonder that caught people's attention for only a brief moment until they sought out the next cause to follow. I wanted to do something that people could follow long-term and get behind for a period of time, allowing them to experience the ups and downs of the journey with me and affording them the opportunity to gain a greater understanding of even a small fraction of the challenges that our military men and women go through every day during and after their service. I wanted to run across America in 100 days!

If my initial conversation with my wife was met with some skepticism that morning, it was with good reason. Tiffany certainly had a sense of pride in our military, but she had also heard me toss around grandiose ideas before—things that sounded fun and exciting but that I never fully pursued. But this was different. And over the next few months, she came to realize that this idea was something that I was passionate about. As she began to embrace my vision, her "Let's do it" response proved to be more than just words. She was now in full support—and belief—of this endeavor.

Tiffany had seen a transformation in me over the past year. A year prior to our dining room table talk, I had begun training for my first marathon. Previously, I had never run further than 12 miles at one time. After completing that first marathon in November 2009, I was hooked. Six weeks later, I ran my first 50-kilometer (approximately 31 miles) ultramarathon in 15 degree temps and six inches of snow.

I was not winning races, yet I felt like a winner every time I crossed the finish line. Each long-distance race I entered allowed me to see beyond my perceived limits. I felt so free and alive during and after the runs, crossing the finish line of yet another race with a sense of accomplishment that I hadn't felt in years. I was learning more and more about myself with each step I took. I had morphed from doing casual 3-mile runs to doing 50-mile overnight races. I had developed a new passion in my life.

Even still, I felt that there had to be more to it, and I wanted to tap into what that *more* was. That's why I felt like I had to undertake a challenge that would not only push me physically, mentally and emotionally, but also encourage and inspire others. To me, running 3,000+ miles across the country without a day of rest for 100 consecutive days made every bit of sense. To others, including some of my closest friends, it sounded insane.

One of the first people I shared my idea with outside of my family was my good friend Dave Rodriguez, who was serving as a Logistics Captain in the U.S. Army at the time. I knew if anyone could understand me and my reasons behind wanting to run across the country, he would be the guy. He and I had known each other for about 10 years and we had the common bond of military service. He loved the idea, but also told me he thought I was nuts. That was the same sentiment of the next people I shared the idea with. Aaron and Sandy Yocum are two close friends who I developed a special bond with through the endurance events I had participated in. As a novice runner, I respected their knowledge and love for the sport that had been developed over many years, so I was interested in hearing their take on my idea.

"You're absolutely crazy," Sandy told me after she stopped chuckling. "You just ran your first marathon last year, and now you want to run across America?"

"That's exactly right," I responded.

Aaron and Sandy talked to me about the fact that not only was I planning on doing something extremely challenging, but I was also planning on doing it in 100 days with no rest days built into my schedule.

"It's doable. I mean, people have done it before," Sandy said. "But they've usually been people that have been running for more than 12 months in their entire lives."

"I know, but it's something I *have* to do," I said. "These men and women who serve and have served our country deserve it. Plus, I feel like there has to be more to this than just going from three-mile runs to overnight races without experiencing injury, and being pretty successful at it."

"You have our support 100%," they both said. "We still think you're insane, though."

I knew that a run across America would obviously require a lot of planning and a tremendous sacrifice from my entire family. Once my family committed to this journey with me, I never once considered failure an option. My training became stricter and the races became longer, but I also seemed happier and more alive than I had ever been. My energy levels increased, as did my miles and lack of sleep, but I found true enjoyment in what I was doing because I realized in my heart that it was for a greater cause. I have a passion for running, but I am even more passionate about the brave men and women who wear our nation's uniforms with pride each and every day. This journey would go beyond me and the feat I was about to undertake. I wanted to make this a story about the true heroes and I hoped each footstep I took would honor and encourage veterans faced with challenges after returning home from the wars.

I thought it would only be appropriate to finish on July 4, a date that symbolizes our nation's freedom. So on the morning of March 26, 2012, I stepped out of the waters of the Pacific Ocean in Coos Bay, Oregon, and for the next 100 days I planned to give our veterans the honor and respect they deserved.

# 1 | Transformations

As I slid my feet out of my sweaty socks and running shoes and slid them into the Atlantic Ocean off Rehoboth Beach, Delaware, the morning tide gripped my tired legs, trying to pull me farther away from the shore. The pull of the water was nearly as overwhelming as the emotions I was experiencing. I was overcome by feelings of jubilation, relief and exhaustion as I allowed my mind to escape into the cool, frothy waters just as the orange glow of the sun was beginning to peek over the ocean's horizon early on the morning of July 6, 2012. It felt good to celebrate the end of my 100-day run across America, capped off by a 100-mile, 24-hour run to the Atlantic Ocean.

Peeling my running shoes off for the final time on my 3,452-mile journey, I couldn't help but think back to when I was putting my sneakers on for the first time three years earlier, when I took the first steps toward running my first marathon, which laid the foundation for this coast-to-coast run across the United States. As I glanced back across the beach at my wife, Tiffany, I reflected back on the first steps of this journey. At the same time, I also asked myself a few questions: *"What had I just accomplished? Where would my life take me next? Where is the nearest bed?"*

It had been just 115 days earlier when my wife, our two children, Nicholas and Shayna, and I left our driveway and comfortable surroundings of Morgantown, West Virginia. We were excited, anxious and nervous about what lay ahead of us as we drove a recently purchased RV west toward Oregon, the starting point of my coast-to-coast run.

The sights I saw, the landscapes I traveled through and the people I met during the trip fulfilled a lifelong desire. As a child growing up in small town America, my dreams always took me outside of the borders of the small, tight-knit community in which I lived. I often dreamed of traveling the world, getting away from the simple life that we had grown so accustomed to. If we drove to Wal-Mart in the neighboring county, it was a big trip. If we drove the hour to get to the nearest shopping mall on the weekend, it was something I bragged about when I went to school the following Monday.

Life was not very complicated in the mind of a kid growing up in Burnsville, West Virginia, deep in the heart of Appalachia. We went to school, took care of our chores and for fun we rode through town on our bikes, feeling as proud as the grand marshal of a parade. We also passed the time by playing pickup basketball on the dirt courts, taking a dip in the swimming hole with my friends or hiking the hills around our home. As an only child, I was very fortunate to live in a community that had a lot of kids my same age to play with.

Most of those kids I grew up with also lived in similar situations as I did. Our fathers or stepfathers traveled away for the week to work. Jobs just weren't that plentiful around home. A common job was laboring as a journeyman lineman, traveling to other counties or surrounding states to work on power lines. These union jobs often lasted several weeks to a few months at each location. In fact, some of my summer vacations were spent at these sites.

Back at home, our weekends were commonly spent helping our dads do labor around the house, such as chopping wood. I still have unpleasant memories of gripping the smooth wooden handle and struggling to lift the heavy head of the ax up over my slender shoulders, barely having enough strength and momentum to get the sharp edge of the ax to split the logs apart. It was not unusual for my stepdad, Roy, and I to cut wood all morning on Saturday and then spend most of the rest of the day in a local tavern. Our small town actually had so many taverns that you could step out of one and trip into another. I wasn't the only underage youth tagging along to the bars, either. In fact, as kids, my friends and I learned to shoot pool in the local taverns.

My limited recreational time with my stepdad was also sometimes spent camping by the river and fishing into the night. Although those experiences were enjoyable, I always longed for more. That wasn't the family atmosphere that I wanted to have, and I was determined that it wouldn't be the family atmosphere of my home when I grew up and married. *"When I become a father, I'm going to be a positive role model and spend quality time with my children,"* I would often promise myself. My upbringing and relationship with Roy was far from terrible, but it was also far from ideal. I realize that we all must make sacrifices to some degree in order to take care of and provide for our families. I just did not want to replicate the experiences of my youth when I became a father. My mom and Roy ended up divorcing a couple of years after I left for the Marine Corps.

My mom was my shelter in the storm and we were very close as I grew up. When I was 4 years old we moved to West Virginia, to the same town where her family lived, after she divorced my adoptive father. Since I was an only child, my mom gave me her undivided attention as often as possible. My mom married Roy when I was 8, so that time spent with her during the four years between her marriages allowed us to build a very special bond, one which we continue to cherish to this day. When my mom got remarried, the excitement of having a father in my life again was tempered by the fact that he traveled away for work each week. That left a void in my life that I resented as I grew up.

I always felt like I had to live up to his expectations even when he wasn't around. I would often worry about not having done something correctly or the way that he wanted it done, and I feared hearing about it all weekend. I often thought, *"I wish he would have to work this weekend,"* because I didn't want to deal with my perceived failure again. I felt like I could never do anything right. And those constant feelings of falling short were factors in decisions I would make later in life, both good and bad.

I always felt as though I had to prove myself, whether it was taking the biggest risks among my group of friends when riding our bikes, being known as the hardest partier or proving how tough I could be by joining the Marine Corps. I was always driven by this notion that I had to prove to others I was better than they thought and that I could do things they didn't think I could accomplish.

My mom, however, was one that I never felt like I had to prove myself to. She was always there for me, encouraging me, letting me know when I had disappointed her, but loving me through it all. Sure, there were times that I knew I let her down with decisions I made as a teenager, but she always pushed me to just be me. As I have raised my children now, her influence on me in that regard has helped me tremendously in loving my kids no matter what and always letting them know that I will always be there for them through the good times, disappointments and struggles. My mom, Brenda, continues to be supportive, having attended my first marathon in 2009 along with my stepdad, Alan. She was also a huge asset and a big part of my run across America.

## BECOMING A MILITARY MAN

I learned early on in my childhood that I was not destined to be a physically gifted athlete. I was usually the smallest child in my class, as well as one of the youngest. I graduated high school at a whopping 121 pounds, and all of about 5-foot-9. I played football in middle school, but due to the shrinking population of the area, our small school was only able to field enough players to conduct intramural scrimmages. My mom often tells a story about me running down the field on the kickoff coverage team and an opposing player literally running over me, knocking me down and causing me to roll backwards three times before I finally came to a stop. With my lack of size, getting knocked down on the gridiron was not uncommon, but every single time, I bounced right back up. I didn't realize it at the time, but that experience taught me to pick myself up and press on later in life, regardless of the situation.

Another sport I enjoyed playing was basketball. I had a pretty good jump shot, but I was small and my form was far from resembling the perfect stroke of fellow West Virginia native Jerry West. I looked like a shooter from an old western movie–I shot from the hip. I didn't really have the strength to shoot a three-pointer from up high, using the proper shooting technique. And because my shots came from the waist, they unfortunately were easier for a defender to block.

Running was a sport that never crossed my mind, so I never joined the track and field team, and at the time, my high school didn't have a cross country team. Most of my running was spent chasing after girls or doing the running man at high school dances. When we would play games at school that involved running, I was never the fastest. Running was just something that never really interested me.

Looking back, the cumulative experiences of my upbringing were catalysts for me making the wisest decision I made as a young man. During my senior year of high school, I was approached by a number of military recruiters at our school about joining the armed forces. I initially balked at the thought. The military didn't seem like the right fit for me, but I also was not exactly positioning myself to be highly sought after by Ivy League universities. I maintained good grades but never really pushed myself that hard in the academic arena. I often found it easy to cram for a test, get a good grade and move on, but I never really applied myself to the best of my ability. I was more concerned with fitting in with the crowd, enjoying life and making the most of my teenage years. The only reason I took the Armed Services Vocational Aptitude Battery (ASVAB) military acceptance test was because a number of my friends were taking it, and it got me out of classes that day at school. My academic aspirations at that time were to do just enough to skate by and spend the remainder of my time hanging out with my friends.

I started receiving phone calls from military recruiters before I ever saw my ASVAB test scores. The Navy was offering me the opportunity to hop on a submarine and join the nuke program. The Army and Air Force presented me with many different paths. But the one that piqued my curiosity the most was the Marine Corps. If I couldn't prove myself on the gridiron or basketball court, maybe I could prove myself with the Marines, right? The thought of being a Marine—one of the few and proud—just sounded cool. They would toughen me up and help me grow into a real man. As an additional benefit, I would wind up with bulging muscles and a high-and-tight (the military version of the buzz cut) that would really impress everyone, especially the ladies. I loved their uniforms, the toughness they displayed and the fact that my friends who were older and had joined the Marines were talked about around town like they were the baddest, toughest men on the planet.

Obviously, at that time in my life, I didn't grasp the concept of what it meant to serve my country. I also had a misconception about how much the Marine Corps would change me physically. My uncle Butch McPherson had served in Vietnam in the Army, but he never talked much about his time in the service. Another uncle, Roger Clark, had been a machinist and cook in the Army National Guard, but I had no other points of reference as far as family members were concerned that could describe to me the military experience.

I had scored high enough on my ASVAB to set myself up for a guaranteed military occupation specialty, East Coast duty station and a signing bonus in the Marine Corps. What could be better for a teenager unsure of his next step in life? I didn't want to go to college, and this was my ticket out of my small West Virginia hometown. My childhood dreams of seeing the world were about to come true. The world was my oyster, with three hots and a cot. I just needed to sign on the dotted line. The thought of finally getting away from the monotony of home, traveling the world and experiencing life outside the walls of the small state I had grown up in was very enticing to me. I would get to work on F/A-18 fighter jets known as Hornets, receive a paycheck every other week, have food and meals provided to me and experience life much different than the childhood I experienced. The opportunity was both exciting and scary.

A number of my high school classmates tried to talk some sense into me. "Are you crazy, Jamie? Why do you want to join the military, especially the Marines?" they questioned. "If you're going to do it, at least join a different military branch. The Marines are just too demanding and you're too small." But at that point there was no changing my mind. I am very stubborn and always have been. That's a trait that has pulled me through many dark nights of running, and through a lot of other challenges in my life.

My recruiter, Sergeant Bubby Sayer, had attended school in Point Pleasant, West Virginia, with my cousin Darren Clark, who I looked up to as my big brother. As soon as he found that out, he reeled me in with stories of he and Darren growing up together, as they only lived a few miles from one another all through school. Going to recruiting meetings with Bubby and experiencing the atmosphere of being around other Marines was the coolest thing in the world to me at the time. And I do stress, *at the time.*

I stepped off the bus full of new Marine Corps recruits at about 3 a.m. on June 21, 1990. Even at that pre-dawn hour, the air was so thick and muggy that taking a deep breath was like trying to swallow a spoonful of peanut butter. We were "greeted" by a crazy Marine drill instructor screaming for all the riders to "get the hell off my bus and get onto my yellow footprints as fast as humanly possible." Despite how fast we moved, it was never going to be fast enough to please this man who had his flat-brimmed hat (known as a smokey) pulled down so low that his piercing eyes were barely visible.

A few minutes earlier, we had driven through the dark of the night onto Marine Corps Recruit Depot Parris Island, South Carolina, across the only entrance and exit to the island, a place we would not leave for the next 13 weeks. If we hadn't been awake when the driver pulled onto the island, we were certainly awakened by the deep, gravelly voice of the drill instructor, who I swear was put on this earth to make men pee themselves. Looking around at the other "boys" who exited the bus with me, I knew that I wasn't the only one standing there wondering, *"Can I go back home now?"*

Just 17 days earlier, as I threw my cap into the air at my high school graduation, I really had no sense of what was to occur in my life less than three weeks later. I only knew I was excited that I was going to be a Marine– a part of an exclusive club of some of the toughest warriors on the planet. Here I stood now completely shell shocked. *"This isn't what I signed up for,"* I thought. I had spent the better part of my 17 years knocking authority, doing just what I needed to get by and applying myself only when necessary. Now there was a drill instructor screaming in my ear that I am not getting off his bus and onto his yellow footprints fast enough, even though I had practically run over the other guys on the bus to get onto those yellow footprints. *"What have I gotten myself into?"* It would not be the last time in my life I would ask myself that question.

### MY TRANSFORMATION

The next 13 weeks spent on Parris Island would shape me into someone I never thought I could become. I was able to push myself further than I ever imagined, in situations that I never pictured myself. Not only was I being shaped into someone different physically, I was also being strengthened mentally to handle things I had never previously faced. This idea of breaking me completely down from this roughneck, pushback kid that grew up thinking I was in control, then changing me into the man I would become in a little more than three months' time was an amazing feat. Looking back on it now, it blows my mind that in what seems like such a short time period in my life I was molded into the man I have become today.

My transformation, however, was not easy. The first few weeks of boot camp were spent with only one thing on the mind of the drill instructors– breaking down the new recruits. The physical and mental stress was so severe and foreign in those first few days my cheeks didn't have a reason to hit the toilet seat. Sleeping was not an option those first couple of days, either, and if you did happen to doze off, you were awakened by the sound of that gravelly voice barking in your ear.

Some of the most difficult times were spent on the quarter deck or in the sand pit. The quarter deck was an area near the instructors' offices where you were physically ground down by being forced to do a flurry of push-ups, pull-ups and other forms of physical activity for several minutes non-stop. The sand pit, next to our barracks, was a place where we had to suffer the typical physical punishment, but we had to do it twice as hard and do it in sand. I still have vivid memories of our squad having to "double time it," drop into a push-up position, and get back to our feet as quickly as possible. What made that even more difficult was when we had to do that while keeping our hands in our pockets. Try dropping into a push-up position with your hands in your pockets without getting a mouthful of sand. It's not possible.

But I survived the physical and mental challenges and was actually named a squad leader for a short period of time. When in that position, when one of my guys got into trouble and was sent to the quarter deck or sand pit, I always went with him and endured the same punishment, not because I had to but because I wanted to display my support for my squad. It's that similar type of support for your colleagues that I love so much about the endurance running community. Much like a military squadron, it's a group that will put individual pursuits aside to lift you up when you're struggling mentally or physically to finish an ultramarathon race.

A week before my graduation from boot camp, I was selected to "perform" on the quarter deck for incoming recruits in order to display just how miserable that punishment could be. It was an honor for me to be selected because it was affirmation to me that our drill instructors saw that toughness and ability in me. By the end of boot camp I had gone from a scrawny 121-pound kid to a tough, 146-pound man.

The character and characteristics I developed during those 13 weeks, however, proved to be good at times, and bad at others. I have been known to train, work, play and party hard. Channeling that passion into something positive and constructive has always been a struggle in my life. I can set a goal and selfishly reach for it, and do it with blinders on. I can get so focused on getting from point A to point B in the shortest amount of time possible that I have taken shortcuts when I should have thought things through better. Whether it's been missing a detail in a project at work that caused an unnecessary delay or pushing myself beyond limits in life situations that have hurt others, I've not always made the smartest decisions.

Stubbornness is a trait that I am glad to carry with me most of the time, however, because it has helped push me through some tough situations in life, whether it's running a 100-mile race or not dropping behind in boot camp when I wanted to give up. One of the things that I often hear from ultramarathon runners is the fact that most of us share that simple trait of stubbornness. If channeled the right way, it will be something that will help us get through those moments in a race or training run when we feel like we can't push any further.

Yet while being stubborn can be an asset to me during my training runs or races, ultramarathon running has also enabled me to learn how to dial back that stubbornness. I have had to learn to listen to my body a lot more, take into consideration the consequences of pushing through an injury, or even plan my training around an event as opposed to waking up and participating. I've had to learn to pull the reigns back instead of pushing through in certain situations, and I've learned that it's a lot more difficult to do that than to simply plow ahead. I've only had a few minor injuries during my short running career, and I believe that they have remained minor due to the fact that I didn't just push through. Far too often I've had conversations with runners who have had to take months off from training because something minor turned into a major issue because they pushed through in order to remain on a training regimen.

Yes, I've been pretty fortunate that I've been free of any major injuries, but I also think that's attributed to my not starting distance running until such a later age in life. A number of runners and triathletes who I run with started doing distance races when they were older and did not experience the body breakdowns that so many people have had from pushing themselves so hard at younger ages. Maturity also helps. I think we become wiser in our physical endeavors, not willing to take chances for the sake of pride. I run races and choose events to see how far I can push myself and to run the race against the trail, not against others. I am convinced that is also why I enjoy running so much. I'll never be the first person across the line in a lot of the ultramarathon events I participate in, but I know if I train properly and listen to my body and my crew that I will cross the finish line.

## RUNNING NAKED

One of the things I have been asked about often is why I don't wear a watch while running. When I started training for the Richmond Marathon in the summer of 2009, I promised myself I wouldn't become a slave to my times. I wanted to do this to enjoy it, to better myself. I enjoy running "naked," as it's termed in the running community, because then I'm not tempted to keep looking at my time and pushing myself for a PR (personal record). I've often told my wife, "The morning I wake up and am not happy with work, that's the day I change careers." That relates to my running as well. I don't want missing a PR by seconds or minutes affecting my mood and minimizing my ability to run for the pure enjoyment of the sport. I want to be happy and satisfied with the fact that I can get out and do it because I love to run, and not be so focused on having to achieve a specific time that, if I happen to fall short of, will cause me to get upset. I'm not wired to run as fast as a lot of the amazing runners I encounter at races, but I think I am wired to enjoy it for what it is—me against the trail and being able to take in what is around me because I just love being outdoors.

I'm also one who never runs with headphones or music playing as a distraction to help me get through a training run. I wasn't always that way, though. When I started training for my first marathon in June 2009, I would not go on a run without wearing my headphones. Based on reading articles and having conversations with other runners at the time, many runners believe that listening to music while they trained was the only way they could get through two or three hours of running as they prepared for a big race. It made perfect sense to me as well. What could I possibly think about during three hours of running that would help keep me sane? There is no way I could go through pounding the pavement for long periods of time without music blaring in my ears or an audio book to listen to in order to help pass the time. So I ventured off on each run wearing my headphones, letting the music kill time and occupy my mind as I set out to train for the Richmond Marathon. I found myself getting lost in the music or the stories being told, and I was proving to myself that it was indeed the only way to get through those long training runs. I also didn't particularly enjoy running with people because I didn't feel like I was in good enough shape to carry on a conversation with anyone while running, so the music became my running partner.

I planned my training schedule for Richmond to work out so that the day I started training was exactly 24 weeks before the race. Because of where I was physically, I knew it was going to take a little bit of time to get a good base under my feet before I kicked the training into high gear. I had never in my life run more than 12 miles at once, which I did two separate times around the base at Marine Corps Air Station Beaufort, South Carolina, where I was stationed. Those runs were just runs to celebrate the retirement or discharge of friends from the Marine Corps. Tackling a run that was 26.2 miles in one shot seemed like an intimidating task, but one I knew I could complete if I could stay healthy. But I also knew I needed to be mentally prepared for what was to come. I did a lot of research and had many discussions with friends of mine who were runners, and most who had completed a marathon utilized training plans that had been put together by Hal Higdon. Hal is a highly respected author, runner and all-around authority for runners worldwide. After looking at the plans, which varied from Novice to Professional, I decided on an Intermediate track. I felt confident that I could handle the training schedule and the miles seemed pretty doable.

For me, running has been much more of a mental than physical journey. I knew that if I could get through the first six weeks of the plan, especially reaching the 12-mile mark in Week 5, then what I would do is start the program back over again from the beginning. That way I had a good base, and also the confidence in my mind that I had already run those initial miles from the first six weeks. For me, running has become a mental chess game against my mind and my body, seeing how far I could push myself. I also learned from previous life experiences that I have to be able to convince myself I can do something, not just jump in headfirst without thinking it through a little bit. This warm-up section through the training program would be great for me. I knew it would only build my confidence.

## SHEDDING POUNDS AND BAD HABITS

In committing to running the Richmond Marathon, I also had to take a look at my lifestyle and examine which things were really important to me. As I said, when I do something I tend to tackle it head on, and I knew that running a marathon required more than just logging the training miles. I had to be all in. One aspect of my life that I had to evaluate and subsequently alter was my sleeping pattern. At this point in my life, I was still very much a night owl. I have never really slept much—maybe four to six hours a night—so I usually would stay up late, many nights way past midnight, then get up around 6 a.m. and really struggle to get myself going in the mornings. My career was also an accomplice to my sleep pattern. I have been in the information technology (IT) industry for most all of my adult working life. With an IT job comes constant concerns with security and uptime, so I always kept my phone or pager by my bed so I could answer the call at any time.

Knowing that I was about to step into a training routine that would require many hours on the trails, I made a commitment to my wife that I would do all of my training early in the morning. My family time in the evening was very important to me. We have two young children who are involved in sports and other activities, and evenings were also reserved for spending time with my wife, and I did not want to sacrifice that time. This was something I knew I would initially struggle with, but as people talked with me about becoming more active, they found that they slept better and it generally made them more productive in life. Tiffany was very happy that I was making this commitment as well, which I knew could only help our marriage in the long run, too.

When I decided to start getting myself into better shape in early 2009, I was at my heaviest weight ever. Just years removed from being that physically fit Marine, here I was standing 5-foot-9 and weighing 198 pounds. The day I stepped on the scale and saw that I was about to reach the 200-pound mark was an eye opener. *"How in the world did I let myself get this far out of shape!"* I asked myself.

I had always worked to stay in pretty good shape throughout the years, but at this point in my life I started to drift away from those healthy habits. I wasn't paying attention to what I was eating. It was common for me to have two or three beers with dinner, or an extra glass of wine with my wife. Snacks had also become a part of my diet that I just accepted. I enjoy eating tremendously, and have learned over the years to enjoy the taste of many healthy alternatives thanks to the encouragement of my wife, but I wasn't doing anything to burn off those calories I was consuming every day.

I made the decision to change my eating habits. When I did snack, I ate healthier foods that were prepared in advance. And based on how bad I felt after eating a cheeseburger from a fast-food restaurant, I made a concerted effort to try to cut out the drive-thru meals we ate as a family. Through research and experimentation, I also learned how to balance my consumption of carbohydrates and protein. In essence, I retrained myself from eating for enjoyment and taste to eating in order to fuel my body, which really is the primary reason for consuming food.

Aside from my desire to keep from tipping 200 pounds on the scale, another reason I altered my diet and began running at that time was because I wanted to be able to keep up with my children. My son was beginning to participate in sports and I didn't want to be one of those parents who sit on the sideline watching their kids, unable to participate with them because I was too overweight or out of shape. I wanted to be able to actively participate in those activities with him, which required some physical activity on my part.

I hated the feeling of being winded after running up and down the soccer field or basketball court with my kids. The sharp pain in my side, the difficulty in breathing and the overall exhaustion I experienced were simply embarrassing. I wanted to be able to enjoy those times and not embarrass my children or myself. I wanted to be able to be an active participant in that part of their lives, and I knew I needed to make some changes in my own life to make that happen. I also reflected back to my childhood, when I made a promise to myself that when I became a father I would spend quality time with my children. I was not going to go back on that promise.

I also had some personal inspiration in my life that helped motivate me to make this change. A very close friend of mine had made some very dramatic changes in his life during the past few years, and I was fascinated at what he had accomplished and was continuing to pursue in his life. Jason Thomas was actually my boss at a job I held for a number of years and he was someone I looked up to tremendously. He was a couple of years younger than me, but was a highly motivated individual, a very hard worker and could inspire those around him in a matter of minutes with his passion for life and learning. He also struggled, however, with his weight, and it was something that he confronted after some pretty hard-hitting things happened in his life. When he left our organization in 2004, he was about my height, but also weighed about 245 pounds. Within a few short years, he was running marathons and completing Ironman triathlons, and he had dropped down to about 155 pounds. He changed his diet, his activity level and most importantly his outlook on life.

I only had a chance to see him a couple of times after he left the company, and at the time he stated that he was going to start working out and running. But many people talk of such things and never follow through. We met for lunch in 2008, and when I walked into the Boston Beanery and looked around the room for him, I figured I must have beaten him to the restaurant. But then I realized that as my eyes scanned the faces of the business men and women and college students that sat at the bar and tables, I had actually looked right at him several times without realizing who he was. It was amazing to see the transformation in his physical appearance. But after talking with Jason for a few minutes, I was equally amazed by the transformation of the outlook on life he now had.

It wasn't necessarily anything that he said that day, but it was the way he said things and the confidence that he exuded that really affected me. It was almost as if I could literally see confidence and a greater self-worth oozing out of him. I was struck by the fact that not only had he lost so much weight, but he had gained a new perspective on what was important in life. The stories he shared about enjoying outdoor adventures with his wife and family inspired me to examine my own life and ponder the things that I was missing out on by being that person on the couch watching the world go by on an LCD screen. Jason's energy and renewed passion for life caused me to reconsider my focus and what it was I wanted out of my own life. I knew I wasn't happy with the direction I was headed. I walked away from that conversation with Jason that day a changed person. I know it was not his intention to influence me, but I couldn't help but be influenced after the changes I witnessed in him. I knew when I walked out of that restaurant that day that I wanted to change the direction of my life and accomplish something greater than I had ever imagined for myself.

Even though I knew that day that I wanted to cast a new vision for my life, I still had no idea at the time that three years later I would have transformed into an ultramarathon distance runner who had completed a nearly 3,500-mile run across America. But it's amazing what the human body and mind are capable of accomplishing if the proper motivation and inspiration are in place. For me, that inspiration was the desire to aid and assist communities in realizing ways to support our military heroes returning home and encourage wounded veterans by showing them the admiration, love and support I have for each and every one of them. I never realized, however, that the message would become so much more than that. What my family and I were about to embark on would make an impact in more ways than we ever imagined.

# $2$ | Rising Before the Sun

**H**ow do you prepare your body to run across America? One step at a time. That answer sounds simple and even sarcastic, but there really is no other way to train for such a monumental task. If you aspire to accomplish greatness, it is not going to happen overnight. An aspiration, dream or vision becomes nothing more until it is fertilized with hard work and commitment. It requires planning and setting a series of difficult but achievable benchmarks. It also requires dedication to reach those benchmarks, and persistence to push forward when things don't necessarily go as planned. So when my idea to run across the country went from conception to implementation, I knew the best way to train for the next 20+ months was to break things down into segments.

I already had a good base when I started thinking about doing the coast-to-coast run. I had recently completed the Highlands Sky 40-mile race in Davis, West Virginia, and the Big Bear Lake 12-Hour Trail Run in Hazelton, West Virginia, and was in the midst of preparing for the Cheat Mountain Moonshine Madness, a 50-mile overnight race that began in Beverly, West Virginia, the night of a full moon in August 2010. I was out on a long, five-hour training run leading up to Cheat Mountain when–partly in an attempt to take my mind off the fatigue I was experiencing as my legs began to feel more like a pair of heavy logs–I began to reflect back on how quickly I had been able to increase my weekly running mileage from the time I began training for the Richmond Marathon.

It became clear that being registered to compete in a challenging distance race was an incentive that helped me to push farther than I had previously run. So I decided that in the 20 months of training that loomed ahead, I needed to set specific goals in front of me that were manageable yet challenging. The benefit of doing that was that I would have smaller, more manageable goals to focus on rather than investing nearly two full years with just one target in sight. Additionally, I knew that each time I conquered a new, longer distance it would give me a needed confidence boost that the ultimate goal was actually attainable.

After completing the 50-miler in the Monongahela National Forest, I did three 50-kilometer (31 miles) ultramarathons from December 2010 through March 2011. The Mason-Dixon Madness in Morgantown, West Virginia, the Frozen Sasquatch Trail Run in the Kanawha State Forest near Charleston, West Virginia, and the Lt. J.C. Stone 50K in Pittsburgh, Pennsylvania, all provided me with distinct lessons that assisted me in my training. But those were only a primer for what awaited me in the summer of 2011–the Laurel Highlands Ultra, one of the country's oldest ultramarathon trail races, which takes place on the Laurel Highlands Hiking Trail in southwestern Pennsylvania's Allegheny Mountains, *and* the Burning River 100 Mile Endurance Run, which also serves as the USA Track & Field 100 Mile Trail National Championship and runs from Cleveland to Akron, Ohio.

Heading into Laurel Highlands in early June 2011, my longest run had been 50 miles. Adding what was supposed to be an additional 20 miles onto my longest run ever definitely presented me with a challenge. I actually had planned on having someone pace me in for the final 20 miles of the run, which is a relatively common practice. But two weeks prior to the race, I decided that I wanted to get through the entire run on my own. This would enable me to simulate the solitude I would experience during my cross-country run, when I wouldn't have anyone to help "bring me in" if I was struggling to reach my destination on a particular day.

Even though seven weeks later I would complete a 100-mile run, Laurel Highlands was actually my most challenging training event. The run presented some steep, rocky climbs on the trail that were technically challenging and mentally and physically exhausting. The race began in Ohiopyle, Pennsylvania, and I was able to run the first couple of miles with the participants at a 9 minute-per-mile pace. But then the course came to a huge mile-long climb that slowed me and most other runners to around a 14-minute pace. It was one of those climbs that runners who have previously competed in the event warn you about, but the horror stories aren't just to frighten rookies. It really was as difficult as advertised! The climb was so steep and challenging that it was simply impossible to actually run, so a brisk walk was all most of us could manage.

The course also took us up through Seven Springs Mountain Resort. When I think of spending time at a resort, I think of being relaxed and pampered. My time running through Seven Springs, though, was obviously not relaxing! Additionally, the Laurel Highlands Ultra is advertised as a 70.5-mile race. But because of a detour due to a bridge being out, an additional 6.5 miles were added to the distance. So this annual 70-mile run was actually a 77-miler on the year I chose to participate. Lucky me! Normally a 6.5-mile run would have been like a walk in the park. But when those additional miles are added onto a 70-mile run and they are on the road in full exposure of the sun, they are definitely noticed! Despite the mental and physical challenges of the 77-miler, I managed to finish in 20 hours and 39 minutes and enjoyed a huge sense of accomplishment after having completed a long, grueling race.

One of the most valuable lessons I took from Laurel Highlands was that watermelon was my best friend. During ultramarathons it is absolutely necessary to consume a considerable amount of various foods and beverages in order to refuel your body. What I found was that watermelon worked the best at hydrating and refueling my body. As a result, water-melon became a staple during my stops while on my run across America. There were times when I was running across the US and the sun was beating down on the back of my neck that the anticipation of popping several pieces of the sweet, juicy melon into my mouth is what pushed me to get to my next aid stop.

I realized early on in my ultramarathon running experiences that I was very fortunate to be able to consume foods and beverages without experiencing feelings of being hungry, bloated or nauseous and having to make frequent trips to a bathroom. But each of these training runs served as another opportunity for me to experiment with different foods so that I could find the best options and combinations when crossing America.

## BURNING RIVER

As I mentioned, only seven weeks after completing Laurel Highlands 77, I competed in the benchmark distance for ultramarathon runners—a 100-miler. This is *the* defining distance for ultra runners, an opportunity to prove their mental and physical toughness. Completing a 100-miler is a landmark moment in a long-distance runner's career and for most is considered the ultimate challenge. And the benchmark for ultimate bragging rights is to complete the 100 miles within 24 hours.

Of course, most runners who compete in a 100-mile race spend literally months gearing up toward this one event. I, however, was tackling this distance just seven weeks after the 77-mile race. It is uncommon for long-distance runners to compete in two ultramarathons of these distances in such a short period of time. Your body and mind simply need time to recover and rejuvenate after such a grueling long-distance run. But considering the fact that I was preparing to run 35 miles a day every day for 100 consecutive days, I thought it would be beneficial to test myself with a shortened recovery time by following the 77-miler at Laurel Highlands with the Burning River 100 Mile Endurance Run.

I knew that it would also provide me with another benchmark in which to measure my progress and offer another mental and physical challenge that would prepare me for my nearly 3,500-mile journey across America. So on July 30, 2011, in northern Ohio, my longest challenge yet awaited me. I knew if I could conquer Burning River, the achievement would be something I could put in my mental arsenal to recall whenever I needed a boost of confidence on my cross-country journey.

Even though I had completed 50Ks, 50-milers and even the 77-miler at Laurel Highlands seven weeks prior to Burning River, there is something magical and, to be honest, a bit unnerving about tackling a 100-mile run. I knew this was going to be the most difficult challenge I had faced since I first got into distance running two years earlier, so I did my homework. I read stories about people who ran 100-milers, hoping to gain even the smallest tips that I could apply in my quest to conquer the defining ultramarathon distance event. I knew that very few ultramarathon runners ever attempt a 100-mile race, and even fewer actually finish. But it was another step–another benchmark goal–that I needed to take in my progression.

My wife had served as my crew and my rock during all of my distance races, and Burning River would be no different, except that because of the demands a 24-hour race would place on Tiffany, I knew we needed a second member of the crew. I recruited my cousin Darren, who grew up with my Marine Corps recruiter, to join the team. Darren joined us at the hotel the night prior to the race, and when he burst through the door at 9 p.m. you would have thought he was running the race. He was full of energy and beaming like a kid in a candy store, but he was able to calm down knowing that he had a 2 a.m. wake-up call in order to drive to the finish line and leave his car there before taking a bus from there to the starting line with the majority of the runners.

My wake-up time was 2:45 a.m. for the pre-dawn start to the race, so needless to say I did not get much sleep that night. Fortunately, I had previously discovered that my adrenaline the night prior to a big race would make me restless, so I learned to get a good night's rest the two nights prior to the eve of a race. Earlier the day before, we actually scouted out the finishing and starting areas of the race, checking in at the finish line at Cuyahoga Falls, near Akron, before making the 40-minute drive to the starting area in Willoughby Hills, near Cleveland.

The start was at a beautiful park called Squires Castle. There was a wedding party there when we arrived that afternoon. We toured around the site for a little bit, took some photos and then headed off to find a place to eat. Fortunately, a few minutes from the castle, we found a wonderful small Italian place called Mario Fazio's, where I could consume my favorite pre-race meal of angel hair pasta covered in garlic, oil and lemon. Mario Fazio's did not disappoint.

Having eaten a great meal the night before and having received a couple of great nights of sleep earlier that week, I felt as though my body was as prepared as possible for the 100-miler. My psyche, however, was a different story. On the way from the hotel to the starting line, my wife asked me what was going through my head.

"I'll tell you what I'm thinking," I said. "I could drive from the starting line to the finish line in 40 minutes. But instead, it's going to take me 24 hours to run to the same spot! Can we just drive there and say I did it?"

"No chance!" she said. So to Squires Castle we went.

## LATHERING UP

I learned from some of my early ultramarathons that you can never put enough Bodyglide and Aquaphor ointment on your skin. At a couple of events when I first got into running, I experienced some serious chafing, which is when a patch of skin becomes red and raw from continuously rubbing against an article of clothing or another part of your body. In a "mild" case of chafing, often you won't notice it until you jump into the shower and the warm water makes contact with the area, sending you briefly hopping back out of the water and howling like a wolf. In a severe case, the raw skin will begin to bleed and become noticeably painful during the run, which leads to you attempting to adjust your clothing or stride and as a result often losing your focus and concentration. I had unfortunately experienced both levels early on during my first few ultramarathons.

I sought advice from more experienced runners about how to prevent chafing. I learned about these ointments and lubricants that have literally saved my hide. So in what has become a part of my pre-race routine, as I prepared for the start of Burning River I spent a few minutes lathering every moving part of my body with lotions and creams. Even parts of me that don't move, I tend to coat really well with these products.

Another routine that I developed after receiving this wonderful tip from a more seasoned runner was to lather up my feet with Vaseline, Aquaphor or lotion, so on this morning I grabbed a bottle of body lotion and applied it generously to my feet. Yes, it feels funny putting on your socks and shoes afterward and walking around with lotion squishing between your toes, but I have been fortunate to never get any blisters or lose any toenails (it's very common for long-distance runners to have toenails turn black and fall off before a new toenail grows in its place) over the past few years, even when I ran across America. Plus, I tell my wife that my feet are soft and kissable!

When I headed toward the starting area to join the 300 other eager runners, it was still dark. But we all looked like lightning bugs floating around because of the glow of runners' headlamps and glow sticks. The scene was energizing, as was the wonderful message we heard from Nick Billock, a former Burning River runner who was bravely serving our country overseas. It was the perfect inspiration for me.

### SLOW AND STEADY

The two weeks prior to Burning River, I really worked on keeping my running at a much slower pace than normal, backing off to a 9- or 10-minute pace. I knew I wouldn't maintain that pace throughout the race, but I needed to get my mindset on moving at a slower pace than normal. I knew my adrenaline would be pumping and I would want to push myself a little faster in the run, but I had to force myself to keep it slow. The pace was a quick one out of the gates for a lot of people. My wife told me that she overheard some of the folks at the aid stations early saying the pace was faster than normal for everyone, but I wouldn't allow myself to get caught up in it. Many runners passed me at the beginning of the race, and I was fine with that. We had a long way to go.

Joe Jurczyk, the amazing race director at Burning River, had talked up the aid workers at the pre-race meal, and his words could not begin to describe what an experience each and every aid station was for me. You could hear music blaring as you approached, tons of food and drinks laid out for us and workers approaching you asking if you needed anything done. Personally, though, I have learned that orange Gatorade diluted with water is what is easiest on my stomach during ultramarathon races. As a result, my crew handled mixing up and refilling my FuelBelt or camelback at each aid station. But I most certainly dipped into the food supplies throughout the day. I wasn't really hungry at the first aid station, still feeling full from all the pasta the day before, but I couldn't pass up some watermelon. The sun was starting to come up through the dense fog, and it was nice to have a few seconds to stop and grab some fuel.

My aid station stops vary depending on the length of the race. For shorter races, I typically run through and grab a drink to slam. For ultras, I will always stop and grab food and drinks, but usually I am in and out within five minutes. The first few aid stations at Burning River I continued my pattern of grabbing some watermelon and grapes and moving on. I did notice, though, that a lot of runners were beginning to hang out at the aid stations a little longer, which gave me an opportunity to leapfrog a few of them.

I did take some time early in the run to do something I normally never do—chat with other runners. I am a horrible talker when I run; I just don't talk. But I knew I had a long day ahead of me, and I was sporting my Run for

Wounded Warriors T-shirt, advertising my run for next year, and a few runners asked me about it. I couldn't pass up an opportunity to promote that, so I jumped at the chance, and running at a slower pace made it easier for me to chat. I had a number of runners say they would keep track of my run across America, which was very encouraging.

After a long, flat stretch, the course began to hit some rolling hills. Remembering how I felt two-thirds of the way through Laurel Highlands, I really wanted to preserve my legs during these climbs and descents, so going slow and steady remained my focus. I remember thinking to myself throughout the first third of the race how pleased I was that we hadn't hit any major climbs. The initial climbs at Laurel Highlands took a lot out of me, so even though it remained relatively flat, I did everything I could to conserve energy.

When I hit the aid station at 33.3 miles, I reapplied lotion to my feet and changed my socks and shoes, alternating between two pair of road shoes throughout the race. The sun had finally burned through the morning cloud cover, so at this stop Tiffany took a towel, dipped it in a bucket of ice water and slapped it on my head and around my neck. Initially the coolness of the cloth on my neck and the cold water dripping inside my shirt and down my back and chest was startling. But within seconds I felt refreshed, and on my neck is where that towel stayed most of the rest of the day.

The next stretch through the halfway point of the race was extremely hot and my pace began to slow. In fact, during stretches on roads that had potholes recently patched, I could see some shoe prints of runners who were ahead of me who had stepped onto the sticky, bubbly black tar. I'd like to think my shoes sticking to the tar was slowing me down, but in reality the heat was beginning to wear me down. About this time I also noticed streaks of blood down the front of my shirt, meaning my nipples had chafed so badly that they were bleeding. In addition to applying Bodyglide, I also did a somewhat common male long-distance runner's trick by placing duct tape over my nipples. The thought is that covering the nipples with tape will prevent the delicate but constant rubbing from your running shirt that ever so slightly bounces up and then falls back into place with each step a runner takes. At the 50-mile aid station, which I arrived at in almost exactly 10 hours (a 50-mile personal best for me) I ditched my shirt, cooled off with an ice-cold sponge, refueled and kept moving.

The heat was relentless when the course left the protective covering of leafy, green trees that were providing shade. In an attempt to cool off, at the aid stations I would reapply more Bodyglide to my chest, dip my shirt in the ice and water in our cooler, and press forward. It turns out that it was the second hottest race-day temperature in the history of the Burning River race. I continued to pound Gatorade, cold foods and salt tablets all day to keep my body moving forward. To a non-runner, consuming salt tablets may sound disgusting, but I especially learned during my cross-country journey that they were essential because they help your body to retain water, thus prolonging your ability to run without becoming dehydrated.

At 63.8 miles, I felt good but knew that I needed to recover for a few extra minutes. A lot of runners came and went during the eight minutes I was at this aid station, but the additional time of rest really energized me. It's funny, though, to watch the video from this section as my crew attempted to document this event. I keep looking up from my seat while my awesome wife is putting lotion on my feet, and as more runners come in and go out, I have this look on my face like I'm mad. *"All these people are passing me,"* I thought. *"I should be up running."* But despite the disturbed look on my face revealed by the video, I knew it was in my best interest to remain patient and take an extended break.

Because of the additional rest, I was really able to cruise through the next couple of sections until I got zapped of energy at the 70-mile mark. Fortunately, Tiffany had planned to go the next three miles at Pine Hollow with me, and her presence was really encouraging, especially since this stretch required a lot of brutal climbs and walking. It was at this point that I really began to question my ability to complete the race. My feet couldn't have been burning any worse had I stuck them in an oven, it was dark and I was becoming disoriented. Having Tiffany there alongside me, however, really encouraged me to keep moving.

After the next aid station, I believe the energy I conserved by running slower during the first third of the run really kicked in. I figured the next section would take me a couple of hours, so I told Tiffany and Darren to get some rest. Turns out I ran the section in 1 hour and 15 minutes, so at the 80.5-mile aid station my crew was nowhere to be found. I did see two familiar faces from races I had run before, Dannielle and Eric Ripper. Dannielle was the race director for the Mason Dixon 50K and I met her husband, Eric, at Laurel Highlands.

"You look like you just ran a 5K," Dannielle told me. It was great to hear that I looked better than I felt. As I entered a covered bridge I found Darren resting on the bridge. He was shocked that I came in 45 minutes ahead of schedule. He informed me that Tiffany was off snoozing in the "sag wagon," which I was very happy about because I knew she was worn out from chasing me around all day. Darren had planned to run this next section with me, but because I was feeling so good I wanted to continue on at my own pace.

The next few miles were muddy with a lot of creek crossings and challenging climbs. I love running on trails like that, just not after logging 80 miles! But my energy level had really picked up and I was actually passing some runners I hadn't seen in more than 12 hours. At my slowest point of the race I was in 78th place out of the approximately 300 runners who left the starting line, and by now I had moved up to 44th. With 15 miles remaining, I had three hours to get to the finish in my target goal of 24 hours. *Woo hoo! I can do this,"* I thought.

At mile 90, however, I hit the proverbial wall. "The Wall," as it is known in the running community, is that point in a long-distance race when your body just shuts down. The muscles in your legs cramp up and start pulsating as if they are pistons firing in the engine of a racecar driving at top speed. It also often feels as though you swapped out your running shoes for a pair of concrete blocks. In a marathon distance, hitting the wall usually occurs around miles 18-20 for most runners. In a 100-miler, apparently the wall appears at mile 90.

My legs began screaming at me about what I was asking them to do. It was all I could do to keep pushing myself forward. Running, or jogging for that matter, was pretty much impossible at this point. At the 93-mile aid station I saw Tiffany, and did my best to put a huge smile on my face when I saw her. Seeing her at any point throughout my races always lifts my spirits, but I know she could tell everything I was doing at this point was forced. My hamstrings and quadriceps were dead.

I passed a couple of runners who were dropping out of the race at this point and were waiting for crews to come get them because of injuries they had sustained. I offered whatever assistance I could provide at that point, which I knew wasn't much, but thankfully they told me to press on. Seeing them in the pain they were experiencing certainly didn't help my psyche, but I continued on with what Darren called "positive forward motion." As I came to the last aid station at mile 96, I was mentally done. Darren had brought a collapsible camping chair that he had offered to let me plop down in throughout the day, but since it was a green Marshall University chair, I refused to sit in it since Marshall is a rival school of West Virginia University, which is located in Morgantown, where I live. But at this point rivalries didn't matter to me, so I planted my butt in the chair and stared off into space. Darren and Tiff did everything they could to encourage me, but Tiff also knew I just needed some time to compose myself on my own before I could move on. I was really having a difficult time convincing myself to get out of the chair because it was so comfortable and warm since we were near a campfire the aid station workers had built.

Finally gathering the strength to lift myself out of the chair, I gave Tiffany a big hug and asked her if she would meet me about 1.5 miles from the finish to run the rest of the way with me. The next 3.5 miles to get to her were extremely difficult. I remembered from videos I watched online from previous Burning River races that there were steps in this last section. I couldn't think of anything else but that dreaded climb as I approached the end. Those were some of the most difficult steps I have ever climbed. My legs were so stiff they didn't want to bend and my feet felt like 40-pound weights. And it wasn't just one set of steps; there was a second set staring me in the face just as I reached the top of the first.

After climbing the steps, I passed under a bridge, thinking it was one I had seen in the video that was close to the end and that this is where Tiff would join me. But as I went under it, I realized I was nowhere near that point. On and on I went, finally coming to a clearing where I saw a familiar SUV parked near a gate with a light shining out the window towards me. I was elated to see Darren and Tiffany there just as the morning sun was starting to creep above the horizon. Tiffany joined me and we walked across a bridge and up our final hill until a clock tower came into view.

"So what do you think?" Tiffany asked me.

"About what?" I asked, grasping for anything to take my mind off of the pain I was feeling in my body.

"About finishing a 100-mile race," she said. "It's a big deal!"

I told her I hadn't really thought about the magnitude of what I was about to accomplish, but later as I reflected back on the race, she was right—it was a pretty big deal!

As we came to the finish, Tiff ran on ahead and I crossed the finish line in 24 hours, 53 minutes and 7 seconds. I made it!

As I ran across the finish line, I scanned the area in search of Darren, who had driven to the finish and planned to film me coming into the finish. He showed up a couple of minutes later, apologizing profusely that after he parked the car nature called and he had to take care of that business. We laughed it off, and at the encouragement of others I ran back through the finish so he could capture it on film. He and I toasted the finish, then headed back to our respective homes, completely exhausted, but very proud of what had just been accomplished.

## SIMULATED RUNNING

After allowing my body to recover from running a 77-miler and 100-miler in the span of seven weeks, I began another important stage of my training. In September 2011, I began a three-month simulation of my 100-day journey. I knew that it was necessary for me to put myself through the mental and physical stress I would endure during the cross-country run prior to the actual run so that I wouldn't be shocked by what my body would experience. It also enabled me to learn some crucial tips that would prove to be extremely valuable.

During this mock cycle, I would typically run 16 miles each morning, stop at the house, and then run the seven miles to the office. I was fortunate that the building I worked in also housed the West Virginia University Police, so there was a locker room with showers that the police chief and building manager allowed me to use. After a day of work I would run the seven miles back home. My pattern was altered slightly on the first and last day of the work week. On Mondays, I would drive to the office in the morning with enough work clothes to last me the week, and then run home. On Fridays after work, I would drive my car back home.

What I found was that putting in 30 miles a day for three months really prepared me more mentally than physically for the journey. The mental challenges of getting up around 3:30 a.m., running, stopping and picking up my day in a high-stress environment and then running home again, all while dealing with the daily duties and challenges of having a family, allowed me to test my ability to manage everything. I knew if I could balance my work and family while running 30 miles each day, I would be prepared to handle the daily grind of running 35 miles daily during the run across America. While at home, I had work and family duties to juggle while running, but during the journey, I knew I would basically just have to eat, sleep and run (a lot).

Another benefit of going through this mock cycle was that I learned that my sleep habits had to change. When I really ramped up my long-distance running, I did alter my sleep pattern to go to bed earlier in order to get my runs out of the way early in the morning. I would typically go to bed at about 10 or 11 p.m. and get up at 4 a.m. But by the end of the first week of this simulated training, I was crawling into bed at 7:30 p.m. in order to be able to get up at 3:30 a.m. the next morning to start running. If I wouldn't have gone through that mock cycle and learned that my body needed an additional two or three hours of sleep each night, I wouldn't have made it the first couple of weeks during the actual journey.

I have always been pretty comfortable at an eight minute-per-mile pace, no matter what distance I was running (I ran my only marathon in 3 hours and 31 minutes, which is an 8:03 pace). But I knew that even an eight-minute pace would not be something my body could tolerate based on the massive amount of mileage I would be logging. So during this mock cycle, I began focusing on purposefully slowing down during my training runs, getting my body used to the slower times. It actually hurt a bit when I started slowing down because my body had become comfortable to the stride and pace at which I had always previously run. Efficiency was what this run across America was going to be about, however, so altering my stride to shorter, choppier steps would be necessary, even though initially it affected my knees and hips. It was admittedly tough to adjust to that, and painful initially, but I wanted to try to put myself through what I was expecting my run to be like when we took off.

In addition to the physical challenges this alteration in my pace and stride caused me, it was also a challenge mentally. No competitive runner wants to purposely run at about a two-minute pace slower than he or she is capable of, so it was difficult mentally to dial back and go slower. I also felt like I was doing the old man shuffle with my stride so short and my leg kick so minimal, but this had to be done. It was going to be a long, long trip.

## LASHCICLES

After completing my simulated training cycle, I continued to regularly run about 16 miles each morning throughout the winter of 2011-12. Living in West Virginia, winters bring brisk temperatures and snow and ice storms with regularity. Running in single-digit temps and several inches of snow presents plenty of challenges, but through trial and error, I found that my Vasque Velocity trail shoes are wonderful in this type of weather, and they helped me power through the snow, with the white powder crunching underneath my feet with each step.

One morning in January 2012, I woke up to what looked like a winter wonderland. I put on my winter running gear, including my balaclava facemask, which covers my entire head and face except for a portion of my nose, eyes and forehead just above my eyebrows, and stepped out into the 7-degree early morning air. But the moisture and humidity created by the balaclava covering my perspiring head, coupled with my watery eyes due to the windy conditions, formed what looked like icicles on my eyelashes. As I came up to the door that morning after my run, Nicholas opened the door and started laughing at my appearance. We both laughed as I gingerly pulled little chunks of ice away from my eyes. From that day forward, those became known as lashcicles.

On that same run, my hands were absolutely freezing, despite wearing a good pair of cold-weather running gloves. I was doing everything I could think of to try to keep my hands warm, and I am sure I looked funny running down the road with my arms crossed and my hands shoved up under my armpits. There are a total of five American flags that fly on my regular morning running route, and I make it a point to salute each of them as I run by. But I'm sure my old drill instructor would have been screaming in my ear with his gravelly voice because of the way I was saluting that morning. I'm sure it didn't look too sharp.

## MENTAL TRAINING

Even though I was gaining confidence in my physical abilities to complete the journey through the various stages of my training regimen, I knew I also had to include some mental training. I was fortunate enough to connect with Chelsea Butters Wooding and Michelle "Mac" McAlarnen, both doctoral students in the Sport and Exercise Psychology Department at West Virginia University. Chelsea, in particular, assisted me greatly in providing me with the knowledge and tools necessary to train my mind to conquer the many mental challenges I would face throughout this journey.

While all of the discussions and meetings with them were beneficial, there were three key things that Chelsea was instrumental in passing along to me that really proved most helpful. Early in our talks, she helped me realize that effectively focusing on running helped me to not get stressed out and put too much effort into the planning and logistics of the journey. That's what Tiffany had agreed to do and I needed to allow her to handle that.

The second tip, I picked up a couple of weeks before the departure for the run. Tiffany and I met Chelsea at a Bob Evans restaurant to discuss last-minute thoughts about the journey, and I told her, "The past few days have really sucked."

"Why?" she asked.

"I was doing an eight-mile taper run and as I was running back to the house it hit me that I'm two weeks away from this endeavor. But after it's over, then what?"

A feeling of depression had begun to sink in with me, mourning the upcoming completion of something I had put so much focus into for the past two years. I had been working so long and hard to achieve this run across America, and before I had even started the journey I was depressed and confused about what I would do after it was over.

"A lot of Olympic athletes go through the same thing," she reassured me. "They train for four years for 10 seconds or one minute of competition. It's just a form of postpartum depression and it is normal. It's important to focus on the *now* and your purpose for running to complete and enjoy your journey."

She allowed me to realize that it's nothing out of the ordinary for athletes who put so much focus and time into one particular event to experience those sorts of emotions. Once she helped me realize it, we were then able to work through it.

Finally, Chelsea provided me with an effective way to communicate with my wife about the pain I would experience on the run without burdening Tiffany with intimate details about the breakdown of my body. Chelsea helped me to use a scale of 1-10 to describe my pain management, with a 10 being I feel great, and a 1 being I feel terrible. She also helped me to manage my expectations and suggested that I not get too caught up in trying to get to a 10 every day.

"If you are a 5 on the pain management scale one day, expecting to get to a 7 or 8 may not be realistic," she told me. "Work on trying to get to a 6. Take baby steps to get to the next level rather than trying to get to a 10 every day."

That scale also gave me a different way to communicate with Tiffany without being too descriptive of the injuries and pain I was dealing with. Tiffany and I used that scale quite a bit the first few weeks of the journey. There were times when I was feeling bad, and Tiffany would ask me what number I was on the scale. What I learned was that I couldn't be too descriptive about the pain that I was enduring because that would add stress to Tiffany, and she also didn't share logistical struggles or issues that came up while being stuck in an RV with our two kids all day because she didn't want those things to distract me. She was strong enough to keep those things to herself and she trusted me enough to allow me to keep most of the details of my pain management to myself. It really created great teamwork. I focused on the running and she focused on the logistics.

# 3 | Mapping Out America

While training to run 35 miles every day for 100 days straight is certainly challenging, there were times when it was honestly the easiest part of the preparation. There were plenty of books, blogs and training plans at my disposal that could assist me in creating a running plan to train for the run across America. Unfortunately, there is no *Running Across America for Dummies* manual that I could purchase at my local bookstore that would provide my wife and me with all of the necessary steps to plan out the logistics of such a monumental trip.

Thankfully, my wife accepted the often overwhelming task of translating this dream into reality by ensuring that all of the necessary preparations were made. And trust her, there were *a lot* of preparations to be made! Without her help, I wouldn't have been able to take even one step on this journey, let alone the estimated six million steps that I took in running from the Pacific Ocean to the Atlantic Ocean.

Fifteen years into our marriage, my wife and I were already aware of the fact that I am the one who sees the start and the finish, and she's the one who considers all of the stops and details along the way in most of what we do. This adventure shined a megawatt spotlight on that fact. She spent hundreds of hours the year leading up to the run ensuring that the logistics of the trip would be as organized as possible. That meant she planned everything from the route we would take to the amount of underwear we'd pack.

Obviously the most important and challenging aspect of planning this journey was literally mapping out America. I told Tiffany where I wanted to start–in Coos Bay, Oregon, where she grew up. I told her where I wanted to finish–in Baltimore, Maryland (at the time). I told her I wanted to finish on Independence Day. And I told her I wanted to complete the run across America in 100 days. All of the other details, I left up to her.

Planning this trip consumed every ounce of Tiffany's spare time. Fortunately, at the time, she was working two days a week as a dental hygienist, which afforded her the time to focus on the infinite details of the trip. She needed every bit of that time to accomplish everything that I was asking her to do.

The first step was determining our mode of transportation during the journey. We had committed to bringing our two children along with us, so we knew that at minimum we would need a van. If we opted for that, it would mean we'd have to find lodging every night and eat most of our meals at restaurants, which after calculating those costs essentially eliminated that option. The best option, it seemed, was to utilize a motorhome.

We contacted several different companies in an attempt to secure a motorhome for use during the trip in exchange for sponsorship opportunities. But after getting rebuffed by multiple dealers and manufacturers, we realized that was yet another expense that we would have to absorb. That would be a recurring theme in our attempt to obtain sponsorship and in-kind donations as we planned for the trip. Tiffany began investigating renting a motorhome. The lowest price she could find for 115 days and 8,000 miles was $17,000. Yikes! That was simply too much to invest in a rental with nothing to show for it at the trip's completion. That left one real option: buying a motorhome. When my family committed to this trip, we knew we needed to do everything in our power to keep our expenses low. Securing sponsorship and donations was a way we hoped to accomplish that. But since no company was willing to provide use of a motorhome, we knew buying one had become a necessity, even though doing so was initially something we resisted.

Yet, the more time Tiffany spent looking at used motorhomes online, the more we could see it becoming a reality. After doing some comparison shopping, we drove to Colerain RV in Cincinnati, Ohio, to purchase our transportation—and home—for the next four months. After buying our 31-foot 2004 Jayco Escapade, equipped with a very necessary shower stall, my wife's mission was to become literate in the understanding and workings of the motorhome from headlight to taillight. She trawled blogs, reading as much as she could about how to operate the motorhome. Once, she even got up the courage to post a question on a blog, but that didn't turn out to be too fruitful.

"I can see in my mind a gray-haired man reading my question and just shaking his head and smirking to himself about the foolishness of what I was proposing to do," she told me. "He's probably thinking to himself, 'Good luck with that!'"

So back to trawling she went. By the time we were ready to start our trip, she had gathered so much information about motorhomes that I believe she could have been hired as a writer for *RV Magazine,* if there is such a tabloid. She, though, was a bit more modest about her knowledge of RVs.

"I'm just trying to stuff as much information between my ears as possible," she said. "And I hope that some of it will stick and I'll be able to remember it when things happen or go wrong on the trip."

## GETTING FROM POINT A TO POINT B

With our mode of transportation now secured, Tiffany was then able to really hammer out the daily route. Much of her time was spent studying maps, routes, highways and elevation gains and losses as she plotted out the course for the run. The shortest distance between two points is a straight line, but unfortunately going from Oregon to Maryland requires a few twists and turns. Tiffany did a marvelous job of figuring all that out, even though it caused her quite a bit of frustration.

"You're far from the first person to run across the country," she told me, "but you definitely aren't taking the path of least resistance." That was due to the run starting in Oregon, where she grew up, because I wanted to pay homage to my wife. It happened to also be the hometown of Steve Prefontaine, a famous runner who tragically lost his life way too soon. Tiffany loved the idea, but after studying the road maps of America, we became a little less thrilled. I ultimately ended up running about 500 extra miles because of starting in Coos Bay, Oregon, instead of southern California like most USA crossers have done. We also organized a few events throughout the state of Oregon as I ran through, which at the time seemed like a great idea, but ended up adding to the mileage.

So how do we get from Oregon to Maryland? This question haunted my wife for a few weeks before she got the courage (and time) to sit down and tackle the route. She had point A (Coos Bay, Oregon) and point B (at the time, Baltimore, Maryland), but she needed to chop it up into 100 bites that I could consume in 24-hour periods while still being able to wake up the next morning and ingest approximately the same distance again, and again, and again. She sat down at her computer in our dining room, said a little prayer for help and then probably spent more time on the Google Maps website than Google's programmers did when designing the site.

Initially, we were under the wrong impression that running on interstates was not allowed in any state. With that being the case, Tiffany set the parameters on Google Maps to pedestrian use only. Gulp! My eyes got a little big when Tiffany broke the news to me that the mileage was about 500 more miles than what I had guessed it would be. Undeterred, I told her to keep planning, and Tiffany began dissecting the route in 1% sections.

After creating an initial route, Tiffany scoured blogs about areas of the trip about which we were a little tentative. She took into consideration the lack of civilization, terrain, elevation changes and other things when refining the course. For instance, on the initial route there was a stretch from Nevada into Utah on Jungo Road. The more Tiffany researched that section, the more she realized we had to find a different route. That path included sharp volcanic rock and it was suggested that trail motorbikes were the preferred mode of transportation. No way was I going to ask my wife, a motorhome newbie, to drive a 31-foot beast on roads on which we wouldn't be comfortable driving a standard sedan.

Tiffany admitted she often felt clueless when refining the course. And in reality, the adjustments continued throughout the journey all the way up to the final couple of weeks of the trip. As soon as we felt like she had a solid route planned, Tiffany placed calls to each of the Transportation Authorities in the 15 (at that time) states in which I was going to run. This process was a frustrating one for my wife. There was so much red tape to cut through with some states and she constantly had to reach out to state employees time and time again just to get a response. And when she did speak with someone, they often made us feel like lunatics that I was even attempting to run across America.

## MY THANKS TO THE CAPTAIN'S MOMMA

*by* **Tiffany Summerlin**

As I planned and plotted the route Jamie would be running, there were quite a few snags and some irritating moments. The irony of the "United" part of the United States is never more apparent than when dealing with each state's Department of Transportation. Assuming each state follows a similar set of rules was my first bang into the sliding glass door that I thought was open. I spent hours calling, emailing, filling out contact forms and mailing permit requests, yet I still felt a little nervous about seeing blue flashing lights somewhere along our trip and learning that Jamie wasn't allowed to legally run on a road we had chosen.

My faith in the system was restored momentarily after talking to Captain Gaylon Grippin with the Colorado State Police. The more we talked about our plans for the run, the more help he offered. He seemed genuinely excited about our journey and the mission. He sent me an email with tips on how to navigate the area we would be going through in Colorado and really went out of his way to help us out. I love it when people do that. Why doesn't that happen more often? I'll just think the best of people and assume their mommas didn't teach them right!

After finalizing the route and receiving clearance from the various states to run on their roads, Tiffany had to come up with a tentative but flexible plan of staying at RV parks, locating grocery stores and laundry facilities and identifying places to take the kids for fun so that they weren't cooped up inside the motorhome all day every day. It was a little bit overwhelming, to say the least. My wife and I often joked that I had the easiest job by doing the running. The details and arrangements necessary to make this epic journey go off without a glitch was a mental marathon for her.

## RV SCHOOLED

Since we wanted our children to be a part of this amazing experience, we had several meetings with their teachers and the county school system administration. Everyone was in support not only of the trip, but of the children coming along. In fact, one of the reasons the superintendent, Frank Devono, was so on board with the run was because his son was in the military and had been deployed overseas several times. He felt it was a great opportunity for our children to visit different parts of the country and see first-hand the reason why I was motivated to run across the country to honor our nation's veterans.

My daughter was in fourth grade and her teacher, Mrs. Duley, decided to incorporate as much of our journey as possible into the class curriculum, utilizing information on our travels in geography lessons and my running mileage totals in mathematics. While we were on the run, they even created a "Where's Jamie? Tuesdays" lesson. Shayna had a great time using Skype with her classmates and it was fun to show them the view of our current location.

My son was in sixth grade and prior to our departure I got the opportunity to speak to his class and answer questions from the students. One of the first questions I received was, "Are you going to shower during the run?"

"We will be staying in an RV, so I'll either shower or I'll end up sleeping outside," I answered.

Other students asked if I would sleep at all during the 100 days, or how much food I could eat during the run. I said that I could eat four pizzas and two dozen donuts every day and I would still be able to burn off those calories during my daily runs. Someone later calculated that I could drink 247 sodas a week without gaining weight based on the calories I burned. Not that I would ever want to attempt that.

One of the last questions I was asked was, "What do you do if you take off running and your wife tells you that you are going the wrong way?"

"You're not married yet are you? That happens a whole lot more often than you think." That retort drew a chuckle from the teachers in attendance.

Nicholas and Shayna did have to do daily journal entries as the main requirement of them being allowed to miss the last several weeks of school. We also worked with their teachers to get workbooks and lesson plans so Tiffany could essentially "RV school" them so that they wouldn't fall behind their peers academically. Everyone was really excited about the opportunity to utilize technology such as Skype to stay in touch with us on the road, and we knew it would be a good way to help keep the kids connected to their classmates back home.

## SPREADING THE WORD

My son's class wasn't my only public speaking opportunity. As the countdown to the run neared, I was contacted by several media organizations and was also afforded the opportunity to speak at some veterans' facilities and functions.

One engagement in particular really affected me, providing me with an uplifting moment and an "aha" moment. I was a last-minute invitee to speak at the West Virginia Veterans of Foreign War (VFW) Mid-Winter Conference in January 2012. I was very excited to share my story with them, explain my mission and get feedback from the people in the room. But when I got to the podium and saw all of the faces of the veterans there looking at me, it was a little difficult to speak initially because I was trying to choke back the tears that were welling up in my eyes. I was overcome with emotion and pride, thankful for all the sacrifices those brave men and women in that room had made for each one of us.

When I was done speaking, it was a very humbling experience to have the roomful of veterans stand and applaud me even though they were the ones who deserved a standing ovation. The event was a reminder of why I wanted to do the run. Their selflessness and bravery was the reason I wanted to raise awareness and funds for veteran-based organizations, and I wanted to honor each of them with every mile I ran.

That speaking engagement, along with similar ones, really made something jump out to me months later. Sometime during my run across the US I thought back to the West Virginia VFW Mid-Winter Conference. *"I'm about 30 years younger than most of the people that were in that room,"* I thought. There were a few veterans in their 20s in attendance, but there was a generation gap that really stuck in my mind throughout my journey. Being out on the open road in isolation allowed me to think about what could be done to get veterans from my generation more actively involved in the organizations set up to serve and assist them.

During a previous speaking engagement, I had the opportunity to meet a fellow West Virginia runner who had also raised money for the Wounded Warrior Project. On Veterans Day 2011, I was invited to serve as a speaker at a gala in Martinsburg hosted by Spenser Wempe, Miss West Virginia. Her platform was the Wounded Warrior Project and Veterans' Welfare, and it was an honor to be invited to take part in this special event. Also speaking at the gala was Drew Miller, who had recently run 2,400 miles from Long Beach, California, to Spencer, West Virginia.

Drew was a very humble guy and knew what he accomplished was remarkable, yet he kept going on about what I was about to do. The insight that he shared with me about his experience running 2,400 miles proved to be invaluable to me. I was able to learn what did and didn't work for him during his journey, and it helped me in crafting my own strategy for crossing the continental United States in a pair (OK, 10 pairs) of sneakers.

When the kickoff to my run drew closer, Drew attended a silent auction put on by my family and friends that raised more than $7,000. Just knowing the suffering that Drew endured during his run was inspiring to me, and there was no competitive demeanor when we talked about our individual runs. Really the entire running community was extremely supportive of my venture. But that shouldn't be surprising. Runners are generally one of the most supportive groups of athletes in sports.

OK, maybe sprinters aren't as supportive of their cohorts. It's pretty common today to see elite international sprinters talking trash like they are heavyweight boxers at a weigh-in. But in the distance running community, generally speaking, it's more about lifting up your fellow competitors rather than trying to tear them down. I think distance runners realize how physically and mentally difficult those long runs can be, and when we see others attempting to accomplish similar goals, we develop a mutual respect and admiration for one another.

## LIP SERVICE

Preparing my body to be able to handle the daily mileage of the run was certainly challenging, but there were other things related to my preparation for this journey that also proved to be difficult. One of them was our attempt to obtain sponsors for the run. The operational costs of the journey were significant, so I knew that soliciting funding and in-kind donations from sponsors was essential. In addition to financing $23,000 for the RV, we ended up spending more than $3,500 in gas during the trip. And while Tiffany and I were both extended goodwill by our respective employers that we would have a job when the journey was completed, there was always a lingering question about what we would do financially if we discovered that wasn't true. We knew we were already stretching ourselves as thin as possible, especially considering we were not earning paychecks during the four months we would be away from our jobs.

Unfortunately, I found that many of the large corporations I contacted couldn't find the time of day to hear my pitch or didn't share my vision, belief and confidence that the run across America would be a success. Others promised to get involved in some way but never followed through.

Fortunately, I had much better success with the smaller local companies. And it was the willingness of those grassroots companies to get behind this mission that really fueled my tank during those times when I would get a little frustrated at the larger corporations that so often quickly dismissed my vision.

Local companies provided some important assistance. Centra Bank CEO Douglas Leech, as well as the Greater Morgantown Convention and Visitors Bureau, were among those that offered financial support. Charles Ryan & Associates, led by Aly Goodwin-Gregg and Jessica Hall, provided unbelievable publicity, connecting me with local and national media before, during and after my run. Asayo Creative provided assistance with the design of my website. HealthWorks provided some medical supplies while Ray Adams offered some stretching techniques designed to aid in my recovery from the daily mileage. Morgantown Printing and Binding did the vehicle wrap on the motorhome, prominently displaying the "Run for Wounded Warriors" theme.

There were some companies that did step up and provide me with some much-needed supplies. The biggest blessing was when 10 boxes of my preferred model of running shoes arrived on my front doorstep courtesy of Dr. Mark Cucuzzella and Two Rivers Treads in Shepherdstown, West Virginia. Others who contributed supplies include Aquaphor, Gatorade, Gold Bond and Gu Energy. One other company, Holabird Sports, located near Baltimore, also came through in a pinch when I truly needed it the most (I'll share more about its assistance in Chapter 9).

Finally, John Brennan from MyAthlete Live gave me one of its newest devices to provide live tracking of me during the run. This was a huge blessing to our family, because it provided a layer of assurance that they would always be able to monitor me when I was off running miles away from the

RV. Additionally, it gave all of my friends and supporters a chance to following my daily progress in real time and monitor my location, elevation, speed and miles traveled.

"If you're following me live on the website and you see that it's tracking me at going 60 miles per hour, you'll know I'm cheating," I joked more than once. In reality, there were some anxious moments for some of my followers when we made last-minute adjustments to the route I was running and the tracker would show me going off the designated course on the map. I know Tiffany and I received more than a few text messages from some of my followers telling us that I was running the wrong way!

I was definitely thankful for all of those in-kind donations. However, as you've probably figured out by now, when I do something I attempt to do it big. I had hoped to get several major companies on board as financial backers. Not only would this help my family to keep our out-of-pocket expenses down (and they ended up being considerable), but the ultimate goal was to raise as much money as possible for organizations focused on providing assistance to our veteran community.

I had literally hundreds of conversations with potential sponsors and supporters of the run in the 18 months leading up to it. I was disappointed to discover, however, that numerous companies that I had relied on to come through with things they promised or committed to, ultimately did not deliver on their promises. Our vets deal with this same type of lip service every day. Many different organizations or federal and state programs have been set up to help veterans, but all too often those groups stray from their good intentions and get off track, thus failing to provide goods or services to the veterans they were supposed to assist and support. That's one of the reasons I have carefully reviewed each of the organizations that has benefited from the funds we raised and continue to raise.

With the realization that major corporate sponsors were not going to back my mission, it caused me to rethink where I planned to finish. Initially my "point B" was Baltimore because it was the headquarters of a major athletic apparel supplier. The company already had a great relationship with the Wounded Warrior Project, so I thought it would be tremendous for all parties if I finished in its home community. The company declined to sponsor me, (although they did offer to give me 40% off of clothing for my journey that I didn't bother using), and as the months wore on and I continued to focus on what the whole run was for, it just made sense to revisit the final stop of the run.

It wasn't until a little more than a month before I began that a new end point was chosen. Knowing that I planned to complete the run on July 4, I thought that the Chesapeake Bay in Annapolis, Maryland, home of the U.S. Naval Academy, would be an ideal finish line. Adjusting the route would also enable me to run through Washington, DC, giving me an opportunity to run past some of the memorials erected to remember our country's heroes. There couldn't have been a better finish line for me to cross.

## DRIVING WEST TO RUN EAST

After nearly two full years of training and preparation, my life had already changed in more ways than I could have ever imagined. But as my family packed into our motorhome and began our trek from Morgantown to Oregon to get to the starting point of the run, I knew the real adventure was just beginning! There were butterflies and feelings of anxiousness as I slid behind the wheel of the RV and began driving out of town on March 16, 2012, but I had invested way too much to turn back now. The road ahead was one that would not only challenge me physically and mentally, but also test our faith and love in one another as a family like they had never been tested before.

The five-day drive from West Virginia to Oregon was eventful at times. By the third night on the road, we were in Wyoming but we had an abrupt end to our travels when we hit a blizzard ... well really the blizzard hit us. Driving into the rapidly falling flakes of white snow with the night sky as a backdrop made for beautiful yet perilous conditions. In what seemed like mere minutes, the snow blanketed Interstate 80 like a fluffy white comforter draped across a bed. The storm forced the state police to shut down the interstate. We managed to pull off in Fort Bridger (we would return to this area during the trek back across America), find a parking lot to park the RV for the night and kick on the furnace running off the house battery. Fortunately for us the small restaurant Will-Yums Turf that was supposed to close at 9 p.m. was still open because of the traffic off of the interstate. The owners let us in to use the bathroom, a welcome gesture since we still had the RV winterized and were without running water.

Still being novices with our new home on wheels, we're not entirely sure what went wrong. But at some point in the night the battery died and my mom, who had joined us on our trip out West, woke me up very early in the morning to tell me the temperature in the RV was down to 49 degrees! Our dog, Emmie, was cuddled up with Tiffany and me in the back of the motorhome, and our two children were tucked away up front, so we hadn't noticed the drop in temperature. Trying to get the furnace back on, I failed to prime the generator and the dull thud when I pressed the start button made my mom's heart drop. When I finally got the generator up and running, I checked and it was 19 degrees and very windy outside.

Later that morning we were able to get back on the road, and we made a stop at the Salt Flats in Utah. Being the adventurous one of our family, my daughter decided to taste a piece of the salt that crusted the ground. Needless to say, Shayna quickly learned that it didn't taste like table salt!

Oregon later greeted us with another snowstorm to go along with high winds and some mountain roads so steep that even this West Virginia native was in marvel. I felt a pit in my stomach as we crept down a 9 percent grade at 15 miles per hour for three miles as I meticulously navigated our 31-foot vehicle down the twists and turns of Doherty Slide, a section of road famous for its steepness, curves and lack of guard rails. You can read travel blogs of drivers retelling their fearful experiences navigating this road in their cars. It was so bad that my mom had to lie down in the back and close the blinds so she wouldn't see the huge drop off the side of the mountain that was visible out the left side of the RV. Later that evening, we slowly crawled down a mountain into Lakeview, Oregon, as the snow provided limited visibility. We pulled into a gas station in Lakeview to spend the night, and the clerk working there offered us use of the heated bathroom so we could get cleaned up. He also informed the manager about our trip we'd be taking back through that same area in a few weeks, and they kindly offered to supply us with snacks and drinks on our way back through.

After successfully driving down these roads in a snowstorm, I was confident there wasn't any situation Tiffany or I couldn't handle while behind the wheel of the RV during the next 100+ days. I wasn't as confident about my ability to run up these same mountains a week or so later!

I typically never pre-run a course when I'm doing a race because I enjoy the unexpected. I was glad, however, that I did get a glimpse of what I would have to be running up a few days later. It allowed me to plan ahead for what I knew would have to be some slower pacing on those climbs. *"If it was easy, everyone would do it,"* I told myself.

We arrived at Tiffany's hometown on March 21, giving us a few days to spend with her family and time to get psyched up for the journey that awaited me beginning March 26. The local community in Myrtle Point put together an amazing spaghetti dinner the night before I took off, and raised quite a bit of money to support our amazing veterans. Tiffany's mom, Kathy, had worked hard to get things prepared for the dinner and our sendoff, and her dad, Tiff, had scheduled numerous events for us those first few days, including the sendoff and interviews I gave the morning of the kickoff to the run.

I had done everything I possibly could have done to get ready to run almost 3,500 miles in 100 days. Now there was only one thing left to do–run!

# 4 | No Turning Back

When I awoke from a fairly light night's sleep at 5 a.m. on the morning of March 26, the stars were still visible in the pre-dawn sky, and the view of space gave me a sense of the sheer vastness of our world. It was a comforting view, reminding me that while my run across America was a major undertaking, the 3,000+ miles I was about to run was just a short distance when viewed from a different perspective. The previous night while lying in bed and this morning as I began to move around, my thoughts, feelings and emotions were swirling around in my mind like liquid in a blender as I tried to comprehend the fact that I was about to begin the most difficult challenge of my life. Physically, I felt completely ready for the challenge. In all honesty, that part of the upcoming journey was the part I worried the least about. I had trained for almost two full years, getting myself ready to take almost six million steps through 16 states over the next three-plus months.

While looking out at the stars, I took in several deep breaths, filling my lungs with the cool, crisp air. The temperature was hovering around 35 degrees, which to me was ideal. During my short time as a runner, I learned to enjoy being out in the cold, feeling much more alert and in tune with my body with each step. I can always add more layers if necessary; in the heat, there is only so much you can take off. For instance, I learned through experience in West Virginia that I was much more successful and my body responded better when running ultramarathons in cooler weather rather than warmer weather. Whenever I was about to embark on a run in cold weather, I could be comforted by remembering the 15 degree temps and snow I ran through while trudging up the mountains at the Frozen Sasquatch, my first ultramarathon. Fortunately, on this first day of my run, I wouldn't have to deal with snow. I was especially grateful for that fact since I had two eager runners joining me that had never experienced the distance or duration that we'd be running.

We pulled away from Tiffany's mother's ranch at 6:15 a.m. Doug Veysey, Tiffany's high school business teacher and one of my running mates, was ready and waiting for us at his house in Myrtle Point. We pulled up to his house at 6:30, headlights shining right at his front door as he stepped out. I had given him fair warning the day before, just as I had shared with others who planned to run with me throughout my journey, that I was happy to have the company while running or happy to share a place to rest while we took our aid station stops along the way, but they would need to provide their own food and drink. We were doing everything we could to spend as little money as possible in order to maximize our donations at the end of the run. I was pleased to see Doug step into the illumination of our headlights with a cooler in one hand and a gallon jug in the other.

To say he was excited would be an understatement. He jumped into the RV, showing no signs of trepidation at what lay ahead. I was sitting in the RV trying to get into the proper frame of mind, but it was sobering to try to comprehend the magnitude of what I was about to set out to accomplish over the next 100 days with no scheduled days of rest. Seeing Doug bounce into the RV like a kid entering a candy store was exactly what I needed. His energy and encouragement erased any negative thoughts I may have had about the daunting task ahead. I would often feed off of the energy of others during some of the toughest days of this run.

We pulled away from Myrtle Point, which was to be the actual location of the finish of my run that day, and drove about 20 miles to the House of

Confusion, an old filling station on the route. It was there that we picked up Kelly Lusha, an old friend and Marine who served with me. Kelly had parked his car here and this would be his stopping point for the day. He wanted to knock out 19 miles with me but still have enough energy to drive five hours back to Portland. We figured the 19 miles, which would be about half of the day's mileage, would be a difficult but achievable challenge for him. We joked as we pulled into the parking lot that we all had to have been in a state of confusion at the House of Confusion in order to attempt what we were getting ready to do.

As Kelly stepped into the RV, Doug asked him, "Are you here to punish yourself, Kelly?"

"I'm here to support my buddy," Kelly responded. "That's *not* punishment."

It was at this moment that I again settled into a place by myself. The energy in the RV was electric; everyone was excited about the launch of this journey. I found myself, however, becoming very distant at that moment. I felt like I was in a quiet, isolated place. This is when it finally hit me that I was about to do something very few others had ever attempted, and far fewer had ever accomplished. *"Who am I to think I can do this?"* I questioned. *"What have I accomplished that makes me think I can do something so difficult?"*

I had never questioned what I was about to do all the way up to this point. Yet there I was, 10 miles away from the start of this journey, and I wanted to be 3,000 miles away, tucked comfortably under my blanket in my warm bed back in Morgantown, West Virginia. I briefly imagined how my life would be different this morning had I never had the idea to run across the country or had I never run that first marathon back in 2009.

In that moment, I snapped out of it and pushed the negative thoughts aside. I didn't want to let anyone sense the concern and fear that I was feeling. Instead of doubting myself, I gave myself a pep talk. *"There is no turning back now. I need to embrace what I am about to do and move forward, one step at a time."*

I was grateful for all of the support I had with me in the RV at that moment. My wife, who had sacrificed so much to be there for me, was not certain what life was about to bring, but nonetheless she was excited about the journey. My children, getting ready to embark on a journey of which the effect, I think, will take years for them to fully comprehend, were there to provide youthful joy and enthusiasm–part of which may have been due to the fact that they were missing the last two-plus months of school. My mom, who had been there for me through so many trying times from my childhood through adulthood, was in the co-pilot's seat and was ready to jump in and assist wherever possible for the time she was on the journey with us. I didn't realize it at the time, but the support of my family would be essential in these first two weeks, in particular. But those were also trying times for them because they would witness every hardship and wince of pain that I would endure as my body adjusted to the miles.

Kelly Lusha is a man I built a bond with going back to our days in the Marine Corps; we shared a kindred spirit about running outdoors and experiencing the many wonders of running various trails and routes as we entered our middle-aged years. Doug Veysey is teacher who had made a profound impact on my wife many years ago when she was in high school, and he had continued to inspire and challenge teenagers. Everyone in the RV, though, had their concerns for me, although I knew that they wouldn't express those. My wife had made up her mind long before we took off, and we had even discussed this fact, that there would be things we wouldn't share with one another on this trip, so as to not burden the other or cause me to worry about anything other than my mission. I'm sure I could have said we're going home, and Tiff would have driven the RV right back to West Virginia without making me feel like a failure. She had every reason to worry about me, but she also knew that this was something that I was capable of accomplishing, so she kept her concerns to herself. I couldn't think about those concerns right now, though. It was 7:30 a.m. and we were pulling into the parking lot at Sunset Bay State Park. The time had finally arrived!

As we stepped out of the motorhome, the sun began to make its appearance, slowly creeping above the horizon as though it was a groggy toddler not wanting to climb out of bed (a feeling I would share frequently during this journey). With the sunrays beginning to illuminate the rippling water of the Pacific Ocean, I began to get energized. The blue sky was fighting its way through the clouds, the air was crisp and fresh, and the energy of the spectators and well-wishers who had gathered at the starting area was electric.

Among those greeting us as we climbed out of the RV was my father-in-law, Tiff, and his wife, Jessie. They had been instrumental in getting the events that had already occurred, and were about to take place that upcoming week, set up for us. Tiff had arranged for the color guard from the Bandon VFW Post 3440 to be there that morning, giving us an appropriate sendoff. The vibrant reds and blues in the United States flag that rippled in the wind that the color guard displayed was a beautiful sight that morning.

Runners from the local Hash House Harrier club were there, as well as numerous other friends that had heard about the event or traveled there to be a part of it. Mariah Valencia, another Marine I served with, and her husband, Carlos, were also there. It meant a lot to me to have many of the friends I had acquired from my days in the Marine Corps there to support me. A local TV station (KCBY) was there to interview me and get footage of the beginning of my 100-day run.

I had planned for months to literally begin my run from the Pacific Ocean, so I had to sink my feet into the soft sand just beneath the surface of the water before I actually began running. I also wanted to begin this journey as a family, so all four of us removed our shoes and socks and walked out into the water. Considering it was 35 degrees and the wind was whipping off the water, it made for a frigid beginning to the kickoff event. But I wouldn't have wanted to start any other way, especially since beginning in the water would take on added significance, which at that time I wasn't aware of, by the conclusion of this endeavor.

After drying my feet off really well and applying a heavy layer of Gold Bond lotion before putting my socks and shoes back on, it was 8 a.m. and time for the kickoff to this run. I wrapped up my interview with KCBY and then Doug, Kelly and I took off. After nearly two full years of preparing myself mentally and physically for what at times seemed like an unthinkable challenge, I was finally taking the first steps of this run across the US! I tried not to get too caught up in thinking about the magnitude of what I was setting out to accomplish. One of the things I had told myself prior to the start of this run was to focus on one day at a time, placing one foot in front of the other, and maintaining positive forward motion.

We ran through a crowd of about 50 people who had gathered to see us off. Included in the group was a family who would write to me later, letting me know that they were walking by that morning and saw what we were doing and just wanted to encourage me as we took off. We passed by the color guard, which was stationed at the exit of the parking lot of Sunset Bay State Park, and as I always do, I saluted the American flag as I ran by it. We then headed out due north along the coastline of Coos Bay.

As we ran those first couple of miles, navigating our way into Coos Bay, Doug, Kelly and I kept our conversation to a minimum so that we could enjoy the beautiful views of the Oregon coastline. We were also constantly waving to people as they drove by, blowing their horns and giving us the thumbs up for encouragement. Of course my adrenaline was flowing, causing me to push the pace at times, so more than once Kelly had to remind me to slow down since I had to tackle nearly 40 miles that day.

### THE FIRST OF 500

When Tiffany and I discussed how we would handle each day of this journey as we were planning this trip, we decided that we would treat this run just like an ultramarathon. For safety's sake, I would run ahead for an hour to an hour and 15 minutes, and then Tiffany would bring the RV up to me to refill my fluids and provide food for me. That would give me the ability to move at my own pace, allowing my family to catch up and provide assistance as necessary. This also gave us the security that with them coming up from behind, in case something happened to me, they would come up on the issue, instead of sitting around waiting for me to arrive at a meeting point.

We knew that due to the numerous weather and terrain conditions we would encounter, my mileage would vary greatly with each stop, but we had learned so much from the ultramarathon running community over the past couple of years about nutrition and hydration patterns that it seemed like a solid plan. Knowing that I would have food and beverage constantly in my system to keep me nourished and hydrated as I ran, and knowing that my aid station workers (family) would be there every hour or so to care for me gave me a calm reassurance.

Five miles into our run the RV passed us and Tiffany parked it up ahead in the nearest spot she could find once she went by. She had already prepared my food and drinks for the stop while she was waiting to take off to catch up to us, so when we got to the RV, I only needed to take off my Fuel-Belt, hit the restroom, then come back out with my bottles filled with Gatorade and sandwiches ready to eat. One of the tricks I read about was to cut the crust off of the bread of my sandwiches because that would prevent some of the strain on my jaw from the constant chewing motions required when eating so much food each day. Even though the crust was usually soft on the bread, Tiff or the kids always cut them off for me. I downed a few peanut butter sandwich squares, washed it down with some orange Gatorade, and off we went on our second leg of this first day. After my first "aid station" stop of what would end up being more than 500 during the entire journey, I could tell this was going to be a plan that really worked well.

Each subsequent aid stop that I made, I was amazed to see how organized, even on this first day of the run, that my wife was. It put a smile on my face to see her taking such good care of me by having food and drinks ready and prepared for me, ensuring the kids were working on their homework and writing in their journals, and managing the RV and all of the other logistics of the trip. I knew she was a great manager and organizer, able to handle many things on her own. But I also knew this trip was going to place a lot of demands and stress on Tiffany, but she handled it like a champ.

During my brief periods in the RV to refuel, I was also encouraged and entertained watching our kids stay in communication with their classmates back in West Virginia. They would use our phones or iPad to give the kids in their classes details about the day. It was funny hearing Shayna relay stories about how her classmates thought it would take me 15 hours to run the 39 miles that day. It would have made for a very long trip if that was the case, but it was great seeing the kids take such in an interest in the run and also turning it into an educational experience.

## RUNNING TOWARD RETIREMENT

As we ran through Coos Bay, it was encouraging to witness a number of the locals out to cheer us on, waving flags or holding up signs they had made to encourage me. I took every opportunity to wave and shake the hands of all of the supporters as we ran by. Throughout my run across America, I made sure I told each supporter not only "thank you" for being out there to encourage me, but I also asked them to take the opportunity to tell a veteran "thank you" as well and let them know they are appreciated.

With Kelly and Doug by my side, we knocked out the first 12.5 miles in a little more than two hours. We were holding steady at around a 10-minute pace, which was about right where I knew I had to be running. Not only was this an ideal pace for me considering the mileage I would be logging, but Kelly had a long run coming up the following weekend, and I didn't want him to push it too hard since he was just getting into distance running. Doug had a marathon coming up soon, so it was also important for him to ensure that he didn't get too fatigued or, worse yet, injured. I was honored that both Doug and Kelly agreed to join me because I knew that asking them to run even a portion of the 39.2 miles that day with me was asking them to make a major commitment and sacrifice.

"When you asked me and I realized you were raising money for injured veterans, I immediately said yes," Doug later told me. "But at that time I didn't even know how far I was going to be running with you. Once I found out, I increased my training schedule to prepare for this adventure and this event really opened my eyes to what commitment, dedication and support can do for a cause."

In fact, Doug shared with me both during the run on this day and months later that he was really able to sort through some things in his head during the run that he had been contemplating regarding the future direction of his life.

"As the miles ticked off when we were running, it got me thinking about my future and what I wanted to do down the road," Doug said. "I had taught school for 31 years and retirement had crossed my mind. During that run, I thought about this in-depth, weighing my options. Running the open roads allows you to open your mind and really think about what may be best for you and that is what I did.

"Because of you and my experience during that first day of your run across America, I decided to retire in June 2012. Now I am free to help other causes in my community. I want to thank you, Jamie, for an amazing experience and for giving me the chance to be a part of your adventure and allowing me the opportunity to look at my future with a clear head."

It was a great feeling to learn that our day spent together on the road gave him the push he needed to follow where his heart was leading him.

## PROMOTING THE CAUSE

Since my reason for doing this run was to raise awareness and funds for organizations that assist veterans, I cherished every opportunity to speak to the news media about my run and the mission. When reporters would call me or chase me down along the road during a run, even if it meant stopping for 10-15 minutes to talk to them about the run, I would always oblige. At times stopping to talk took me out of my rhythm a little bit, but in the grand scheme of things, I realized that falling 10-15 minutes off my pace usually didn't matter that much. I had 100 days–or 2,400 hours–to finish this run. The veterans were far more important than keeping to a strict schedule so I never concerned myself with finishing my run a few minutes later or missing out on a few minutes of sleep here and there.

On this first day of the run, I was approached by a reporter from the local newspaper in Coos Bay as we ran through town. We allowed them to take pictures and get a few quotes from me about the trip. Any chance I had to share the story of what we were doing also enabled me to give thanks and attention to the veterans that this run was all about. After the interview, we made our way to the House of Confusion, which was a little more than 19 miles into the run. This is where Kelly had left his car, and I was extremely proud of him that he had run almost the entire 19 miles, taking just a short break to ride in the motorhome and rest his legs. His will to push through and run a distance that he hadn't run before was so inspiring to me. It was bittersweet to say goodbye to Kelly after having spent only a short time with him, but the time we had together was special.

While we were stopped, I did an interview with a radio station back in West Virginia. As I was preparing to head out on the next leg of the run, a family that had seen the wrap on our RV advertising my Run for Wounded Warriors approached us, introduced themselves and asked for more information about what we were doing. I explained to them that I was running across America to raise money for wounded veterans.

"I bet you're excited to be finishing up aren't you?" asked the gentleman after taking a photo of me with his grandkids, obviously thinking I was finishing, not starting, on the West coast.

"I wish I was wrapping this thing up!" I laughed. The whole crew got a good laugh out of that, and the family just stared at me in disbelief as we ran off.

Doug and I had a little more than 20 miles to go to wrap the day up and make our way into Myrtle Point, so off we went, running against traffic. But here in Oregon we not only had to be aware of cars and trucks, but also log trucks hauling huge loads. It was then that I realized why Tiffany would laugh whenever she saw a log truck in West Virginia loaded with tiny "toothpicks," as she referred to them. The one smell I will remember forever from this trip is the strong odor of freshly cut logs as the trucks blew by us. Every log truck that barreled past forced me to lower my head to keep my hat from blowing off my head. But as the trucks blew past, the scent of those logs burned through my nostrils and almost seemed to sharpen my awareness of everything else around me. I also had to deal with the little shards of bark or small limbs and needles that seemed to jump off the trucks and onto me, but after the first couple of experiences getting pelted with wood, I quickly learned to watch out for debris.

We also had to deal with the lack of a shoulder along the road at times through the last half of this run. As we continued to tick off the miles, the road at times seemed to close in on us. Going around some of the turns and curves, the hillside bumped right against the white line on the side of the road. We had to pay close attention while running through those sections, turning our heads to listen for oncoming traffic when we couldn't see it because of the blind left hand turns we ran into.

Throughout the day, after an initial rise in temperature, it steadily began to drop as the number of clouds increased and the wind began to come at us in bursts. Sometimes the clouds would send a few sprinkles down on us, but 35.6 miles into the run, with just four miles to go, the wind really picked up and the rain came down a bit harder. Wet, tired and hungry, we climbed into the RV for our final aid stop and the aroma of warm macaroni and cheese really energized me. Our legs were definitely feeling the effects of pounding the pavement for the past 6 ½ hours, but Doug and I only a few more miles to go. Doug was really pushing himself at this point, running several miles longer than any distance he had ever previously gone. But the conversations we shared and the encouragement we offered each other really helped us both get through the miles.

As we approached the end point of the first day, a number of residents in Myrtle Point came out to cheer us on and congratulate us on completing our first day. Doug and I exchanged hugs and congratulations on knocking out nearly 40 miles together. I didn't have much down time immediately after finishing the run, however. After dropping Doug off at his home, we had to get to the Veteran's Memorial in Myrtle Point at 7 p.m. for a ceremony they had organized. These opportunities to let local veterans in the towns I was passing through know how much I appreciated them were some of my most cherished memories of the entire journey.

I was so honored and humbled to be standing there in front of the memorial with veterans from the Myrtle Point VFW Post 2928, posing with them for photographs. The stories they shared with me about the battles they participated in, friends who never returned home from battle and the long periods of time they were away from their families, not knowing if they'd ever see their loved ones again, made me appreciate even more the foundation the older veterans had laid for veterans from my generation. What was even more amazing to me was the fact that they all spoke of their service with great pride, especially considering how they were greeted when they returned home from Vietnam and other conflicts. Our society was not kind to these men and women, yet here they stood, proud to have served and unabashedly expressing their love for their country.

After that ceremony we went to my mother-in-law's house to grab some dinner and get me off my feet. I knew I needed to allow not only my body to recover, but also my mind. I still had plenty of adrenaline from the day's events, so it was difficult to get some quality rest. But I had 33 miles staring at me the next morning, with an increase in elevation from the 100 we were currently at to just over 1,000 by the end of the day. I fell asleep that night with a smile on my face, satisfied that the first day had been a success and pleased with the amount of encouragement and support that I had received in the first 24 hours of this 100-day journey.

# 5 | One Day at a Time

Unlike the opening day, which included festivities and fellow runners accompanying me, I knew Day 2 was going to be relatively uneventful. I was pleased that I felt very little muscle fatigue or soreness that morning as I slipped on my No. 2 pair of running shoes. (I numbered each of my 10 pairs of shoes using a small piece of tape on the shoestrings and rotated them daily so the tread would wear evenly and I would have a consistent feel when running in each pair. This also prevented me from having to break in a new pair of shoes every few weeks.) I headed out on the open road and was accompanied only by the steady drops of rain. It didn't take long for me to find some inspiration. About three miles into the run, I witnessed a beautiful bald eagle flying overhead. The majestic beauty and grace it displayed as it soared along the mountaintops was symbolic of America's freedom. A little further into the run, there was a herd of elk along the roadside, which while not really inspirational, was still an interesting sight to behold and it particularly excited our kids.

Shayna used Skype to communicate with her classmates and she was able to share some views of the gorgeous mountains, which seemed overwhelming in size to the children in comparison to the mountains we have in West Virginia. I was even able to chat with the class for a couple of minutes during a stop, which seemed to excite the kids while also lifting my spirits since I enjoy the opportunity to inspire others, especially children.

My family's spirits were also lifted later that day. Typically when a police officer pulls up behind you, it means you are in trouble. But today the officer who pulled up behind the RV while my family was stopped on the side of the road and I was out running wasn't there to issue a citation, he was there to offer words of encouragement. A.C. "Rock" Rakoski is the chief of police for the Myrtle Point Police Department and is a retired Marine Corps 1st Sergeant. He spoke with Tiffany, briefly sharing his experience in the Marines before his retirement from the military in 2002 after 20 years of service. "I read about your run in the local newspaper," he told her. "I was hoping I'd be able to find your support vehicle, say hi and show you my support." It was great for Tiffany to receive his words of encouragement and later I was equally inspired when she relayed the story to me.

I felt really good through the run that day and enjoyed the opportunity to see the country on foot, one step at a time, giving me a view of America unlike anything I had ever experienced. A reporter from KMTR in Roseburg, Oregon, caught up with me about 19 miles into the run that day. The interview began with him asking me, "Did you just get started today? You don't seem too winded." I chuckled at the reaction on his face when I told him I was almost 20 miles into the run.

I had some climbs to tackle during the last portion of the day's run as I made my way toward Camas Valley. At one point, the climb was so brutal that I pulled my hat down over my eyes, kept my focus about five feet in front of me and plowed ahead. I finally took the opportunity to lift my hat and head and look back at the 500 feet in elevation that I had climbed over the past mile. Viewing the portion of the climb I had just conquered gave me a sense of accomplishment and awe but also a realization that the hill was nothing compared to what awaited me in the coming days. I was grateful that I had trained myself to focus on putting one foot in front of the other rather than getting too caught up in looking at the challenges ahead of me. The peak of the climb also offered an amazing view of the mountains and landscape below. After only two days on the road, this had already become a life-changing experience for me.

## SETTING THE TONE

I still felt good when I woke up the morning of Day 3, but I had no idea that this day would end up defining my entire journey. Just as it had been 24 hours earlier, it was a rainy and damp morning. The fog was beginning to lift over the mountains in Camas Valley, so I suggested that Tiffany spend some time taking photographs of the landscape while I was out on the first leg of my run. I tried to always keep in mind that my wife and kids were making a huge sacrifice in accompanying and assisting me with the run, so they deserved to take any chance they had to get out of the motorhome and do things they enjoyed. My wife is passionate about photography and is extremely talented. I am very grateful that she was able to so skillfully visually document our trip. In fact, for various reasons, the experiences of our journey across America reignited her passion for photography and allowed her to focus more time on growing her photography business once we returned home.

Early on in my run that day, as I made my way through a small community called Ten Mile, a motorist passing by slowed down and told me to have a safe journey to Maryland. He must have seen the news clip from KMTR the day before. I ran by a small gas station in town, and a guy walked out of the station applauding, wishing me well and thanking me for what I was doing. More people stopped and spoke to Tiff and the crew in the RV as I was out running, even making small donations as they heard more details about the purpose for my run. That not only provided encouragement for me as my family relayed these stories to me when I would stop for food and drinks, but I know it was also encouraging to my crew. No matter how difficult this run would be, experiences like those were what I learned to rely on to help me push through anything I faced.

The clouds began to break as I made my way into Winston, Oregon, where Tiffany and I stopped to get a picture of me with the Winston Wildlife Safari Cheetah statue. I made the comment that I was out "cougar hunting," which drew a small chuckle from Tiffany. Thankfully I have a wife who, if not appreciates, can at least tolerate my sense of humor and wise cracks. Later, my son joined me out on the road to run along with me. The kids wanted to be able to run with me from time to time so they could get a sense of what I was doing all day while they were in the motorhome. While this was only the third day of the run, we had already driven five straight days to get to Oregon, so the kids were already wanting to get out of the RV as often as possible. We would later joke that instead of traveling across the country in an RV, we were "living in a box on wheels." It certainly gave us an opportunity to literally get close together as a family, as well as get on each other's nerves.

## A CHANCE TO SAY 'THANK YOU'

After my running was wrapped up I had a couple of newspaper and TV interviews, and then we had a scheduled visit to the VA hospital in Roseburg, Oregon. This caused us to adjust my route on the fly that day so that we would come into the hospital from the opposite side to an easier and more accessible entrance. It was funny, because my wife and I received several phone calls and emails from concerned people who were following me via the MyAthlete Live online tracker. People also expressed their concern with Twitter and Facebook posts. There was a map showing my route, and since we had adjusted our course it looked to those following me online that I unknowingly took a wrong turn and had veered off course. It not only provided us with some laughs, but also made me aware that there were many people across the country who were following my progress in real time. I just hope they didn't spend too much time watching the virtual Jamie Summerlin move slowly across the map on their computer screens when they should have been working!

Tiffany's dad worked with Carrie Boothe, the public affairs officer at the VA hospital, to coordinate our visit. As we entered the entrance to the campus we were greeted by a policeman who was also a veteran of the Marine Corps. It felt great to hear him say how proud he was of us for undertaking this journey and raising funds for veteran-focused organizations. "I know your visit here is going to be so uplifting to the patients," he said.

The officer got in his police cruiser to lead my escort to the hospital entrance, and I was followed by my family in the RV. As I wound through the campus and made the turn leading to the front of the hospital, the scene I witnessed was simply overwhelming. Along the roadway, standing on the sidewalk and sitting on the lawn, were about 100 staff and patients, cheering and clapping for me and holding up signs that they had made to greet me. I caught a glimpse of several American flags that were waving in the air, including one extremely large flag flapping atop a flag pole, and I saluted each one.

It was difficult for me to look too closely at the faces in the crowd because I had tears welling up in my eyes and I was trying to retain my composure. The primary purpose of this journey was to honor and say thanks to the brave men and women that I considered my heroes, yet there they were lined up and giving me applause. It was a very humbling and emotional experience. As we got to the end of the parking lot, just past the hospital buildings, the police officer climbed out of his car, walked up to me with a huge smile on his face and as tears streamed down my cheeks he said with a chuckle, "Suck it up, Marine."

Tiffany and I were the only ones from my family who received clearance to enter the hospital, so after I took a moment to compose myself we joined Carrie and she escorted us through the corridors and into a meeting room, where I would be speaking to patients and staff. As soon as the room became visible, I saw the patients—a group diverse in both age and ethnicity—sitting in plastic chairs that formed a semi-circle in the middle of the room. But when I walked into the room, the patients and staff all got out of their chairs and gave me a standing ovation. So much for composing myself! I tried not to break down in front of everyone, but it was difficult not to since I was so humbled that these veterans were displaying appreciation toward me when it should have been the other way around.

I opened up my talk with one statement that I stuck to during this journey—one that I emphatically shared with people I met along the way and news outlets that interviewed me. As my eyes scanned the room, looking at these injured veterans, I told them, "This run is about you." In front of me were men and women who had honorably served our country and had sacrificed in so many different ways. Each of these men and women had their own personal stories and experiences that they could share. While each experience is unique, we could all understand and relate to what the veterans in the hospital had, were and would continue to endure. Many in the room had been scarred both physically and mentally, had dealt with the different challenges we face in the military lifestyle and had been forced to learn how to cope with the hand they had been dealt. I told them that I had been very fortunate to exit the military with both my physical and mental capacities intact. They laughed, though, when I tried to convince them that someone running nearly 3,500 miles across the country in 100 days was not crazy.

After my talk I answered tons of questions about how I was coping with the challenges of the run, how long my training had been and what I most looked forward to.

"Are you looking forward to getting back to your home state?"

"Are you excited about making it to the ocean in 97 days?"

"Do you look ahead at some of the challenging routes that you will have to run in the days ahead?"

"I can't," was my response. "I have to stay focused on the now. I have to just take each day as it comes and remain completely focused on getting through that day, keeping alert and mindful of everything around me. Let tomorrow worry about tomorrow."

"That's exactly what I have to do," stated one of the patients. "I am excited about waking up each morning, and looking forward to getting through another day. I just hope when I lay my head down at night I can wake up to witness tomorrow. I know that I've got to live one day at a time."

This really hit home with me and allowed me to realize that my journey across America and life's daily journey for wounded veterans paralleled in a way. Neither of us can look too far ahead. It was a beautiful moment that became burned in my memory and one that I frequently recalled for motivational purposes throughout the rest of my run. I often replayed in my head a lot of the things the veterans told me that day. It always helped to give me a morale boost.

"I don't know any of you personally," I said as I looked around the room while wrapping up our visit, "but I love each and every one of you like you were my brother or sister, because you are as far as I'm concerned. You wore that uniform with pride, served this great country without question and now that you need assistance in dealing with whatever challenges you may face in life now, I want you each to know that there are a lot of us that care about you. We want you to get better; we want you to succeed. We are grateful for everything you have done for us, and where there are gaps that need to be filled from the government programs that are out there, understand that there are people and organizations that want to help you."

We left the hospital after spending about an hour inside with the patients. As we strolled down the halls and back outside toward the RV, I was filled with pride—but not in an arrogant manner—about what I was doing. I was also humbled by the welcome and support that these veterans and the VA hospital staff gave to us because these were the folks I was doing this run for.

A couple of days later, my wife received a phone call from Carrie, who wanted to give us some feedback. One of the things she shared with Tiffany, who later shared it with me, enabled me to push through some of the toughest challenges I would face on this run, and lift me up whenever I truly needed some encouragement. I had the opportunity to talk one-on-one with a few of the patients in the hospital during my time there, and was able to personally let them know that I was taking each step for them. I wanted them to know that my goal was to make sure the rest of the world understood how special these servicemen and women were. After our visit, one of the men I talked to shared something with the public affairs officer that I will never forget.

"It was the first time I ever felt like someone outside of these hospital walls really cared about me," he told her.

I could have ended my journey right then and there. We were only on Day 5 of this run, and we were already able to have a profound impact on some veterans. I knew right then that what we were doing was worth all of the effort that had gone into this trip. No matter what challenges I would face on the remainder of the run, nothing would stop me from completing what we had set out to do.

# 6 | The Naked Truth

I was informed before I embarked on the trip that not only would I witness some of this country's great natural beauty, but I would also see some of the peculiar people that make up America's great melting pot. It didn't take long for that to happen.

After enjoying a great free dinner and complimentary room courtesy of the owners at the beautiful Steamboat Inn along the North Umpqua River, whose roaring waters lulled us to sleep the previous night, Day 5 was off to a relatively uneventful start. The rain was pouring down during the first 15 miles, but as I began to climb the mountain through the verdant Umpqua National Forest, the air became colder and the snow drifts from the previous week's snow were still piled high along the road, which shifted back and forth in tight S-curves, winding its way up to Diamond Lake. The air was so brisk that I was expecting the precipitation to turn from rain to snow at any moment.

As I started up the climb, Tiffany drove past me to make her way to our next aid station stop, ringing the cowbell as she drove by. I also could hear the sounds of engines and heavy equipment over the embankment to my left, where a road led to a construction site on the side of the mountain. Along that road, I noticed a man and his dog walking in the same direction that I was.

As Tiff pulled over, he and I made our way to the RV at about the same time. The man's dog stood only about 10 inches off the ground, probably didn't weigh more than 10 pounds and had a bark to match his diminutive stature. The dog started toward me, yipping with all its might, and jumped over a puddle of water. But the dog didn't quite make it, nor did he realize how deep or wide the puddle was. I actually laughed out loud when the dog landed in the puddle and sank below the surface of the water. As the dog resurfaced, I tried to act concerned, but the whole scene made me laugh that much harder. The owner checked on his pooch and then asked us if he could catch a ride up to Toketee Falls just a few miles up the road. It was pouring rain at this point, and he was just as soaked as I was, but the first thought that went through my mind was to ensure the safety of my family—my wife, our two children and my mother. As the man stood there in front of me wearing a drenched pullover hooded sweatshirt and jeans, I wanted to help him out, but something made me say no. I also wanted to keep our RV from smelling like a wet dog, so I politely declined his request. We watched from the RV as the man and his four-legged companion marched on up the mountain.

I changed into some dryer and warmer clothes during this aid stop, and then began making my way up the mountain towards Diamond Lake. A mile or so up the road I caught up with the stranger and his dog, passed them and wished him well. A couple of minutes later, I heard footsteps running behind me, so I turned around quickly and was startled to see him running up the road, now without his grey hooded sweatshirt, which had probably absorbed so much rain that I figured it had just been weighing him down. Now shirtless, he was making his way up the mountain at a pretty rapid pace.

"Hey man," I said to him. After he reciprocated my greeting, I told him, "You are going to catch a cold running like that out here." He shrugged his shoulders and kept on moving up the mountain, now in just a pair of rain soaked jeans and work boots, with his dog running right alongside him.

Over the next quarter mile, he continued to pick up his pace, and made his way around the mountainside without slowing down one bit. At this point, however, I guess he decided his boots were slowing him down, so he stopped, pulled his brown work boots off, and I was taken aback as he tossed those, along with his socks, down the mountain into the woods. I have run with a number of barefoot runners over the past couple of years, so I just blew it off and watched him now take off flying up the hillside. As I rounded a corner where I could see him again, I noticed he was slowing down again before coming to a complete stop. It was at this point that the man's bizarre actions became even stranger.

I slowed to a walk as I watched him take his jeans off, and with what looked like a move from an Olympic shot putt gold medalist, he tossed his pants into the woods. So now he was down to only his blue and white polka dotted boxers in the cold, pouring rain! I wasn't sure what to make of it, but I kept my silence and watched him run rapidly up the road. I also wasn't sure how far he would go with the undressing, and I hoped he had reached his limit. As he ran off around a bend in the road, I could not help but laugh at the situation, thinking to myself, *"I hope that's as far as he goes, but man, what a great story this will be."* But as I came around the start of the curve, there, lying in the middle of the road, right in front of me, were his blue and white polka dotted boxers. I stopped dead in my tracks and shook my head in disbelief. *"These can't be his,"* I thought to myself. But what were the odds of another pair of boxers exactly like the ones he had been wearing lying there in the road?

As I continued to round the corner, I saw him in his birthday suit, running naked up the road in the rain! And there was his loyal dog, still by his side, running right along with him without a care in the world. I just laughed, thought to myself, *"Well, it is Oregon,"* and let him go on. I didn't want to slow my run up any, but I also wanted to keep a good distance between us. As cars and trucks came down the mountain past him, they would slow down, and as they approached me, I just threw my hands in the air and shrugged, trying my best to make it obvious that he was not with me. The faces of the drivers varied from laughter to incredulous disbelief. I knew exactly how they all felt.

He eventually started walking and I caught up to him and his wet dog. At that point I'm not certain who was panting more, the man or his dog. Fortunately, they were still on the other side of the road. I couldn't bite my tongue any longer. "You're going to catch pneumonia," I shouted, both as an admonition and a friendly warning. After I got about a half mile ahead of him, I glanced back over my shoulder in time to see the pale-skinned stranger and his dog heading to the left down the road to the hot springs to which he had initially requested a ride. During that last half-mile stretch before he veered off the road, several cars drove toward me from the opposite direction. All I could do was wave and laugh at the thought of the sight those drivers were soon to witness!

During this whole excursion up the mountain, I hoped that my family would catch up with me and that my wife would have her camera ready in order to capture the tale, but it was not to be. When she did catch up to me, she told me a story about a passerby who stopped by the RV, marched up to the door with a purpose and banged on it until she opened it.

"Is it normal for one of your guys to be running up the road without a stitch of clothes on?" he asked.

*"Oh my God,"* she thought to herself. *"We're five days into the run, and Jamie's already lost it."*

"My husband is wearing an orange jacket," she told the stranger.

"Oh, we saw that guy running. But there was another guy who was completely naked running up the mountain. With a dog."

"That guy's not with us," she said, breathing a sigh of relief.

"OK, we just wanted to make sure!"

At this point, Tiffany started up the mountain after me but she was too late to capture the stranger in all his glory. I relayed the story to a dumbfounded crew, who wasn't sure whether to laugh or shake their heads as I tried to keep my composure while telling the tale. A little while later, as we were parked for another aid stop, a man pulled over in front of the RV and asked if we had seen the naked stranger. They told us that a number of people were out looking for him. They had found his car (which we had unknowingly seen earlier that day) along the side of the road with a couple of empty pill bottles inside, and nearby they found his keys, wallet and cell phone tossed into the woods. If they had looked a little further down the road, they would have found his clothes, too.

The men who were out looking for the naked man became very interested in our mission. The older gentleman was a farmer who was a throat cancer survivor. He became very emotional as we told him why I was running. He offered to help out any way he could by taking wounded warriors out on guided hunts on his property. It was a great example of the many people we would meet on the journey who expressed their desire to honor and support our veterans in whatever way they could.

## RUNNING TOWARD RECOVERY

While the naked man's roadside striptease provided me with some humor, his actions led me to believe that he was suffering from stress or was dealing with some mental issues or addiction. That got me to thinking about our veterans who are commonly affected by mental anguish and stress, commonly referred to as post-traumatic stress disorder (PTSD). Whenever mentioning that my desire with this run was to help wounded veterans, the images that typically came to people's minds were soldiers suffering from ailments such as lost limbs or physical scars that are visible. But the mental anguish many veterans experience can often be just as painful and difficult to recover from.

The U.S. Department of Veterans Affairs estimated that 20 percent of the veterans returning from serving in Iraq suffer from PTSD. In my home state of West Virginia, which has an extremely high participation rate in the military per capita, the percentage of veterans suffering from PTSD is even greater. Dr. Joseph Scotti, a professor of psychology at West Virginia University, conducted research that revealed that for West Virginia veterans who have recently returned home from Afghanistan or Iraq, nearly 50 percent show signs of suffering from PTSD, yet only 15-20 percent seek treatment for their mental health.

Richard "Brett" Simpson is someone who not only overcame his own struggles after serving in the military, but now helps fellow veterans deal with the same issues that he endured. Brett, a 2000 graduate of the United States Military Academy at West Point, spent his entire life after high school serving his country whenever and wherever he was needed.

Brett spent more than a decade in the military in various leadership positions. But the only life he knew was gone when he was honorably service-connected medically retired in 2011 as a Major in the U.S. Army after undergoing a lengthy process with the Medical Evaluation Board and a brief time in the Warrior Transition Unit in northern Virginia.

Brett always planned on making the Army his only career until retirement. Yet, still in his early adulthood, those plans had to change.

"Making the transition from military life to civilian was extremely difficult and frustrating," Brett told me months after the conclusion of my run across the US. "I served a non-profit, helping veterans, but the work was sporadic. Leaving behind a way of life where your day is consumed with duties, it was extremely difficult for me to have so much free time. I didn't know what to do with myself and the lack of structure, regimen and certainty in my life was driving me nuts. I couldn't find solace or peace within myself, yet at the same time, I knew I wasn't helpless. I could think, move, walk and, as I eventually learned, run."

Brett stumbled upon a story about my run across America. Much like everyone else who first heard about my run, he initially thought I was crazy. But when he learned more about the purpose of the mission, he was intrigued that I was able to take something I was passionate about–running–and use it to make a difference for veterans.

He admitted to despising running, "but looking to fill a void, and fill time in my day, I decided to give it a try, because that's one of the things I knew I could do. What I found was that running, or any type of physical activity, was helping my sense of awareness, focus and mindfulness while also getting me in better physical shape than I had been in a long time.

"Above all, however, running made me feel good about myself," Brett continued. "I finally looked forward to getting up in the morning and seeing if I was going to get my personal best time, be able to run farther without feeling fatigued or be able to run eight miles instead of six. Running became a passion. I began running at least five times a week. I was feeling better, thinking more clearly, enjoying life again and recognizing things about myself and my surroundings that I hadn't noticed in a long time."

Brett followed my progress daily via Twitter or Facebook and as I progressed across America, he, too, began to push himself further than he previously thought possible.

"Seeing how you were progressing provided motivation for me in my personal journey," Brett told me. "It made me realize that pushing myself through what seemed to be the impossible was, in fact, possible."

Now that Brett had found a new purpose as a civilian, he began to thrive in his position as program manager of Operation Welcome Home, a non-profit organization that assists veterans in north-central West Virginia. Through that organization, he helped spread the word to fellow veterans of just how therapeutic exercise can be as they attempt to acclimate themselves to a different lifestyle. Brett's message to all who will listen is simple.

"There are forms of physical fitness that are beneficial and suitable for veterans who have suffered short- or long-term physical injuries, including amputations, for those who are battling PTSD and for veterans dealing with just about anything else imaginable," Brett says. "Wheelchair sports, water aerobics and specialized treadmills are just some of the ways veterans can remain physically active and regain their sense of self-worth.

"The bottom line is that while times may seem tough or even hopeless, they are never too tough to fight through. Veterans are tough enough to fight through anything. The first step, literally, is to get up and move. I firmly believe that physical activity can make all the difference in the world for those going through some of the same struggles that I faced. And the great thing is that it's not something that has to be overcome alone. There are organizations to assist veterans, there are plenty of fellow veterans who are trying to overcome similar challenges and there are 'battle buddies' who can help those in need take that first step toward recovery."

## MILE HIGH CLUB

Thinking about the naked man provided me with some giggles as I continued to climb up the mountain. But this was no normal climb. When I read about Marshall Ulrich's journey across America, when he attempted to break the record for the fewest days needed to make the trek, I remembered that he had specifically mapped out the journey to include no climbs of more than 1,000 feet in a single day. I started this day at just over 1,000 feet in elevation and would wrap up at just over 5,200 feet.

*"What in the world was I thinking when I OK'd this route?"*

The rain continued to pour, the temperature continued to drop and the road continued to ascend up the mountain. I was also entering a stretch where there were sizeable snow drifts. It was not an enjoyable experience and I wanted desperately to get out of my wet clothes, get off this steep mountain and get off my feet, so I just continued to push onward and upward. I had no way to simulate this type of climb back home, even in the mountains of West Virginia, because the highest elevation in the region was 4,800 feet and I would climb that in about 25 miles of running this day.

I think being distracted by the naked guy diverted my focus from the fact that I needed to make sure I was stretching my legs out and not climbing while running on my toes all day. By the time I finally climbed to the top of the mountain and came over the last ridge, I could see the RV waiting for me and I just lost it. The tears were streaming down my face not only because I was happy to have finished this grueling climb, but also because I had developed a very sharp pain in my left shin. With every step that I took the last portion of that climb, I felt a twinge of pain in my shin that reminded me of some of the worst shin splints I had experienced when I first started distance running.

I was hoping once I finished the run that day, got off my feet and warmed up that the pain would subside. But as the evening progressed, my leg continued to tighten up and the pain grew worse. Little did I know just how bad it would get.

***Left to right from top:*** My football glory days, 1985 • U.S. Marine Corps bootcamp graduation, 1990 • Tiffany and I ready for the Marine Corps Ball, 1995 • My mom and I celebrating my 3:31 finish, Richmond Marathon, 2009 • Trying to stay cool during the Burning River 100 Mile Endurance Run, 2011

Day 1, starting with my feet in the Pacific Ocean, with Nick and Shayna by my side • Saluting Old Glory as I make my way to the Roseburg VA Hospital • Saying thanks to the Myrtle Point, Oregon VFW at the end of Day 1

The end of Day 5, approaching Diamond Lake, Oregon • An inspiring visit from World War II veteran Frank Vaughn, Lakeview, Oregon • Handling the twists and turns as I make my way out of Oregon into Nevada • Standing at the top of Doherty Slide, Oregon

Our dinner in the middle of the Salt Flats, Utah • Running with Shayna and Nick on the Salt Flats • Dirt roads, pastures and foot paths were sometimes the only available way to travel

At the top of Emigration Canyon, Utah • Celebrating the first 1,000 miles, Echo Canyon, Utah

One of many tanker trucks that kicked up dirt and rocks, Colorado • Pictured with Captain Gaylon Grippin (second from right) in Sterling, Colorado • Posing with some Mother's Day Parade participants in Imperial, Nebraska

Meeting fellow USA crosser "Joe on a Bike" in Kansas • Celebrating our 16th wedding anniversary, Kansas • A stray dog joined Shawnee McClanahan and me in Missouri

Fellow Hash House Harrier Heather Auman rode alongside me outside of Lexington, Kentucky • Doing an interview with Chris Lawrence of WCHS in Charleston, West Virginia • Arriving at the West Virginia State Capitol in Charleston with members of the Tallman Track Club

# 7 | Snap, Crackle, Pop

**M**any times during our trip across the country we received gracious gestures such as a free meal, a complimentary spot at an RV park or a free room in a hotel. The owner at Diamond Lake Resort, Steve Koch, was just one of many to do so. He provided both a free meal and accommodations. The hospitality was appreciated, but because of the pain in my shin I got a horrible night's sleep. I'm sure there had been many previous sleepless nights in that honeymoon suite, but for a different reason than why I didn't sleep.

When I got up the next morning, my shin was still in severe pain and it was also extremely swollen. The first thought that went through my head was that I had suffered a stress fracture. In all of the research I had done about people who had attempted but failed to run across the country, many of them had to drop out after suffering some sort of stress fracture. I tested what my limits were, gingerly walking around inside the room, but I quickly realized that there was no way I could run.

Before we embarked on the trip, Tiffany and I had agreed that if I ever needed to take some extra time through the day to log my miles that would be fine. I wasn't out to break the crossing record, and except for a few events that were scheduled in the first couple of weeks, I didn't really have an agenda that I needed to stick to. So before I stepped outside that morning I told my family that I would just walk off the miles, and jog when I could, so that I could continue moving forward.

We opened the door up and were greeted with an almost whiteout condition outside. A snowstorm had come through the night before, and the snow was continuing to pile up. The snowdrifts alongside the road were literally higher than our RV, and the snow was not letting up at all. It was snowing so hard that I couldn't even see a quarter of a mile in front of me. The conditions were such that even if I was healthy I wouldn't be doing much running that day because I would have to be very careful out on the roads. Tiffany headed up the road in the RV but only made it about a mile before she pulled over. As I came up to the RV I saw my wife lying underneath the motorhome putting the snow chains that we had just purchased the day before on the tires. She was proving once again why I sometimes call her Superwoman.

I continued to push through in the snow, and the pain grew worse and worse with each step. But I knew that I could not stop moving forward. Typically it had taken me about 6-8 hours to complete my daily miles. But over these next four days, I was out on the road 12-13 hours each day and I was still beginning to fall well behind our planned pace. I just couldn't manage anything more than three miles per hour. Tiffany's sister Lesley and brother-in-law Rich drove down from Washington state to join us during this stint, along with their two children, Jonathan and MacKenzie. I was disappointed that they had to see me laboring and in so much pain. In fact, a couple of times they saw me stop moving and bend down, stooping over along the side of the road. They thought I was folding over in pain, when in reality I was stuffing packed snow up into the lower portion of the left leg of my cold gear running pants. At that point I was attempting anything I could to ice my leg and try to reduce the swelling in my shin.

We had a few events going on in the Klamath Falls area that had been scheduled long before our arrival, so the logistics and driving plans we had were quickly thrown out the window. The Linkville Lopers, a running club in Klamath Falls, and the Rip City Rider motorcycle club had organized a run through Klamath Falls for my arrival, so I had to cut short my day to drive in to make it to the event. The group run was a little more than seven miles, and even though adrenaline was pushing me through, the pain continued to worsen in my shin. A number of veterans were among the group of runners and I knew I couldn't let them down by slowing down or walking. With each story they shared with me about their friends who were wounded or killed in battle, I was motivated to press on. I knew that my pain was temporary, while the physical and emotional pain many veterans and their families experience is long-term.

Over the next few days, the pain continued to prevent me from doing much running at all. In fact, I used walking sticks for a few days, which helped me quite a bit. But it also prevented me from being able to wave at every car that drove past, which is something I enjoyed doing. Less than two weeks into this 100-day run I was already 28 miles—or nearly one full day—behind schedule. The snow also wasn't letting up much, and because of some events that were scheduled based on our projected pace, we had to drive the motorhome seemingly all over creation to get me up ahead to appear at an event, and then back to where I had left off. Literally hundreds of extra miles were driven in the RV to escort me back and forth in order to attend these events and then get me back to my spot on the route. This was not only frustrating and time consuming, but it also put a dent in our budget since an RV goes through gas like a family with a newborn goes through diapers. But one thing I absolutely would not do was cheat the mileage, so we always made certain that I began running right where I had previously stopped.

During this time of commuting to events we were fortunate that some of Tiffany's dad's friends allowed us to stay in their homes and attempt to nurse my leg back to health. The first night we arrived in the Klamath Falls area, we stayed at Mike and Sophia Homfeld's home and I was able to soak in a bathtub with Epsom salt for an hour. The next couple of nights, Dan and Cindy Kinsman took great care of us, providing warm beds, good food and a hot tub for me to use as I tried to work the knots out of my leg. Unfortunately, I allowed the pain and frustration of my injury to affect my disposition during these trying days, and it not only led my family and friends to worry about me, but it also made me unpleasant to be around at times. It wasn't until after the run was complete in July that Tiffany and I discussed this period of the trip, but she told me afterwards that it was at this point that she was just waiting for me to say the words, "I quit."

I've been asked many times since I finished if there was ever a point when I wanted to quit and give up my dream. But at no point, even when I was dealing with the intense pain in my leg, did I ever have a desire to quit. What most upset me was the fact that I thought there was no way I could finish on July 4. I had put so much into achieving the goal of finishing on that day, and with each passing day I was slipping further behind the schedule and I had no idea when, or even if, my leg would heal.

I received so many prayers and encouraging words from so many people during this stretch. While it was uplifting, it was also almost burdensome to realize that so many people were following my journey. I knew I had to do everything in my power to not let them down. But I also didn't want to let myself down. Below the emergency contact information on my Road ID bracelet it says, "Quitting Lasts Forever." For the last two years, my life had focused on preparing for this run, so even though I still had 90 days to get to the finish, I felt as though I was too close to accomplishing the goal to not see it through to the end, or at the very least exert every ounce of physical and mental energy that I had trying to get to the finish line.

The frustration and worry swelled up inside me so much that it overflowed and on two successive mornings I sat on the edge of the bed in the motorhome and sobbed as Tiffany engulfed me in her arms. When we talked about this stretch later, Tiffany told me that if I would have uttered those two words there would have been no argument or discussion about it; she would have driven the RV home toward West Virginia. I'm glad I didn't allow those words to come out of my mouth or even the thought to cross my mind.

By the end of the fourth day of dealing with severe pain in the shin of my left leg, large knots had formed in the area, it had become swollen and it felt so tight that I wouldn't have been shocked if my skin split open. I hadn't been able to move my foot or ankle much because of the swelling and pain, and I knew I wouldn't be able to continue much farther unless I was able to regain some mobility in my ankle. I told my wife that I needed to try and stretch my shin out and attempt to work out the knots that had developed. Tiff agreed to try to stretch my leg, so we headed to the bed in the back of the RV.

Anyone who has ever eaten Rice Krispies will recognize the popping sound the cereal makes as you pour milk into the bowl. As Tiff stretched my leg out, grabbing the top of my foot and pulling my toes toward her, she ran her knuckles firmly up the front of my shin. When she did that, we heard the popping sound like milk being poured into a bowl of Rice Krispies. I had a pillow over my face to drown out my screams of agony as she pressed the knots out of my leg. It was one of the worst pains I have ever experienced. I discovered that since I had not fully extended my left foot for four days, as my leg began the healing process, adhesions in the front of my shin were knitting the muscle tighter, and in a set position.

I did my best to sleep through the pain that night, and as I stepped out of bed, the pain shot through my leg just as it had the previous few mornings. I immediately thought that I may have to visit a doctor, which had always been a last resort to me because I knew a physician would tell me not to continue running across the country. But after I took a few more steps, I noticed that I could at least partially extend my ankle without too much discomfort. I sat down on the couch and Tiffany grabbed my ankle and amazingly extended it to where my toes were pointing straight down, resembling the perfect form of the pointed feet of a ballerina or gymnast. I hadn't been able to flex my foot like that for a few days.

Not only did it physically feel better, but emotionally it lifted my spirits tremendously. I could tell it helped lift everyone else up in the RV, too. My mom was growing more and more worried with each day, and the kids were watching me go through some of the worst pain I had ever experienced. I gave them a thumbs up and smiled as I stepped off that day, still determined to walk it out, but at a much quicker pace if possible. When they weren't around to see me, I attempted to jog a little bit, but the pain was still there.

## A PROUD MOMENT

I made my way through the first 20 miles that day, moving along at a quicker pace, but also keenly aware that I couldn't push it too hard. I was scheduled to get 31 miles in that day, but since I felt a little better I hoped to start making up some miles after falling behind. At the 20-mile mark, the sun was starting to come out, the temps were warming up, and we were finally out of some of the higher elevations where the snow had been piled up on us. Nicholas wanted to get out and do some miles with me. For the past four days I had been out on the road by myself, so I was able to let out some screams of frustration and pain. But whenever I got around my family, I tried to put on a positive front. But I was glad that I was able to spend three miles out on the road this morning with Nick.

We had a good talk and I also did a short interview with WCHS-AM in Charleston, West Virginia, updating their listeners about my progress and the pain I had endured recently. After wrapping up the interview, Nick and I walked a bit further and then he said a few words to me that I will never forget.

"You know, I just never thought my dad would ever run across America," he said. "That's pretty cool."

His words almost stopped me in my tracks. My son, who was 12 years old, was proud of me for what I was doing. He recognized that this mission was about others, that we were doing it for some amazing people, but he thought his dad was pretty cool for doing something like this. I think it's every dad's desire to be a cool dad in his children's eyes. We don't have to run across America to make that happen. Even doing small things to help others is a great thing to teach children. Even though they may not acknowledge it verbally like my son did that day, they will recognize the selflessness and learn from it.

Nick saying what he did allowed me to see that I was making an impact on my kids' lives. It made me feel proud that we were planting a seed that would eventually grow into helping them do things in their lives for others, always remembering that there are people from all walks of life that we need to support and encourage. It was one of the most impacting conversations I had on the journey. At the end of the three-mile walk, the RV passed us and pulled over, and I told Tiff, "If I am going to do this, I have to do this now."

The road I was on that day had a fairly wide shoulder, with soft dirt that provided good support, but enough cushion to take some of the jarring pain I would experience on the pavement away as I took each step. As I moved away from the RV, I thought back to the words that Nick had just shared with me, and I also thought back to the men and women I had already met along the way who deal with far greater pain every day. This was 100 days of temporary pain for me. I would hopefully heal up from this and go on about my life in a normal fashion. A lot of the members of the military, however, do not have that luxury. With that in mind, I decided I was going to start jogging the last 12 miles as best as I could. With each step I took and with each mile that passed, I continued to build within myself the confidence I had when I started this journey. The pain was still there, but it was nowhere near as bad as it had been. The RV caught up to me an hour later, and I had knocked out six miles and was back at my pre-injury pace. When they pulled up by me, ringing the cowbell out the window, I gave them two thumbs up and a smile I'm sure you could see 100 miles away. I was going to do this!

At one point over the last six miles, the shoulder was covered with little rocks that crunched with each step, so I decided to call my buddy Kelly, who had run the first day with me. He and I had chatted a few times earlier that week about the injury. When I called, I got his voicemail, but I had to leave him a message.

"You hear that Kelly?" I yelled over the speakerphone, as I held the phone down by my legs. With the crunch of the rocks under my feet, I yelled out, "That's me running, buddy!"

He called me back a couple of minutes later, literally laughing about my message but ecstatic that I was able to run again. "You nut," he said when I answered. "I'm so happy for you, but be careful. Don't run and talk at the same time."

"It's OK, I'm on speakerphone."

I also called my cousin Darren, who I had talked with a lot the preceding days. We both cried when I called to tell him I was running again. My cousin was my rock at times during the run, especially when I needed to share something that I couldn't share with my wife, whether it was a painful experience or frustrations that I didn't want to burden her with.

### PAIN FREE!

I woke up the next morning needing to run at the highest elevation of the journey so far, 6,000 feet, which was the Doherty Slide area that we had driven down on the way out. I was amazed that I felt great that morning. I literally had no pain in my shin. The stiffness in my leg was gone, the swelling was down and I could fully flex my foot. The weather was also warmer. It's as if the clouds that had hovered over me the past few days literally and figuratively parted.

Being 28 miles behind schedule, I decided to add a few miles to the run that day in order to chip away at the total distance I was behind. I knew it would take a couple of days to regain the conditioning that I had lost after walking so much the past few days. But I also believe all of the walking allowed me to adjust to the thinness of the air, keeping me from dealing with any elevation-related sickness.

Shortly after running through the small town of Adel (population 78), where we learned at the gas station that there was a wedding scheduled in town later that evening, I was back out on the deserted road, with just the sounds of my feet clapping against the road and the rustling of the many jackrabbits I encountered running through the underbrush. But then I heard a noise that startled me and the jackrabbits.

BOOM! BOOM!

I don't know if it was due to my military training, but instinctively I dropped down low on the road. I knew that what I heard were gunshots directly east of me. I looked around cautiously because I was literally in the middle of nowhere. About 30 minutes prior to hearing the shots, a truck had passed me heading east, and I lost them as they rounded the turn. As I scanned the area from the where the shots came from, I saw the truck parked out in the open area of the high desert. Some shrubbery and fencing around the land almost concealed the truck from view. I then saw a man in an orange vest, then another in a bright yellow vest and finally a third man in an orange vest. They were walking through the area near the truck, spread out with shotguns in their hands. A jackrabbit scurried across the road in front of me, hopping around the carcass of a dead coyote on the side of the road and away from the area where the hunters were. I wasn't sure if they were hunting jackrabbits (if they were, they weren't good marksmen), hunting coyotes (if so, they had good aim) or hunting runners, but I didn't want to stick around long enough to find out.

I waved at them as I ran past, and fortunately they all waved back. I suspect they were probably thinking to themselves, "What is that nut doing running out here in the middle of nowhere?" I had the same thought about myself just then, considering there was gunfire going on around me. I heard a few more shots as I made my way down the road, and as I ran I laughed when I imagined that the men were probably rounding up some food for the wedding reception that night.

Blizzard Gap was approaching, at an elevation of 6,122 feet at the summit, and I was feeling really good. Shayna and Nick had both run with me some that day and we were all relieved that I miraculously appeared to be getting back into the groove. After crossing over Blizzard Gap, I knew I had one more big climb to tackle that day–Doherty Slide. Whenever I faced a large climb that coincided with an aid stop, I told Tiffany I preferred that she stop at the top of the hill rather than the bottom. I just preferred to knock those climbs out at the end of a leg so that after I refueled and stepped out of the RV to run again, I wouldn't be faced right away with a difficult stretch of road. In this case, I was about to wrap up the day of running, so it would be great to have Doherty Slide in our rearview mirror the next morning.

As I made my way up the mountain, I could see for what seemed like at least 100 miles out. I stopped a few times to get photos and video with my phone. I really learned to appreciate the beauty of this country on the trip, and the view from the Slide was one of the best. The RV went by me as I was about a mile up the mountain, and I noticed that one of the kids was in the front seat with Tiff. My mom has never been a fan of heights, so it was no surprise when she told me later that she had been lying down in the back of the RV so she wouldn't have to look out the window as Tiff motored up the mountain.

At the top of the Slide, there was an area where the state road had huge piles of gravel to put on the roads for inclement weather, so we parked behind one of the piles and stayed the night. The water in the RV was running low and the laundry was piling high since we had been in the middle of nowhere for a couple of days. We were finally feeling good about the mechanics of living in our box on wheels, but it sure wasn't easy. I knew I was getting close to the Oregon/Nevada border, so we were excited about making our first entry into a new state.

I woke up the next morning, which happened to be Easter Sunday, and stepped out into the most beautiful sunrise I had seen in a while. We were still at a pretty significant elevation, but the land was so flat you could see forever. Eight miles into the run, the RV went by me, and I rounded a turn to a beautiful sight. The RV was parked alongside the road, right in front of the Nevada state line sign. Everyone was out getting photos, and I just couldn't hold in my excitement as I approached the crew and yelled, "First state down!" What a momentous occasion for all of us.

We came into Denio Junction later that day, where the town (of about 40 people) had put up a sign welcoming us. The children in the town made the sign to encourage me and display their support for the troops. It was definitely a moment to remember and I was thankful that the message was getting out there. The town held an Easter dinner and invited us to attend. We celebrated my daughter's 10th birthday in the restaurant that evening, and also swapped out a crew member. My in-laws met us in Denio Junction, where Tiffany's mother, Kathy, replaced my mom, who was flying back to West Virginia.

Having my mom with us helped out in so many ways, as did our upcoming time with Kathy. Tiff had so many demands, taking care of me, the RV, the kids and dealing with the logistics of everything. With our mothers taking turns being there with us, Tiff was at least able to get some time to decompress. I was also very grateful that my mom had been able to see me begin running again the last few days she was with us. I know it really bothered her to see me go through all the pain I was in with my leg, so I think it eased her concerns as she left to see that I was feeling good again.

The next couple of days through Nevada were pretty uneventful. Civilization in the area was sparse, and the small towns we did travel through appeared to be once-prosperous towns that were now boarded up. I joked with my kids that it looked like this is where the animated movie "Cars" was filmed.

We were heading into the Battle Mountain area when, before I headed out to begin my run that morning, there was a knock on the RV door. Numerous times on this trip, my wife had arranged for old friends that we hadn't seen in years to meet up with us, and this morning I was greeted by Matt and Kathy Ewoldt, along with their children, who had driven eight hours up from Las Vegas to spend the day with us. It was great seeing them, and it also gave our kids an opportunity to get outside and play with other children, something they desperately needed. At one point, the kids found an old tire along the roadside and had an absolute blast rolling the tire up the mountainside, cheering it as it bounced back down the mountain. You could tell they had been cooped up in a motorhome too long.

Things didn't remain cheerful for long, though. For whatever reason, as the temperature rose that day, I continued to get colder and colder, adding a couple more layers to my clothing just to keep from being too chilled. I had felt fine the night before, even though that day I had a difficult time eating much and I also didn't drink as many fluids as normal. On this day Tiffany helped me try to be more conscious about refueling, but I wasn't feeling well enough to eat and drink everything she put in front of me.

At the end of the run that day, I was freezing and I asked Tiffany to run a hot bath for me in the hotel room that the Ewoldts had set up for us. That was mistake #1. I also immediately turned the heat up full blast. That was mistake #2. When I crawled into the bath, I just kept telling myself to run more and more hot water into the tub. *"This will certainly help take the chill off of me,"* I thought to myself. That was mistake #3.

I finally got out of the bath, having thoroughly cooked myself, and crawled into bed. I was shivering, and just couldn't get warm, but Tiff felt my forehead and said that I was burning up. She sat on the edge of the bed and forced some beef stew down my throat, getting me to drink and eat as much as I could. She let me rest for a while, but Tiff and her mom took turns checking on me. This is the one time of the trip I think Tiff had the most concern about me. She could tell something wasn't right.

Then all of a sudden it hit me. I remembered reading in Marshall Ulrich's book about how the body would heat up during the run, making it almost impossible to sleep at times. They had to keep the living quarters cooled off to get his body to cool down enough to get into a recovery mode. Whatever bug I had certainly wasn't helping matters, but I also wasn't doing the proper things to take care of myself. I crawled out of bed, turned the AC on and then got back in bed, this time just placing the bed sheet over me. I was cold, but I knew that I needed to stop cooking myself the way I had been. I fell asleep a few minutes later, and woke up around 2 a.m. feeling like a new man. I never did figure out what caused me to catch whatever bug I had in my system, but whatever it was, it was gone. I'm also not sure who was more relieved, me or Tiffany, but I was happy to feel 100 times better than I had just a few hours prior.

I met Matt and Kathy downstairs the next morning before they left, apologizing that I didn't get a chance to spend a lot of time with them, and what time I did spend with them was not very pleasant.

"No worries. We came to see Tiff and the kids anyways," Matt joked.

After having a rough time the previous day and evening and being pretty dehydrated, I was determined to flood myself with Gatorade on this day. By the time we had driven the six miles from the hotel to the start of my route that day, I had already drunk a full 32-ounce cup of Gatorade, and made sure that by the first stop, all four of my FuelBelt bottles were empty. If there was one thing I could not do on this trip, it was take in small amounts of liquid, especially as it began to get warmer.

As the day wore on, my system continued to feel replenished and alert, so I pressed on at a fairly good pace, only stopping long enough to refill my drinks and shove lots of food down my throat. Everyone seemed to be in better spirits after having spent a day with some great friends, and also seeing that I was feeling a lot better. But difficulty was brewing on the horizon.

## SMALL TOWNS, BIG HEARTS

As we made our way toward Elko, Nevada, the generator stopped working in the RV. As the weather was getting warmer, we found ourselves running the AC in the RV more often to keep the crew cool, which also gave me some relief as I stepped in from my run. It was also becoming critical for me to be able to sleep comfortably at night, getting the RV down to a very cool temperature, which often froze everyone else. We knew that being without air conditioning was not an option. Tiffany started calling ahead to service stations in Elko, and being a Sunday, we found most repair places were closed. I had about eight miles left to go to finish the day, so I told Tiff to head into town and I would meet the family there. This gave her more time to try to find a place that could take a look at the generator.

As I continued running along the freeway, I met a couple of bicyclists and struck up a brief conversation with them.

"Where are you off to?" asked one of the cyclists.

"Annapolis, Maryland" I replied.

"What?" responded the other cyclist, dumbfounded and uncertain that he had heard me correctly.

"Annapolis, Maryland," I repeated. After a 30-second explanation of my mission, they headed off and as I watched them ride away, I could see both of them shaking their heads in disbelief.

I made my way into Elko, tracking Tiffany and the crew down by phone as I jogged through the streets. She had found a parts store in town, where she bought a new spark plug and fuses. She replaced all of the parts, but still had no luck firing the generator. We found out there was a Cummins Service Station in town, so we decided to try our luck there in the morning. I took the opportunity that evening to catch up on the phone with several good friends who I went to high school with, including Palmer Stephens, who is a radio DJ near my hometown back in West Virginia. He and I spoke often on the journey and he would give me time to keep his radio listeners updated on the progress of the run. One of the things that I was most thankful for was the fact that when I would call one of my friends back home, they were always willing to listen when I needed to talk.

Tiffany called the Cummins shop when we woke up the next morning and, fortunately for us, one of the two mobile technicians they employed was there that day. Usually they were both out on the road servicing vehicles. We explained what we were doing and expressed our desire to do whatever necessary, within financial reason, to get the generator running again. Within 45 minutes the technician identified the problem. Tiffany and the kids had started geocaching and rock hunting as we came into Nevada, and some of the roads weren't necessarily made for a 31-foot RV. The technician suspected that is what caused a wire to become loose on the starter, and once he clamped it down and made sure contacts were good, it fired right up. The workers at the store then thanked *us* for what we were doing, and told us the labor was on them.

It wasn't really a surprise to me, but more of a reassurance and a confirmation of the true American spirit. We may be strangers, but people understand the sacrifices the men and women in the military make every day, and when they see others giving everything to help them out, the true American spirit really starts to shine. People came out of the woodwork to take care of us when we needed it, and to just shake our hands or throw us a wave as they drove by. It wasn't surprising at all as far as I was concerned. I knew that spirit was out there, I was just giving people the chance to let it shine.

And did it ever!

# 8 | Road Closed Ahead

Just as I needed some smaller, attainable goals during my two years of training for this run across America, during the actual run it really helped me to identify various benchmarks that I could use to mark my progress or to offer me a sense that the end goal was within sight. Crossing into a second time zone was one of those milestones. We were leaving the Pacific time zone on Day 25, so it also meant that 25 percent of my journey was complete.

My body was now settling into the run quite nicely, and the injury I sustained to my left leg that set me back early on was healed. A phenomenon that I had read about from runners who had done similar journeys across America or the Appalachian Trail was starting to take place. My "long distance legs" were finally getting under me, which enabled me to run for long distances, day after day, without experiencing the tiredness or pain that normally occurs after running extremely long distances. When I would wake up each morning, it felt as though I hadn't even run the previous day. That was a strange but exciting feeling for me.

I remembered how I felt after many of the ultramarathons I ran the previous two years, especially the 40-Mile Highland Sky race. The day after that race, I flew with my wife to Las Vegas, where she was attending a conference. For the first four days of the trip, I could barely walk down any steps without wincing in pain. The Laurel Highland and Burning River races wiped me out for a couple of days afterward, forcing me to spend those days resting on the couch. I wouldn't have even thought about lacing up my running shoes for a few days after those races. But here I was on my 25th consecutive day of running an ultramarathon, and I was waking up to very little stiffness or pain in my body.

I shared with Tiffany that I was really feeling strong physically, but the run was still a mental challenge. *"Only 75 more days of this,"* I told myself while out on the run. But instead of serving as a comforting thought, that phrase just made the remainder of the journey seem even more daunting. I laughed as I said out loud to no one in particular, "Only 75 more days!"

After my final full day in Nevada, I was still about 12 miles behind our scheduled stopping point at the end of that day, so we went ahead and drove to Wendover, Utah, which was right on the Nevada-Utah border, to spend the night at a casino RV park. I never really liked it when we would drive ahead in the route because I would rather not know what challenges the route would present each day. But logistically, we had to do it often in order to fulfill obligations, be at scheduled events, or simply because oftentimes that was the closest place we could find to stay the night.

That evening we walked back into Nevada because we thought it wouldn't be right to leave the state without doing a little gambling. The RV was literally parked a few feet across the state line in Utah at the campground, so the walk was a relatively short one. The adults hit the slots and blackjack tables while our children had fun in the arcade. Lady luck wasn't on my side at the slots, but she was later that evening. Even though I was pushing my body to its breaking point physically each day, being isolated out on the roads while running really increased my desire to be with my wife. That desire actually increased more and more as the days passed. I'll never forget the conversation Tiffany shared with me that she had with her mother when she pulled her aside while we were out at dinner that evening.

"Can you keep the kids at the arcade for a little while?" Tiffany asked her mom.

"Is everything OK?" Kathy asked.

"Everything is fine. Jamie and I just need some time alone, back at the RV."

"Oh," Kathy said with a laugh.

The next morning the sun was beginning to break through the clouds and the wind was gusting. I was invigorated not only from the previous night's intimate activities, but also by the fact that early into the run I would be crossing into my third state. The initial leg of the run that day was about nine miles of straight, flat road and I knocked it out at a pretty quick pace. The climb up the hill just prior to entering Wendover was very windy, and slowed me down some, but I had learned when running in similar conditions earlier in the trip to take short, meaningful steps. Just as in boot camp, short choppy steps were necessary a lot of times just to keep positive forward motion. I crested the top of the hill, which offered an incredible view of Wendover and the salt flats just beyond the town down into Utah.

After taking some photographs at the summit, I headed down the mountain, spending the last couple of miles in Nevada running along the interstate. Based on conversations my wife had with the Department of Transportation, I knew that I wouldn't be able to *legally* run along the interstate in Utah. I coasted into the RV park where we had stayed the previous night and there was a painted line down the middle of the road marking the Nevada-Utah state line. Once the rest of the family arrived, we took turns straddling the line so that we'd be standing in two different states simultaneously. The previous night when we came through here, we joked that on the Nevada side of the line were casinos and right across the line on the Utah side were chapels where you could marry multiple partners.

The kids also got a picture with Monti Bear, a stuffed animal bear that somewhat resembled the Mountaineer mascot from West Virginia University. The kids brought the bear along to photograph him in each state. They walked on each side of the line, holding onto Monti's hands, as he hung in the air right above the state line. Nick was happy that he was on the side of the line where he could marry multiple wives.

## SALT DRIFTS

Having driven much of my running route on our way from West Virginia to Oregon for the start of the run, there were a few stretches that really stuck out in my mind. Among them were the long climb in Oregon out of Lakeview into the mountains, going up and over Blizzard Gap and of course driving down and then running back up Doherty Slide. Another memorable stretch awaited me this day. It would be the longest stretch of straight, flat road that I would encounter during the entire trip—38 miles of road that was straight as an arrow and surrounded on both sides by white salt flats.

In Nevada I ran 13- and 22-mile stretches of straight road coming into Denio Junction, but that was nothing like the isolated and seemingly endless stretch of frontage road that lied ahead. On the way out to Oregon we drove on Interstate 80, which runs parallel to the road I would be running this day, and we drove about 30 minutes without having to touch the steering wheel because the road was so straight. When we were standing on top of the overlook coming down into Wendover, I could see this stretch of freeway looming ahead, and remembered that long drive across the flats on the way out.

I have learned to embrace the ups and downs of trail running, understanding that my entire body gets a workout on those types of runs. Long, flat runs are not the most enticing to me because you continually work the same muscles over and over again, and the repetition of the movements and the monotony of running along the same stretch of road for miles and miles is not something that I enjoy. To make my way across America, however, I knew I would encounter some long, flat stretches of road. Another thing that concerned me this day was that as I was preparing to start my run on the salt flats, we could see some ominous storm clouds nearby and I knew that out on this stretch of road there would be nowhere for me to seek cover if the weather got too nasty.

Prior to heading out on this seldom-traveled frontage road, Tiffany and I debated about what we should do when I wrapped up the run for the day. I would finish right in the middle of the stretch, so we were faced with the decision to either back track to Wendover for the night, or drive approximately 17 miles ahead to another town. We decided to settle that debate when the time came; I just needed to move forward.

With the RV parked alongside the road behind me, and the temperature starting to climb, I made my way out onto the frontage road. It wasn't too long before I saw the first of many signs on this stretch that read, "Road not maintained, travel at own risk." The farther I ran, the more I understood why the signs were installed, because the condition of the road continued to get worse. There were tons of potholes and buckles in the pavement. In addition, the salt and sand from the salt flats was blown up onto the road, with drifts of sand piling up in sections. It looked more like I was running along a beach of white sand, although there was no blue ocean water for me to jump into to cool off.

To make matters worse, there were pieces of old fencing that were scattered across the sandy road. Knowing that the RV would be driving up from behind, I spent a lot of time picking up pieces of fencing and fencing staples that had blown onto the road and tossing them off to the side. I knew Tiffany would have enough of a challenge navigating the RV around the potholes and through the salt drifts, so I didn't want her to be concerned about dodging fencing staples and risk blowing out a tire out in the middle of nowhere.

As Tiff and the crew got closer, I looked back and noticed that the RV looked like it was on an obstacle course. Tiff was weaving the rig back and forth on the road, avoiding potholes and driving over huge chunks of salt that caused her more than once to think the RV was not going to make it through. I called her at one point to warn her to watch out for a shrub that was growing up in the middle of the road. Tiffany later compared driving on that "non-maintained" road on the salt flats to being out on a sand rail in the sand dunes in Oregon. We laughed when she told me that at one point she thought she would have to get out and put the snow chains back on the RV just to make it through the drifts.

I continued to monitor the weather and the huge black clouds that were nearby. It certainly looked like the storm that was brewing was making its way toward us. Fortunately there was a strong wind from the north that ended up blowing the storm clouds south of us. Once the storm clouds blew out, the temperature really started to spike and there were no trees or buildings to provide any shade relief for me. Tiffany had been spraying sunscreen on me for a few days now, as I encountered more and more sunny days. I remember her that day spraying my legs down well, but I didn't pay too much attention to the fact that she missed a few sections on the back of my legs. I would pay for that the next day.

I took things relatively slow that day, making a few stops to ensure that I was getting enough fluid and food but also to just enjoy the uniqueness of the scenery and take some photographs. Nicholas again joined me to run about three miles after our first stop on the salt flats. It was a nice break for me, taking the time to talk about the sights we were seeing and answering his questions about the salt flats and how they came to be. Shayna remarked that Nick and I looked cute out there running with our desert hats on, with the flaps that covered our necks blowing in the air as we ran along.

As I was getting to the end of my mileage for the day, both of the kids got out and ran the last 1.5 miles with me. Shayna wasn't happy at all with the fact that the closer we got to the RV, the faster Tiffany would drive to stay ahead of us. It reminded me of a prank friends play when one person gets close to opening the car door to get in, and the driver drives ahead a few feet, repeating that several times before allowing the passenger to finally open the door and hop in. The sun was beating down on us, and by the end of the run I was getting a look from Shayna that could cut right through me, but she held back the tears and pushed on. I was so proud of her for getting out there and joining us. Stepping out to run on the salt flats with them was an experience I will never forget.

Tiffany pulled the RV over to an open spot on the side of the road, and we discussed the fact that we were now out in the middle of the frontage road. It was about 18 miles to go back the way we came, or another 20 to go to reach the end of the road and meet up with another main roadway. Considering the treacherous condition of the road, Tiffany didn't want to drive the RV on it any more than we had to. With some initial hesitation from me, we decided it would be best to stay put. All of the maps and information about the salt flats that we had with us mentioned there was no camping allowed on the salt flats. Tiff assured me we would be fine out there and that no one could get to us anyway, so we leveled the RV up and set up camp. Interstate 80 looked to be about a mile away from us, but there were no roads from I-80 to our road, so we had plenty of separation between us and any major traffic.

The closest thing to us was a railway that ran parallel with the road, which we had almost became numb to by now. It seemed like a lot of the railways that traversed this great country ran parallel with my running route, which gave me a chance to wave at the passing trains. One drawback, however, was that the passing trains also often kept us awake at night, especially during the early legs of the trip. I eventually learned to sleep pretty well through the sounds of the trains, but the rest of the crew wasn't so lucky. It became a running joke with us concerning our overnight sleeping location and the proximity of the nearest train tracks.

After a shower and a quick interview with Tony Caridi of Sportsline, a sports radio talk show in West Virginia, I headed outside to figure out why everyone was laughing. When I saw Shayna I figured out why–she had buried her feet and legs in "mud," which was a mixture of salt/sand and standing water. The recipe not only created a squishy substance, but also an odor so repugnant that it immediately gave me a queasy feeling in the pit of my stomach. But watching Shayna giggle at the tickling sensation of the gray-ish-brown mud oozing between her pale toes had everyone else cracking up. Any concerns about a residual odor that may cling to her feet was worth the tradeoff to see the pure, innocent joy on her face as she waddled around in the mud. Plus, I knew I couldn't complain about the smell since, for the past four weeks, my family had put up with my stench that was built up over eight-plus hours of sweating every day.

The remainder of the evening was spent sitting in the four red folding chairs set up around a white card table outside the RV, just enjoying the stories we all shared about our individual experiences on the journey thus far. It was great to hear how our children opened up about the thoughts and emotions they had about what we had been through this first month on the road. I was physically exhausted from the run earlier that day, but that time spent around the card table really rejuvenated me physically and emotionally.

We watched as the sky that was draped over our heads like an awning turned from sunset orange to purple to a deep black with sprinkles of brightly lit stars that looked more like white paint splatters on a black canvas. We were in total isolation out on the salt flats, and as the chatter and laughter died down, we soaked up the stillness and quietness of the night. It was amazing how quiet it was out there, even with the freeway within sight off in the distance.

Until, of course, the first train passed through that night.

## FREEZING IN 90 DEGREES

It was not until I woke up the next morning that I realized Tiffany had missed a few spots on the back of my legs as she was applying the sun screen. As I stepped out of bed, it felt like the skin on my calves was tighter than a bed sheet on a bunk at boot camp. From the top of the back of my knee to just below my calf on each leg, it was blood red, minus a few spots where sunscreen had actually made contact.

One of my morning rituals since I suffered my injury included spraying Biofreeze on my left shin prior to taking off on my run, just to make sure I experienced no recurring pain. This morning, I also sprayed some on the backs of my legs to try to alleviate the pain of the sunburn. That sent shockwaves through my body as the coldness of the Biofreeze met the hotness of the splotchy, red skin. After a few seconds, however, it felt much better. And Tiffany also made sure I had plenty of sunscreen applied all over since the forecast called for temps above 90 degrees.

The first 17 miles of the run were spent on the frontage road, enjoying a few short stops as the kids got out to play in the flats and sandstone that was alongside the road. We encountered an area called Knolls that was inhabited not only by lizards and other wild animals, but also adventure seekers out on sand rails and four wheelers. It certainly would have been nice to hop on one of the machines to help get me through the day, but nobody offered me a ride, so I ran on.

Halfway through the run, the frontage road switched over to the north side of I-80, and we stopped to take some video of me describing my run so far. We tried to make a point of recording my thoughts as I left each state and entered a new one. Since the heat continued to climb, the words I shared were brief, but it was nice to recount all that we had seen through the Pacific time zone, and how excited I was to be moving on to the next leg of the journey.

During the second half of my run, Tiffany spent most of the time searching for a place for us to dock the RV that night. Since we had camped out in the middle of the salt flats the previous night, we were eating away at our utilities and water. She wasn't able to find a place with an RV hookup within a 60-mile radius, so she settled on a rest area where we would camp. Since we wanted to conserve water, Tiffany and her mother also ended up using the rest area restrooms to wash our dirty dishes and clothes later that night.

As I was running up a fairly steep hill along a gravel road that ran behind the rest area at the end of my run that day, I heard a vehicle's tires rumbling across the bed of gray rocks from behind. I turned to see a truck approaching, and was glad to see the driver had slowed down and moved over into the opposite lane in an attempt to keep the dust from kicking up as he passed me. The truck slowed up even more as it got alongside me, and then I heard two of the best words that can be uttered to a Marine.

"Semper Fi!" yelled the driver, as he gave me a thumb's up. "You're doing a great thing!"

Semper Fidelis is the motto of the Marine Corps and it means "always faithful." The shortened "Semper Fi" is a greeting used by all Marines when we encounter one another. As the truck drove on ahead, I noticed Marine Corps bumper stickers on the back of the truck. He had obviously seen the RV along the side of the road with the wrap promoting the Run for Wounded Warriors. It was great to receive that appreciation for what I was doing for our fellow brothers and sisters. Moments like that occurred frequently when I ran through heavier populated areas, but after being around very few people those past few days, it was certainly a very encouraging moment for me.

## DUSTY ROADS

I began the morning running along the gravel road, eventually encountering a farm that had about 1,000 roaming sheep. As I made my way farther down the road, I saw a gate up ahead that blocked the entrance to a dirt road that looked to be sparsely traveled. I called Tiffany and told her to drive up and meet me so that we could discuss a plan. There was no way the RV would make it on that "road," and we didn't want to drive it onto gated property anyway. We decided it would be best for Tiffany to backtrack to the interstate entrance, drive on ahead a few miles to the next exit, and wait for me there. I would continue on along the dirt road and meet them. My only concern was not knowing what type of animals I might encounter. More specifically, I hoped I wouldn't see any snakes!

I was only on the dirt road for a few miles, and thankfully the only animals I saw were a number of cattle, some of whom decided to jog alongside me for a bit. After meeting the crew at the interstate exit, we were presented with our second navigational challenge of the day. I again had to cross over the interstate to follow the frontage road, but the road went backward almost a mile and a half before it turned and headed east again. There were some motorcyclists and four wheel riders on the road, but we could tell the road was not traveled much at all. Tiff drove on over to ask the guys if they thought she could navigate the RV on the road, and they said it was passable but to be very cautious. They told her it actually used to be the main road that went through the area, but it was replaced by I-80 and was not maintained at all anymore. A couple of miles into the run on that road, I called her to let her know navigating the RV on the road became tricky ahead, but she would be able to make it through.

The temperature continued to rise, as did the clouds of dust as my running shoes stirred up the dirt with each step. I felt certain that I resembled Pig-Pen, the character from the cartoon Peanuts, who was always followed by a cloud of dirt. When the gang caught up to me in the RV for an aid stop, it looked as if a dump truck had unloaded its haul of dirt all over the motorhome. And when I stepped inside, it looked as if a dust bomb had exploded *inside* the RV. Dirt found its way into every nook and cranny of the RV, even up underneath the bed in the back. Being the RV newbies that we were, we had left the bathroom exhaust fan on to circulate the air. It also sucked dirt in from every possible entry. It was a messy lesson to learn!

When we arrived in Delle, we asked some people inside the gas station for advice on the path that we needed to take. They informed us that the frontage road stopped again just past the exit. I told Tiff to drive on ahead on the interstate and I would make my own path to the next stop. As I crossed to the north side of I-80 again, the road turned into nothing but a very desolate area of flats to run for the next few miles. Early on in that stretch I came upon a young man in a truck with a motorcycle in the back.

"Excuse me," I said. "Do you know how far it is to get to the next road?"

"I'm not sure. What are you doing running out here?"

"Running across America for wounded veterans," I replied.

With a skeptical look on his face, he shook his head and said, "What?"

"Running across America," I repeated. "I'm making my way to Annapolis, Maryland."

"Very cool!" he said. "I'm originally from Baltimore."

I told him I would be running through my home state of West Virginia on my way to Maryland.

"I've spent some time in Morgantown with some friends of mine at West Virginia University," he said.

"That's where I'm from," I laughed.

"No way! What a small world."

By this time, some friends of his in another vehicle approached us. "You guys have got to get out here and meet this guy," he told them. "He's running all the way across the country!"

It was a neat experience to be able to share my purpose for the run with them. And I was amazed by the fact that out in the middle of nowhere on a seemingly deserted section of back roads, I could cross paths with someone who had friends in my hometown.

As I closed in on the finish of another day, we encountered another area where the RV had to take a different route. This time Tiffany would have to meet me on the other side of a mountain, and the maps weren't very clear about what roads were in the area, so we just had to gamble that Tiffany would find a good place to park and wait for me. I was confident, however, that as long as I continued to head east I would eventually connect with them.

There were numerous hiking trails that went up the side of the barren hill, with rocks jutting out at all points, so I had to run this section a bit cautiously. But it was a nice diversion, breaking up the monotony of constantly running on pavement and alongside passing vehicles. I have always enjoyed trail running, so even though the climb was somewhat challenging, it really energized me. As I crested the mountain, where I could see the RV parked on the other side waiting for me, I took a moment to just take in the beauty around me. I could see the Great Salt Lake, and looking back could see where I had run most of that day. It really gave me perspective as to how much ground I was covering with each passing day, and it was a reminder of how beautiful this country truly is.

Later that evening, Tiffany said she felt like she had an understanding of what storm chasers do. Based on the limited weather information they have at the moment, they just have to make an educated guess on where the storm will appear and how to best get to that point. With her, it was making an educated guess on where I would appear from behind a mountain and figure out how to get the RV to that point to meet me. We didn't have too many of these moments along the way, but when we did they were always very anxious moments for everyone.

## SNAKES AND A TRAIN

As I continued to count down the miles until we arrived in Salt Lake City (the first sign for the city I saw said: "Salt Lake City, 410 miles" and that was nearly two weeks ago), we continued to encounter "roads" that were impassable in the RV. Leading up to the final day before we entered the city, we were forced to decide how to conquer another detour in the route. This time I learned that it is always best to listen to the crew chief, especially when that person is your wife!

I remembered this section as we drove out to Oregon, not because of the mountain I would possibly have to go around, but because of the fact that the Salt Lake was literally just a few feet from us on the northern side of I-80, and how beautiful and vast the glittering blue body of water was. Having never traveled to this part of the country, I could not get over how majestic the lake was, and seeing the snow-capped mountains behind it made it just that much more incredible. "I can't wait to run by here," I remembered telling Tiffany on our way out. This was going to be one of those sections where the "five miles an hour, one mile at a time" USA crossing would be most enjoyable.

As I approached this mountain on foot, however, we realized that other than the interstate, there were no other roads going around the mountain. On each side of the mountain, there were roads that approached it, but no connections between the two. Aside from the interstate, it was a 17-mile journey around a different roadway to get to the east side, which of course didn't sit well with me. There was no way I was going to just add an extra 17 miles onto the run, so we decided to do as we had done the previous few days and have Tiffany approach the mountain as closely as she could in the RV, let me go on my own and meet me on the other side.

At that point I had two options. Option #1 was to run along the railroad tracks that ran parallel to the interstate on the southern side of the mountain. Option #2 was to navigate around the mountainside off-road and have to battle brush, rocks and a steep slope. With the second option, I was also worried that I would be faced with one of my greatest fears–snakes.

I don't like snakes. I never have, and I never will. My son developed an interest in reptiles when he was young, even once boasting that he wanted to be a herpetologist when he grew up, but I couldn't embrace them as he has. One of the biggest (and to me bravest) things I believe I have ever done was let Nicholas buy a pet snake when he was about 9 years old. It was one of those moments when I had to swallow my pride (and fear) and allow him have the responsibility to care for his pet snake. I wasn't happy about it, but I allowed it, because that's what dads do, right?

Looking at the path that was in front of me, which really was no path at all, and fearing that I would almost certainly encounter a snake if I went that route, I thought it was in my best interest if I headed toward the railroad tracks and followed them the mile and a half around the edge of the mountain to the other side.

The dilemma reminded me of the scene in the 1980s movie *Stand By Me,* when the four boys decide to walk on the railroad tracks that spanned a wooden bridge 100 feet over a river rather than taking the safer route that was 10 miles out of their way. I had seen a couple of trains come through the area as I had approached it on my run earlier that day, and one had just gone through about 15 minutes prior to my arrival, so I believed I had a good window to run along them without issue. Tiff, however, preferred that I take the off-road, rocky path. She did not want me on the railroad tracks because there wasn't much "shoulder" on either side of the tracks for me to jump off if a train did come through.

Since I had already seen a freshly killed rattlesnake along the road earlier that day, my fear of snakes won out and I headed up the hillside toward the railroad tracks. About 50 feet up the hill, I stepped over a rock and a light brown snake covered with many darker brown splotches slid out from under it, right under my foot. My foot came back up just as fast as it started down, and I ran back down the hill toward the RV in record time. When I saw Tiffany I announced, "I'm taking Option #3. I'm running the interstate!"

Initially that wasn't one of our options because Utah doesn't allow pedestrians on the freeways, so I knew that I was taking a risk. I had seen some bicyclists on the interstate, so I figured I could push it hard during this small section and hope that no police officers stopped me as I ran along the shoulder of the road. I hopped onto I-80 and ran the next two miles faster than I'd run during anytime in the entire trip. I did see a state trooper drive by in the opposite direction as I ran along I-80, but he apparently didn't notice me or didn't care. When cars zoomed past me at 70 miles per hour just a foot or two to my side, my heart pumped a little faster, which made my legs pump a little faster, too.

About four minutes into my run on the interstate, a train went barreling down the tracks that I would have been running on had I not been spooked away by the snake. The first thing I did when I got off the interstate and into the RV was look at Tiffany and say, "You were right. Running along the train tracks would have been a bad idea. From now on, I'll listen to my crew chief."

# 9 | Salt and Wind

Making my way through Salt Lake City, I faced high temperatures and even higher mountains. The temperatures were in the 90s almost every day and I had several serious climbs. Typically that's a combination that will really zap the energy out of a runner. But my body was adapting not only to the daily miles, but also to the warmer weather. Plus, Tiffany was doing a great job of keeping me hydrated by ensuring that I gulped down plenty of orange Gatorade to go along with salt tablets.

I was growing more and more comfortable with this routine of rising early and putting down 35 miles by mid-afternoon. While this routine allowed me to settle into the run, I could tell it was beginning to become a bit of a bore for our children, who had been trapped in the box on wheels. That's why when we entered the heart of Salt Lake City I suggested to Tiffany that she allow her mother to take the children to a park or go do something fun in town. The kids were obviously excited to be able to stretch their legs and it also gave them some special time with Kathy.

As I entered the heart of downtown at about the midway point of my run for the day, I approached a red light. As I was standing there waiting for the crosswalk light to change, I caught a familiar face out of the corner of my eye. It was George Weekley, a good friend of mine from West Virginia who now lived in Salt Lake City with his wife, Jennifer. We had been communicating earlier in the journey and George offered to allow us to stay at his home that night. But I had no idea he was going to surprise me in the down-town area. He was tracking me through MyAthlete Live, and it was accurate enough to allow him to hunt me down. We chatted for a few minutes, he gave us his home address so we could meet up there after the day's run and then he headed back to work.

I was pumped that George was able to track me down, but I was equally excited by two other encounters that I had out on the road that day. Earlier, a cyclist came upon me and slowed down to ride with me for a couple of miles. I shared my mission with him and he shared his own journey with me—one that had enabled him, by riding his bike, to lose 100 pounds and change his outlook on his life. He was an older man, but as he told of his own transfor-mation he had a youthful exuberance about him. I was so glad that he had slowed down to ride alongside me, because his story reminded me so much of my own transformation.

Later, as I was refueling during an aid stop, a car pulled up behind the RV. A man jumped out of the driver's seat and introduced himself to me as a fellow runner by the name of Wayne. He explained that he had seen me run-ning a few weeks earlier at the Oregon/Nevada border when he was travel-ing on Route 140. He looked up my story online and started tracking me as I was making my way to Salt Lake City. He said he had changed from his work attire into his running clothes and hoped he could run with me during his lunch break because he thought what I was doing was so awesome. I was happy to oblige, so we headed off towards Emigration Canyon and he began peppering me with questions about my health, the logistics, sponsors, etc.

As we made our way towards the base of the canyon, he told me I had a heck of a climb ahead of me, and would encounter a lot of cyclists along the way. It turns out the mountain is used for training by some of the best road racers in the world. His words proved to be true because a lot of bikes (and very nice ones at that) passed me as I headed up the road. Wayne dropped off, thanked me for letting him run with me, and I told him it was completely my pleasure.

Having his company really helped me to take my mind off something that had really been grinding away at me earlier in the day. When I was running out of downtown I passed the Salt Lake City VA medical center. We attempted to reach out to the hospital days prior to our arrival, and my friend George's neighbor, who worked there, also tried to get something set up so that we could speak to and meet some of the patients. Unfortunately, we never heard back from anyone at the hospital, and that really drove me nuts. The primary purpose of this run was to pay homage to wounded veterans, so it really bothered me that hospital staff didn't return our correspondence. Tiffany tried to remind me that it was no fault of ours that connections couldn't be made, so I shouldn't feel guilty about running on, but it still bothered me for quite a while.

Back on the mountain, the temperature was above 90 once again. I saw some cyclists zooming past me on their way down the hill, and others inched their way ahead of me on their way up the hill. I was inching my way up the hill, too. I was intentionally taking the climb slower because I didn't want a repeat of Oregon, where I injured my left leg on an ascent up a mountain. This time, however, I went slower and made rest stops to refuel every 30 minutes. At one of those stops Tiffany climbed out of the RV and we took the time to just stand there arm-in-arm together, looking back out toward Salt Lake and talking about how fortunate we were to be doing this. It was a very special moment.

I finally made my way to the top of the Canyon, overlooking the Little Dell Reservoir, where I had a chance to talk to a couple of bikers about the climb and what I was doing. Since they were familiar with the area, we talked about my running route the following day. They mentioned this climb was a good warm-up for the next day's journey. I cringed as they described how climbing up Big Mountain would take me up to over 7,400 feet in elevation.

I was fortunate to talk to them because they also informed me that since I was going through the area at this time of the year, the roadway heading up and over Big Mountain was closed to vehicle traffic. "Another opportunity to revisit the maps," Tiff said. I only had a couple of miles to go to get to the gate where the road was closed, so I decided to head on down the mountain to the lake, then onto Route 65 to run up to the gate. Tiff stayed back to get a few photos, then headed on up to the gate to meet me. It was another successful day with some beautiful scenery and inspiring moments.

That evening we enjoyed a relaxing night at George's house catching up with his family as well as chatting with a neighbor of his who was also an ultramarathon runner. I was thankful for the good night's rest because the next morning I knew I needed fresh legs for the climbing that loomed ahead.

George was going to run three miles with me before he headed in for work that morning, so he drove up to the starting point since Tiffany couldn't get the RV up that road. When we got there, I saw another familiar face. William "Three" Corley, another Marine I knew from back in West Virginia, had flown his airplane into the area the night before with his wife, Crystal, and their baby daughter, Claire. I was glad that we were able to set up this visit with Three and his family. As George and I set off on the run he warned me to keep my eyes open for wildlife as I made my way up the mountain. Unfortunately all I saw that day were deer and rabbits.

This section was one of the most peaceful and quiet runs I had on the entire journey. It did go straight up Big Mountain, but it was amazing to just have this 12-mile section nearly to myself. A couple of cyclists passed me on the way up, and we shared greetings, but aside from that, it was just me alone out on the road. The road wound back and forth up the mountain, so it wasn't as steep as the climb I experienced back in Oregon on my way to Diamond Lake. I actually made some great time to the peak of Big Mountain. The evergreens along the mountain provided a gorgeous backdrop to what had been a very memorable trip through a beautiful state.

We had a little celebration at the end of the run this day. I passed the 1,000-mile mark that day, and at the end of the run Tiffany's mom took a photo with myself, Tiff, and the kids forming our arms into the numbers

1,000. It was the first time I had taken the opportunity to celebrate a true milestone on this run.

Leaving Echo Canyon on my final day in Utah, I ran along Echo Canyon Road, which ran parallel to I-80, on a road that seemed to be very lightly traveled. There were markers all along the road describing the red rocks that were to my left as I ran along. I was running along what was the Mormon Trail, with markers describing certain encampments and fortifications used by the Mormons as they made their way west. It was an amazing cluster of rock formations.

About 10 miles into the run, I caught up to the RV. My next section of the route was about 17 miles that took me on the north side of I-80. I'm thankful Tiff drove up ahead earlier in the morning to scout the road, because she discovered a showstopper for the day. The road I was supposed to run on had a private property sign at the gate, and the gate was closed. I chuckled to myself because this last day in Utah was just typical of my entire time in the state. There was one curveball after another thrown our way and we simply had to adjust our route one more time.

We looked at the map and realized we had a couple of options. I could backtrack and get to another road that took me to my finishing destination for the day, which would have added almost 30 miles to my run, or I could run along the interstate. If I jumped on the interstate, I would have a total of 12 miles to run on it before I hit the Wyoming border. Knowing that it was illegal to run along the interstate in Utah, I wasn't crazy about that option. However, when compared to adding another 30 miles onto my run, it was an easy decision.

Tiff drove on up to the entrance ramp of the interstate, where I met her for a quick aid stop. I had about six miles to run before the next exit on the interstate and I told Tiffany I would run those six miles as fast as I could and then text her when I got close. My family later named this section of the journey "The Citation Run." That's because I ran those six miles so fast that when I texted Tiffany, she thought I had been picked up by a state trooper.

I wasn't a fan of running where I wasn't supposed to, but there was no other reasonable option (as if any portion of running across America would be considered "reasonable"). First and foremost, I had no desire to get stopped by a police officer. Second, I wanted to be a good example for my children by obeying the law. I just had to write this off as one of those "do as I say, not as I do" moments so many parents have with their children.

On this last section of I-80, I had to run past a weigh station. I was running as fast as I could and also trying to stay down off of the interstate as much as possible in order to stay out of sight from the patrol car at the weigh station. Fortunately, I made it through this section and got off the interstate without any incidents.

While running into Wahsatch, which is right on the Utah side of the Utah-Wyoming state line, I came upon an Army National Guard facility, so I poked my head into the office. As I stepped in, a young man at the front desk greeted me, and a number of senior enlisted men were also in the room. They all gave me the same look I received as I entered other facilities: "Who is this sweaty guy and why is he in here?" I introduced myself and handed the sergeant behind the desk my card, and spent a couple of minutes explaining my story. Another soldier came up to me, and just listened with a look of disbelief as I described the reason behind my journey. I held my hand out, and said the words that I would share every time I met a current military member or veteran: "Thank you for your service."

The looks on the faces of the men before me immediately went from disbelief and curiosity to appreciation. I remember how it made me feel when I served in the Marines and someone took the time to thank me for my service, and I wanted to make sure I took every chance I could on this run to give that back to those in the military. And I was always met with the same response—a warm smile, a shake of the hand and a sense of gratitude from those who sacrifice every day. As I headed out the door of the facility, my chest was sticking out with pride in what we were accomplishing. It felt good to give of ourselves to help these brave men and women know that there were a lot of us out there who were very grateful for all they were doing for us.

### 'WIND'ING THROUGH WYOMING

My time spent in Wyoming can be described in one word—windy. The best part about it, though, was that most days the wind was at my back and almost literally carried me through some areas. I was able to run on the interstate the whole way through Wyoming, which enabled me to become more comfortable doing so. I became very in tune with the rumble strips, prepared to jump over a guard rail or into a ditch if I heard the vibration of a car veering out of the right-hand lane. I was grateful that nearly all of the large semi-trucks that passed me by as I ran would get over into the left-hand lane to give me a bit more space on the shoulder.

The first day into Wyoming, as the temperature dropped and the snow rolled in, I told Tiff that I should have known it was coming. I was about to finish my day in Fort Bridger, the site of our encounter with crazy snow and weather on our way out to Oregon where they shut down the interstate on us due to the conditions. It just seemed there was no way I was going to go through this area again without getting snowed on. The snowfall wasn't as bad as it was on our first trip through, so I was able to push through at a pretty good pace. I was feeling better and better each day on the run, my times were coming down and at the end of the day I felt like I had more energy.

Little America was our next stop the following day, after another day filled with howling 40-50 mph winds and blowing snow. After leaving Salt Lake City, I hadn't seen many trees with green leaves, so when we came upon a truck stop on I-80 surrounded by trees overflowing with bright green leaves, it was almost as if it was an oasis in the desert. It was certainly a welcoming sight.

We pulled in for the night and Tiffany headed over to the truck stop laundry facility to wash the heap of dirty clothes that we had accumulated. Since we packed light for the trip, Tiffany usually had to hand wash my running clothes every night and wash the rest of the family's clothes that way from time to time as well. Being able to use a washer and dryer every once in a while was a nice treat. But using this laundry facility ended up being more of a trick than a treat. When Tiffany headed back to grab the clothes from the dryer and fold them, she discovered that a pair of her jeans was missing.

I just looked at Tiff and said, "I bet that trucker sure will look good in your jeans at the next truck stop."

The wind howled and shook the RV pretty good all night long, so it made for a miserable night's sleep. The next morning as I groggily searched through my pile of clothes for my Koenig rain/wind pants that I had been running in the past couple of days for warmth, I couldn't find them. I asked Tiffany and Kathy to check to see if they were in with their clothes. While I continued to search for them, I realized that I was also missing a pair of my running shorts. The thief the night before had not only taken my wife's jeans, but had also pilfered my pants and shorts that I wore just about every day. If there is one thing I can't stand, it's a thief.

Tiffany went back over to the office and they said that no clothes had been turned in, so I took off on my run that day wearing my Nike ColdGear pants with a different pair of running shorts over top of them. Not only was the wind pushing me along, but I had a fire burning in me from having our clothes stolen. I considered it not only a slap in my face, but a slap in the face to all of the veterans I was doing this run for.

In preparation for this journey, I was in communication with Kathe Flynn at Holabird Sports in Baltimore, Maryland. They offered to support me and try to drum up support from other national clothing brands. While they experienced the same results that I did—getting no interest from any national companies—Holabird Sports did support me in any way they could. A couple of days after the laundromat incident, Holabird Sports delivered a package to us in Wamsutter, Wyoming. The timing could not have been more perfect. In the box they not only included first aid and nutrition supplies, but also a few new pairs of shorts and shirts for me to wear during the run. That shipment not only helped to replenish my wardrobe, but also my spirit.

Just as small companies like Holabird Sports came through for me, it was the small communities that I ran through that really offered the greatest encouragement, support and warmth. That was the case all through Wyoming. Countless people came off their front porches or out the front door of their local retailers to offer words of encouragement, talk to me or the crew in the RV and sometimes give donations. We also received some good publicity through local newspapers like the *Rawlins Times* and the *Saratoga Sun* as we passed through Wyoming. Each day as I got farther into the state the mountains continued to get higher, but thanks to the local support of those small communities, those mountains seemed more like small hills because I had more spring in my step.

When we arrived in Elk Mountain, population 275, we stopped at the Elk Mountain Trading Post to inquire about dinner and a place to park our RV. The owners, Ken and Nancy, said there was an RV park nearby, and called the owners, Peggy and her husband, to get us set up. Once the RV was hooked up, we walked back over to the Trading Post for dinner. Ken and Nancy were great ambassadors for the little town of Elk Mountain. They welcomed us, provided great food and shared stories of their comfortable, small town. It was almost as if we had gone back in time. Nick and I played a game of pool, and when a song came on the jukebox that had a nice little beat, I grabbed Shayna's hand and danced with her across the room. It was a nice break from the normalcy of running across America.

When we left Elk Mountain we knew I had a few larger climbs as we headed toward Laramie. Heading out from Elk Mountain, I was faced with three consecutive climbs that day peaking at elevations of 7,579, 7,597, and 7,716 feet. I was feeling really good, though, and the wind continued to push me along. I encountered some prairie dogs and prong horned antelope, which I thought were one of the most majestic animals I had ever seen. Even with the climbs, the wind and sight of the animals really made the time pass quickly.

My climb to the highest point of the entire run was in Laramie, where I peaked at 8,640 feet. I actually got to the top of the climb about half an hour quicker than my crew expected because I was feeling so strong. I ran 34.5 miles that day, with the last six miles climbing to the peak, and I covered the entire day's leg in just less than six hours.

While we were in the Laramie area, we stayed a couple of nights with Dr. Edward Bradley, a professor at the University of Wyoming. His son is a Marine who was stationed overseas at the time, and one of his Marine friends had been following me on the run. He contacted us and worked out our stays with Edward. As he told us, "Marines stick together, and you are a part of my family, whether my son is here with me or not."

Prior to heading into Cheyenne, I did everything I could to pack on three or four extra miles each day so that once we hit Cheyenne I could have my shortest day of the run. Kathy would be flying back to Oregon from Cheyenne, and I wanted to make sure we spent as much time as possible with her prior to her flying out. The day I headed into Cheyenne, I only needed to run 10.5 miles to get to my scheduled stopping point for the day. A cold front had pushed in, so I ran the first eight miles in a heavy snowstorm, but the weather cleared up as I made my way into the city.

As I stopped at the RV, a sheriff pulled up behind us to make sure everything was OK. After a short conversation about our run, he revealed that he was retired from the Air Force. He then paused, and I could see tears beginning to well up in his eyes. He swallowed the lump in his throat, and then rolled up one of the sleeves on his uniform. He showed me a hunter green wristband that was woven out of paratrooper rip cord.

"I wear this for my wife," he said, his voice trembling. "She's a medevac pilot and she's doing her third tour in Afghanistan right now. She deals first-hand every day with wounded men and women in the military, so I really respect you for running for wounded veterans."

This moment reminded me exactly why I was making this journey. There are so many heroes out there, and I love hearing their personal stories.

We had an enjoyable last day with Tiffany's mom. Kathy had been with us for almost four weeks and had been a big help. She helped out with the kids and allowed Tiffany to focus on my needs and the logistics of the trip. It was also great for our kids to spend some quality time with their Gramma because they don't get a chance to do it often since we are separated by three time zones. We all looked forward to her and Dick joining us again when we arrived in Washington, DC, as well as bringing our sweet Golden Retriever, Emmie, back home to us as well. When she flew out from Cheyenne, it felt awkward without her or my mom with us, but I knew we had an incredible crew chief in my wife who could handle anything thrown her way.

## ALL DOWNHILL FROM HERE (WELL, ALMOST)

Looking at the elevation map that was created by MyAthlete Live based on our planned route, it looked like someone could trip me coming out of Laramie, Wyoming, and I could roll all the way into Kansas. Coming down into Cheyenne, it seemed like I was almost heading straight downhill, and there was really no end in sight to that. Besides the Appalachian Mountains in a couple of months, it was pretty much all downhill from there.

While my elevation was decreasing, the amount of media coverage was increasing. I did my first regional interview since the kickoff of the run with K2TV in Cheyenne. Jeff Schuman interviewed me at Holliday Park in Cheyenne and provided me with the chance to meet some of his friends in the Air Force that were stationed locally at Francis Warren Air Force Base. It was great to share stories of my journey with them, and to hear what it meant to them for us to do this.

My first day in Colorado was met with wide open dirt roads and a lot of time spent alone. It was about this portion of my trek across the country that I began to pick out a silo, water tower or clump of trees off in the distance and keep my eyes on that marker in order to pull me in to that point. Once I reached that landmark, I would look ahead for another one. I could literally see 10-15 miles in front of me in most of the areas in the Plains and Midwest.

On this run, I spent 30 of my 37 miles on the dirt, which was a nice break from the pounding of the pavement. Unfortunately, I encountered about 10 snakes on the road that day, but thankfully all of the rattlers I saw were dead. I really hate snakes.

This was also the only day that I really had any major issues with large tanker trucks. I told Tiff at the end of the day, it seemed like they were playing games with me. Each tanker seemed to go past me faster (50-60 miles per hour) and closer to me than the previous one. The road was wide enough for two lanes and even though no other vehicles were approaching from the opposite direction, when the trucks passed me they failed to get over to the left to give me room.

Due to the heat quickly approaching 90 that day, I had my shirt off for most of the run. Since I was running on a dirt road, each truck that roared past me would kick up a ton of dirt and rocks. Little pebbles kicked up by the tires felt like BBs being shot from a gun as they pelted my bare chest, arms and legs. After the first truck passed, whenever I heard another rumbling down the dusty road, I tried as quickly as possible to toss my shirt on to at least provide a buffer between the flying rocks and my skin.

## HELP FROM THE CAPTAIN

One of the most helpful people as Tiffany was planning our route and checking with all of the states was Gaylon Grippin, a captain of the Colorado State Police, who lived in Sterling. Not only was he extremely helpful during the preparations for the trip, but he said he would help us out in any way possible when we came through his town. He certainly lived up to his word.

When we got about 40 miles outside of Sterling, we took him up on his offer and drove ahead into town to stay at an RV park.

"We've made it into Sterling for the night, Captain," I told him when we called after getting settled in.

"Yes, I saw your RV coming through earlier," he said. "It's great to have you here, and we all support what you are doing."

Not only did Captain Grippin offer to take our family out for dinner the following night, but he also set up interviews for me with KPMX-FM and the *South Platte Sentinel*. When I ran into Sterling the following day, finishing up in 90-degree temps right in front of the courthouse, Captain Grippin was there with two more of Colorado's finest police officers. Gaylon and his wife, Lora, treated us to a wonderful meal that night and we enjoyed some excellent conversation and company. It was interesting to hear stories about the history of their town, while also sharing some of the more interesting and trying times that we had experienced thus far on our journey. As I was relaying the details of one story, however, my mind went blank and I completely lost my train of thought. It was evidence that not only was this run physically exhausting, but it was mentally draining as well. The moment did, however, provide a nice laugh for everyone at the dinner table.

## NO SYMPATHY

As I headed out of Sterling the following morning, there was a 50-degree drop in temperature. After running in 90-degree heat more than 12 hours earlier, I was now trudging along with temps in the 40s and a cold wind that had shifted from being at my back to being in my face. I was not having a good day running on the rolling hills, and the cold wind smacking me in the face was reminiscent of my lashcicle runs during the previous winter. I got into the RV at the first stop and as was usual, everyone smiled and asked how I was doing.

"The wind is right in my face, and it sucks!"

That sucked the joy right out of the RV. The kids just kind of hunkered down and didn't say a word. Tiff handed me my food, sat down across from me and in the most encouraging way said to me, "Sounds like you just need to refuel and keep moving forward."

I wolfed my food and drinks down, said bye to everyone and stepped off in a huff.

*"Where is the sympathy for what I am going through?"* I thought. *"I'm out here getting beat up in the wind, it is 50 degrees colder than it was yesterday, and you just tell me to keep moving forward?"*

I took off trying to push my frustration out on the road, getting madder and madder at the wind and the weather conditions that were being thrown my way. After a couple of miles of wearing myself out struggling to cut through the wind like I was swimming without the use of my limbs, I just decided to settle in and not exert too much energy. I was getting a chance to enjoy this beautiful country and experience America in a way very few ever had, and I was complaining about a little wind. I also wasn't showing much gratitude to my crew in the RV for what they were putting up with from me. I made a conscious decision that when they caught back up to me, I needed to apologize right away. With my chin up, I pressed forward, just as Tiffany had told me to do.

No more than five minutes after adjusting my attitude, a truck traveling east on the road pulled up beside me. A young man rolled the window down and asked me to come over for a minute. Running over to the vehicle, I noticed a C&T Hauling label on the side of the truck, and the young man introduced himself as Cody Iverson, from Gillette, Wyoming. He had stayed in the same RV park as us the night before and saw our RV, so he wanted to hear a bit about our story. I told him what I was doing and why, and he asked if we had any corporate sponsors helping us along the way. I shared with him a few of the challenges and frustrations in our attempt to secure sponsorship. He just shook his head and then reached into his wallet.

"Take this and use it to help yourselves out a little bit. It's not much, but hopefully it'll help get you along some when you need it." I looked down and he was handing me a $100 bill.

It was at that moment that I realized that I just need to do everything without complaining, especially on this trip. When I least expect it, someone will lift me up when I need it most, and it reminded me exactly why I was on this run. I was out there to encourage others, not looking for anything for myself. If I made the run about me, the whole mission would be a bust. When I focused on others and how grateful I was to be doing this, things just seemed to work out. This day was proof.

When the RV caught back up to me, I walked in with a much different demeanor. I could tell Tiff and the kids were very guarded when I walked in, but I did my best to alleviate their concerns and make amends for the horrible attitude I had earlier. I told them about the encounter I had with Cody out on the road and I promised that I would have a more positive attitude the rest of the journey.

Later on that week, I shared the story on my blog about that day, and how I had reacted to the weather and road conditions I experienced. The comments posted in response by readers were quite humorous. "Let it out!" one person commented. Another person wrote, "You need the negative moments to make the recovery of your spirit grand. Ever hear of makeup sex? You just did that with your mind."

# 10 | Watching the Corn Grow

*"If I can just make it to the Central time zone, I know I can make it to the finish."*

That thought would often run through my mind both before I started this trek, and many times throughout the first few weeks of the run. Approaching my third time zone and the 50-day mark was something that really provided sincere belief that the final destination and the 100-day goal was within my grasp. Aside from a few moments of mental weakness–which often coincided with physical weakness–I never doubted my ability to finish. My ability to finish within 100 days, however, was something I questioned from time to time.

But at this point I knew that I had already conquered what I thought would be the toughest legs of the trip. I dealt with freezing temperatures and heavy snowstorms in Oregon and Wyoming, dime-sized hail in Colorado, pouring rain throughout the early states, the deserts of Nevada and Utah and the highest peaks of the entire trip in Wyoming.

Cutting through the corners of Colorado and Nebraska saved me from even higher peaks through the Rockies and it provided sections that were flat. The downside to that route, however, was that it meant we would be passing through populated communities infrequently. And one of the purposes of this run was to get out in front of as many people as possible in order to spread the word about our mission.

Those concerns were quickly dispelled, however, because there were many times when we were out on the road or near a small town and people would stop by the RV to learn more about the run, donate money and share their own stories of triumph or tragedy. Having the vehicle wrap on the motorhome promoting the run was a tremendous avenue for enabling us to advertise the run and its purpose.

No matter what town we passed through, we were always greeted with smiles, waves and tremendous hospitality. This hospitality would be none more evident than when we passed through the Colorado/Nebraska border and into the small town of Imperial, Nebraska.

The wind was still brisk as I crossed the border into Nebraska, and looking at the map, I had about eight miles of straight road to tackle before the end of my day. Prior to the slight right I made on US Route 6 coming into Nebraska, I had run the previous 28 miles on an extremely flat road, with only a small left-hand turn that I saw coming at me for about 10 miles. With the various crops (primarily corn) still in their infancy, there was really no barrier to block the wind that was whipping across the plains. Living in West Virginia, I'm not accustomed to these types of winds because the hills tend to break the wind up. But out here, the wind was able to charge full steam ahead. Even though the temperature was rising, I still couldn't shake the chill that hit me with each gust of wind. But having learned my lesson in Kansas that I shouldn't complain, I knew there was nothing to do except continue to press forward.

One of the things I always do when I run is take note of vehicles approaching me or passing me along the road. For whatever reason, I have always been good about remembering the make, model and color of cars that I see while I'm on a run. It tends to keep me from getting too bored at times when my mind can wander. On this long, straight stretch, I took note of a large red truck (in this region, most of the vehicles that passed me were large pickups) that was hauling an all-terrain vehicle (ATV) in the bed of the truck. I jokingly told myself that I wished the driver would have stopped and allowed me to ride the ATV to my finishing point for the day.

I finished my run that day a short while later at the intersection of Route 6 and 315 Avenue. Since the nearest town, Lamar, didn't have an advertised RV hookup location, and the closest town to that was Imperial, we decided to just find the nearest place to park the RV. It just so happened that at the intersection, there were two large farm buildings and a number of grain elevators.

Sitting in the parking lot of the property was the red truck that passed me about an hour earlier, minus the ATV in the back. The owner had a loading ramp hanging off the back of the truck, which I told Tiff hopefully meant that they would be returning soon so that we could seek permission to park the RV in the lot for the night. Our fingers were crossed that the owner would also have a power outlet that we could use to power the electricity in the RV for the evening as well. Asking for assistance is one thing that we became very straight-forward and open about on the trip, something that was not second nature to us before.

About 15 minutes after we parked, I heard the ATV approach, so I stepped outside the RV to greet the owner. Tom Arterburn introduced himself and listened to my story as I explained our mission and that we hoped to be able to camp here in the RV tonight. Tom told us it was his family's property and that he would call his father, John, to check. But he mentioned that he didn't think his father would object, and he pointed to the back of our RV.

"That right there means a lot to our family, so there shouldn't be a problem at all," he said as he pointed to the license plate.

When we registered the RV, one of the things that I wanted to do was show our pride in being veterans of the armed forces, so in bright red letters the West Virginia-issued license plate read "VETERAN" just above the license plate number.

"We really appreciate it a lot," I said to Tom as he headed toward his truck.

A few minutes after I showered and cleaned up, John pulled up in his truck. We stepped out to introduce ourselves, and he told me his son had already explained everything to him and it would be no problem for us to stay.

After thanking him, I shared some of the stories of people we had met and how encouraging it was to encounter people like his family who went out of their way to help us out.

"We appreciate the men and women in the military, and will do what we can to support them," he said.

As John pulled away, his son, who had been washing his truck and ATV, came back over to the RV and asked if the kids would like to get out of the RV for a while. He said he had talked to a good friend of his who had a bunch of horses and cattle on their farm, and wanted to see if the kids wanted to go for a ride.

"Yes!" exclaimed both of the kids. I asked Tiff if she wanted to go, and she declined, saying it would be good for her to just get some time alone to clean up the RV and have some quiet time. Understanding completely, the kids and I jumped into the truck with Tom, who took us to his friend Colton's farm, where there was a horse outside. Seeing both of the kids with smiles on their faces, eyes beaming brightly at the view from atop the gorgeous animal they were on was something that felt really good. I knew the trip had taken its toll on the kids and they had grown tired of being inside the "box on wheels," but they rarely complained. The fun time they had riding the horse, playing with the farm dogs and "chatting" with the cattle really lifted their spirits.

Tom took us to another part of the farm and pulled up next to a big combine tractor. He allowed the kids to climb inside the tractor–a behemoth of a machine with wheels that easily were taller than our RV. Nick described to me the amount of circuitry and computer equipment inside the tractor, and Tom explained that they program the combines by GPS and can get down to the inch as far as where they need the tractors to go in the fields. I watched in awe as Nick and Shayna both took turns driving the tractor, raising and lowering the forks on the front.

I learned a lot about America and its terrain on this trip, and this part of the run through the Midwest was no exception. Having flown over the Midwest numerous times, I often wondered how those large, perfectly round plots of land were created as I looked down from the plane above. Not having any flat land like that back home in West Virginia, nor having spent any time in the Midwest, it was always one of those mysteries to me. I'll never forget the day on one of my runs through the Midwest when I realized exactly what caused those circles to be formed. No, it wasn't the work of aliens or pranksters. Massive irrigation systems that looked like they were a quarter mile in length, attached to a massive motor with wheels about every 50 feet or so, connected to a base that would complete a half circle, and sometimes a full rotation, on a plot of land that spanned acres. It honestly took about three or four days of running by these systems before it even clicked with me what type of pattern they were creating on the surface, and when it did click, I shook my head at myself for not solving that "mystery" sooner. You learn something new every day, especially crossing America on foot.

Tom drove us back to our RV and while we were thanking him for giving the kids and I a great time on their farm, this 21-year-old reached into his pocket and pulled a $50 bill out of his wallet, handing it to me.

"I want you to take this money to help out with your cause. I really appreciate what you're doing and I want you to know that my family and I are grateful for all those who have served in the military and what they have done for our family."

His gesture and words were signs of his maturity and the good values that his parents had instilled in him.

## MOTHER'S DAY PARADE

The following morning was Mother's Day, and as the kids and I awoke, we saw an absolutely gorgeous sun peeking over the horizon of farmland. It was difficult to try to celebrate special days during this trip, but we tried to make do with what we had and Mother's Day was no different. A couple of weeks earlier, the kids and I had bought some cards and a necklace for Tiffany so we would be able to give them to her on this day.

Tiffany had purchased a French press coffee maker to bring on our trip and had become pretty proficient at using it to make some great-smelling coffee. I had just a few sips of the brew on the whole journey, so I hadn't really used it at all, but on this morning I did my best to make her a cup. Nicholas fixed her some cinnamon-sprinkled toast. "Nothing but the best for mommy on Mother's Day," we told her. Even though it wasn't the most special of breakfasts or ways to celebrate the day, Tiffany really made us feel like we had made her feel special on this morning.

As I climbed out of the RV to begin my run that morning, Colton, whose family owned the farm where our kids rode the horse and drove the combine, pulled up in his pickup truck. I told him again how thankful I was for allowing our kids to have a great time on his farm. "It's nothing compared to what you guys are doing," he said. He then handed me a $100 bill to be added to the funds we were raising for veteran-based charities. I ran back to the RV, beaming as I went inside, to give Tiffany the money.

As I started to head out again, John Arterburn pulled up and asked if we needed anything else before we got going. I told him we were fine and thanked him again for allowing us to stay on his property. I also shared how wonderful his son was to all of us the previous day and how proud he must be of his son.

"That's just the way we are around these parts," he said.

I headed on down the road, with about 20 miles of straight road in front of me before I entered Imperial. The highway was very kind to me. The road was wide and the shoulders were soft, giving my feet and knees a break from the pavement I had been bouncing on for the past 50 days. I took my time and just marveled at the vastness and the beauty of the fields that surrounded me. I was amazed at how fortunate we are to be able to enjoy the fruits (and vegetables) of all of the hard work so many farmers do each day. I had the chance to see it in action as well. As I ventured into the lower elevations out of Colorado, I encountered fields that had been freshly plowed, and was now witnessing the corn and other crops coming out of the ground. I've often heard and used the term "watching grass grow." Well, I literally saw corn grow on this trip.

About 13 miles into my run on Route 6, a truck came toward me and pulled over to the side of the road. A man stepped out of the truck and introduced himself as Dwight Coleman, the mayor of Imperial, Nebraska. He told me that one of his council members had called and told him we stayed in his lot last night.

"I know you'll be headed into town in about an hour," Dwight said, "and even though I don't have much time, I wanted to let you know I'm going to try to put something together for you before you arrive."

I had just got back on the road from a stop in the RV, so I told him that Tiff was less than a half mile behind me in the RV and that he could swing back to coordinate any plans he may have with her. He spent about three minutes talking with Tiff and the kids, and then blew the horn as he drove past me, heading back toward Imperial. I was feeling really energized at this point, excited about what was to come and the outpouring of support that people were giving us.

About seven miles later I approached a right-hand turn and on the right side of the road were two teenagers and a man standing there waiting for me. As I approached them, the man told me he was the coach of the local high school cross country team, and the two teenagers were members of his team. He apologized for not being able to round up other runners, but he wanted to get some of the boys out to run with me. We rounded a corner, and I couldn't believe what was in front of me.

Parked alongside the road was the RV, and across the road were a police car, a fire truck and numerous other vehicles, including a couple of motorcycles. Standing near the RV were Tiffany, the kids and about 20 other people. I made my way to the group and was introduced by the mayor to members of the city staff and a local reporter for the *Imperial Republican*, Jan Shultz, who we had spoken to the previous night. In less than an hour, the mayor of Imperial had managed to arrange an impromptu parade through town. This just blew my mind!

With the police cruiser leading the way, myself, the two high school runners and my son ran through the town of Imperial, followed by the motorcycles, the fire truck and the RV. My head was held high as we ran down the street. I knew it was nearly noon and realizing that it was Sunday, and Mother's Day, I didn't expect many people to be out on the streets. I was dead wrong!

Many families who were returning home from church had pulled their vehicles off to the side of the road to wave at us, cheer and offer words of encouragement as they hung their heads out their car windows. Many others were standing, lining the streets. Several were waving small American flags attached to wooden sticks and saying, "Thank you" as we ran by. The scene seemed surreal–like I was in a scene of a movie where a soldier returns to his small hometown from the war and is greeted with a hero's welcome. The amount of pride I felt at that moment was indescribable. I believe you could have seen my smile all the way in Kansas, and as flat as the terrain around us was, that was probably true.

At the end of our two-mile run through Imperial, we pulled over to allow everyone to part ways and wish us well. John Arterburn had Tiffany drive the RV back into town so he could pay to fill up the gas tank (with the price of gas and the size of the tank, spending $150 to fill it up became commonplace). The whole experience was unbelievable and we could never thank them enough for how they welcomed us into their small town and treated us as though we were family. Even though I ran 37 miles that day, it felt like a seven-mile day because I was so energized by the experiences we shared with the amazing people in Imperial, Nebraska.

We ended the day at Enders State Park, enjoying a nice stroll along the lake and grilling hot dogs with the kids over the fire pit. The kids treated

Tiffany to a backrub that night and Shayna brushed her hair. What began as coffee and cinnamon toast turned into an amazing Mother's Day.

## COMMON BONDS

My final full day in Nebraska was rather uneventful. I wrapped up the run just outside of McCook with temperatures hovering around 90 degrees. About a mile from the end of my run, I noticed another runner approaching me from the other side of the road and he crossed over to greet me. His name was Justin Walker and he explained that he was on a "running sabbatical." He was an ultramarathon runner and was in between jobs, so he wanted to travel around for a couple of months and take the opportunity to run in some beautiful areas of the country.

Justin reversed course and we ran the last mile in to the RV. We talked for a little while about both of our journeys and how cool it was to cross paths like this. He wanted to get a few miles in with me the next morning, so we set up our RV that night at the city park and he set up camp in his truck next to us. The next morning Justin drove his truck 11 miles ahead into McCook and then rode back in the RV to our starting point.

We ran at an enjoyable pace and shared some good conversation as he ran with me the first 15.5 miles. We remained in touch after that day and he sent me several encouraging text messages throughout the rest of my trek. During my training the previous two years I preferred to run alone since I wasn't confident enough in my conditioning to be able to talk with fellow runners. But I was beginning to realize that I had transformed into a runner who pretty much wouldn't shut up when someone joined me. I wasn't running out of breath as I talked and ran, which was a testament to the conditioning that I had built up. I turned into such a chatter box that when people ran with me, I typically apologized for talking so much. Those who ran with me, however, always said they enjoyed listening to some of the incredible stories that I had to share.

As I neared Oberlin, Kansas, the temperature continued to climb and the wind picked up. The wind shifted a lot across my body, which put some strain on my knees. As the day wore on, the pain in my right knee around my iliotibial (IT) band, which runs along the outside of the leg from the hip to below the knee, continued to worsen, but I kept moving forward as best as possible. During my aid stops I would ice it and stretch it out, and I tried to run as gently as possible. By the time I reached the Oberlin airport, I had navigated a number of rolling hills that continued to put more pressure on my knees. The wind was also blowing directly into my face and, combined with the 92-degree temperature, slowed me down to almost a crawl.

## DIPS IN THE ROAD

We camped that night in Oberlin at Terrace Gardens RV park. The owner was a disabled veteran who had spoken to Tiffany prior to our arrival. He put us up for the night for free, and it was just the first of many ways that the people of Oberlin cared for us during our short stay.

During our trip, when we did go out to eat dinner, we always preferred to find a "mom and pop" restaurant so we could enjoy the true experience of each local community. In Oberlin, we found a small place on the GPS called the Frontier Family Restaurant, which sounded perfect.

As motorhome newbies, one of the things we were most concerned about was having a major catastrophe mechanically with the RV. We knew one problem could put us completely behind schedule. The very first thing we noticed as we traveled through the old residential neighborhood, especially as we made our way through the small side streets following the GPS directions, was that at each intersection, the road had deep divots at each crossing. It looked to us like they were there to allow for runoff and drainage from heavy storms. Crossing the first one, Tiffany took it really slow and crossed it with no problem. Our GPS, just like the online maps we'd used before, didn't always turn out to be perfect, so we made a couple of turns that weren't necessary, slowly navigating the deep sections of the roadway in an attempt to avoid dragging the bottom of the RV against the road, but we heard it bottom out and scrape a couple of times.

We missed the entrance of the restaurant the first time by, so we had to circle back around the block again. As we made our way through the first turn, everything seemed normal. But when Tiffany made the turn on the street directly behind the restaurant, she noted what looked like a fresh stream of water on the road, and it was following the same path we had just driven. Around the next turn, sure enough, the same pattern of water led the way. By the time we made the last turn and pulled into the restaurant parking lot, we knew we had a problem.

We both jumped out of the RV and could immediately hear water pouring out from under it. I ran to the back, looked underneath and saw that the gray water pipe, which carries water from the sink and shower to a holding tank, was cracked and spewing water. Panic began to set in as we realized we were in a small town where we didn't know a soul, and we were concerned about what was wrong, how quickly we could get it repaired and how we would be able to afford the cost.

About this time, the manager of the restaurant stepped outside, almost assuredly because he was concerned we were dumping sewage into his parking lot as if I was Clark Griswold's cousin Eddie in the movie *Christmas Vacation*. We assured him the leak was water coming from a busted pipe from the gray water tank, and then voiced our obvious concern about getting it repaired. At this moment, an angel stepped out of the restaurant to show us exactly what small town America was all about.

"I see you have a problem," the lady said as she walked out. "How can I help?"

I explained our situation and our mission to her.

"Let me call my husband," she said.

She stepped away from the RV for a moment, made a quick phone call and came back over to us. "My husband, Jim, is on his way." She introduced herself as Ruth and tried to ease our anxiety, assuring us that the RV could be repaired.

Five minutes later, her husband arrived and said that he had placed a call to a plumber who would be there shortly. Jim was a member of the local American Legion, and just as his wife had done, he assured us that everything would be taken care of. After another five minutes, a young man pulled up in his truck and immediately got under the RV to inspect the problem. Within minutes, he pulled out his tools, including a reciprocating saw, climbed back under the RV, cut out the section that had cracked, replaced it with a new pipe and fittings and verified everything was in working order. The whole process could not have taken more than 30 minutes from the time we pulled into the parking lot to the time the repair was completed.

As he put his tools back into his truck, I asked him what we owed him for his service.

"Don't worry about it," the man said. "Because of what you're doing, I'm donating my time, and the American Legion is picking up the tab for the parts. I'm just happy to help you guys on your way."

I shook the man's hand, thanked him for everything and turned back to Jim and Ruth, who while the plumber was working had listened intently to the story of our journey and shared stories of Jim's own service in the military.

"Now go on inside," Ruth said, "and get yourselves a bite to eat. Dinner is on us."

What we witnessed that evening was the reaffirmation of the American spirit, and how so many are willing to step up and help out when someone is truly in need. We enjoyed a great meal that night, reflecting back on all of the great folks who had been so generous to us in so many ways. We were so thankful and inspired to be able to get a first-hand glimpse of the true American spirit. It was also a great reminder that while at times it seems like the US has forgotten about the sacrifices being made by our men and women in the military, the vast majority of Americans have a genuine appreciation for the sacrifices made by veterans.

We had only been in this state for a few hours but had already been pleasantly surprised by the hospitality. Little did we realize that Kansas would provide us with even more surprises in the days to come.

# 11 | Singing Off Key

I had to endure a variety of elements while running from Oregon in late March to Kansas in mid-May. We never knew what we were going to experience from one day to the next. The next 10 days through Kansas would offer another challenge with extremely strong winds, combined with the warm weather. I felt like I had to exert twice as much energy just to keep from being blown backward, let alone move forward, all while standing in front of a blast furnace.

There were still, however, several enjoyable and inspirational moments as I passed through Kansas. Early during my first full day in Kansas, as I was about to go back out on the road following an aid stop, I saw a man riding a bike coming toward us from behind. His bike was loaded down with what looked like all his worldly possessions. He stopped as he rode up and introduced himself as Joe.

"Where are you riding to?" I asked him.

"Cape May, New Jersey," he said with a smile. "Where are you running to?"

"Annapolis, Maryland" I replied matter of factly.

"That's awesome!" he responded. "How cool is it that two transcontinental travelers meet up like this?"

"Are you riding for a cause?" I asked Joe.

"No. I promised myself that if I lived to see 50 I would ride across America, and I made it, so now here I am living out my dream."

I listened intently as Joe told me the story of his service in the Navy, when he felt like he was on top of the world and in great shape. After he was honorably discharged and entered civilian life, he struggled to maintain a healthy lifestyle. His weight ballooned and his health worsened, causing him to have to take multiple medications daily. At the age of 42, he weighed 300 pounds and his self-esteem had bottomed out. He decided to begin riding his bike regularly and he promised himself that if he made it to the age of 50, he was going to ride across America.

Eight years after he made that promise to himself, here he was, making his way across this beautiful country on his bike. "I'm still not at the weight I want to be, but I'm alive at 50," Joe said proudly. We talked about the strong winds in Kansas, the incredible people we had met along the way and just how awesome it was to experience America like we were able to. The more we talked, the more I was inspired by his drive and motivation.

So often we commit to something in life, yet it doesn't take much to get us off track. Even when the goal we set for ourselves is something easily attainable, it is often difficult to stay focused because of all of the distractions in life. Our children, our careers and everything else tend to pull us in different directions, resulting in us drifting off course from our goals. Here was Joe, however, who eight years ago made a commitment to pursue a healthier lifestyle and as a result he was achieving greatness by riding across the US at the age of 50. I found the story of his own transformation incredibly inspirational and thanked him so much for sharing it with me.

We promised to keep up with one another along the way (we both made blog entries that evening about our encounter and posted a photo of each other on our respective blogs, his on www.joeonabike.com) and said our goodbyes. He hopped back on his red road bike with red saddlebags flanking each side of his seat and I lowered my head and began to plow my way forward through the wind. I was able to keep him in my sights for the next few miles since the roads were fairly straight, but I eventually lost sight of him after he crested a hill a couple miles ahead of me. I continued to follow Joe, who actually donated to our cause, from time to time on his blog and was excited to read that he completed his journey in 50 days, arriving in Cape May, New Jersey, as planned.

## A PAIN IN THE WIND

I had always been under the impression that Kansas was a very flat state with no real hills. While the roads were perfectly straight for miles at a time, the first few days in the state presented me with plenty of rolling hills coupled with winds that just wouldn't let up. Running on rolling hills has never really been a problem for me. But in West Virginia, the hills typically blocked the wind and I was also usually under the cover of trees.

In Kansas, however, every gust of wind those first couple of days seemed to find the valleys in between each rolling hill and blew in a direct northern direction, right into my right side. Each day the weather forecast predicted sustained winds of 20-30 miles per hour, with gusts up to 50. The National Weather Service even issued warnings during this time for sustained winds in excess of 35 miles per hour.

As strange as it may sound, for two straight days the wind literally beat me up. I had to fight to stay upright and the extra effort exerted, combined with the crosswinds, put some major pressure on my knees. I had a problem with the IT band in my right knee when I first started training for the Richmond Marathon, and that flared up a day earlier when I first arrived in Kansas. Back when I was training for Richmond, I purchased a compression sleeve to wear to keep pressure and warmth on my knee. It helped tremendously.

Aside from my shin issue, I hadn't really experienced any leg pain until I hit Kansas, when the wind really wore me out. Well, the wind and the 2,000+ miles I had put on my legs the past 50 or so days. I'm thankful that my wife packed the blue compression sleeve because at this point I needed it, and it stayed on my right leg the remainder of my journey. After a couple of weeks wearing it, I believe I could have run without it because my knee was feeling much better, but it gave me some mental comfort knowing that it was providing support for my knee, so I didn't want to risk changing anything up that was working. Plus, at that point I had about an eight-inch section of pale skin above and below my knee that was underneath the sleeve and concealed from the sun when I ran. I didn't want to look any goofier than I already did running along the side of the road by showing everyone my knee-sleeve tan.

As I ran into Phillipsburg, Kansas, my route turned directly south on Route 183 for the last three miles of that day. The wind that had been beating up my right side for the past couple of days was now dead in my face. And it wasn't letting up. The temperature read 93 degrees on a bank sign as I ran through town, and now I had 45+ mph winds that were blazing hot and blowing directly in my face.

It literally felt like I could walk faster through the wind than run through it. Hunched over, I pushed forward as hard as I could, with the wind drying the sweat from my forehead and the tears from my eyes as quickly as they formed. I had my hat pulled down low to try to keep the wind out of my face, and about every 10 steps I would look up hoping I would see the RV on the side of the road because Tiffany had already driven past me to the finish spot for the day. I would crest a rolling hill, look for the RV and dejectedly put my head down and literally weep from the pain when I wouldn't see her.

I enjoy running in all types of weather, but this was ridiculous. It just seemed that with each step I took, I almost felt like I was going backwards, not just physically, but mentally. The wind was beating me up in more ways than one. When I finally crested the last hill and could see the RV, I tried to pick up the pace to get to the RV as I typically did each day, but there was no picking the pace up on this day.

I crossed the road to get to the same side as the RV and walked slowly up to it as Tiff looked out the window at me. She knew something wasn't right.

I had been complaining about the wind all day, but never had she seen me so defeated on the run. Even when I had the shin injury, I felt like I was still making progress, but this had me shut down mentally, which I was finding very difficult to overcome.

I hopped into the RV, completely spent, and was greeted with encouragement and cheering for having made it through the day. My wife and kids knew how much the positive reinforcement from them would help me through some tough stretches, and they didn't let me down that day.

## CHASING THE WIND

There's an old saying that states, "You never get a second chance to make a first impression." I'm eternally grateful that proverb didn't prove true when I began chasing after Tiffany when we first met. I first noticed her while we were working in the same division when stationed in Iwakuni, Japan, while in the Marine Corps. Initially, she wanted to avoid me like the plague.

Tiffany was dating someone else at the time that I began to make my intentions of getting together with her very clear. Initially, that bold talk turned her off. She would walk through the division and purposely avoid my work center, avoiding what I considered to be my magnetic personality. But I was a pest that wouldn't be swatted away easily.

Since we had the same core group of friends–the self-proclaimed "Fun Bunch"–we were frequently around each other. Fortunately, she slowly began to warm up to my personality, gradually realizing that I was harmless. As she would learn later in our relationship, I talked a good game but you usually couldn't take everything I said seriously. Maybe that's why when I threw out the idea of running across America, she initially thought my desire to do so was just harmless chatter.

I pulled one stunt during a weekend camping trip while stationed in Japan that I knew sealed our fate together. Early in the morning, still a little woozy from a night of drinking, I snuck into the tent that Tiff was staying in while she grabbed some breakfast at camp central. I grabbed a pair of her underwear, put them on my head, pulled them down over my ears and wandered around the campsite saying, "Whose are these? Whose are these?" I've since told people that when she didn't turn and run as fast as she could in the opposite direction at that moment, I knew we were destined to be married.

On May 18, 1996, it took only $90 and 30 minutes to fulfill that destiny in the living room of a Justice of the Peace in San Diego, where Tiffany was stationed at Marine Corps Air Station Miramar. Immediately after the ceremony, we called our parents and told them we had just gotten engaged. It wasn't until Thanksgiving that I revealed the news to my parents. When we walked through the door of my mom's house, I dropped my luggage and said, "We've got some news."

"You're pregnant?" my mom asked, her eyes focusing on Tiffany's tummy.

"No," I said.

"You're married?"

"Yes," I said proudly but with some hesitation.

"Welcome to the family" she said enthusiastically as she gave Tiff a huge hug.

At Christmas time we shared the news with Tiffany's family and were similarly relieved when, upon learning that his daughter was already married, her father bellowed out in his deep and intimidating voice, "Well, you just saved me a bunch of money!" Her parents welcomed me with open arms, but also gave me a little of what I deserved for stealing their daughter away.

I'm certain that neither of us imagined that on our 16th wedding anniversary we'd be waking up at 5 a.m. so that I could run 35 miles and she could chase me down while driving a 31-foot motorhome. Yet here we were in the middle of Kansas standing on the edge of a cornfield on our special day posing for a photograph with a dry erase board that had the number "16" written on it. When we met in Japan and later were married in San Diego, I told her I would take her places. She probably never imagined I'd take her to a windy and blistering hot Kansas cornfield in a box on wheels.

Throughout the rest of our time in Kansas, I kept my feet moving east while the kids and Tiffany began to get into geocaching. She was encouraged to join the geocaching culture by a fellow Marine who she had served with, and it proved to be a good suggestion. The kids were obviously starting to get really tired of being in the RV all the time, and being able to track down the little treasures that people would leave behind seemed like a great way to get them outside. They became obsessed with geocaching the rest of the way, and it was a wonderful way for them to stay engaged and keep from getting bored in the motorhome.

I had a few other veterans stop me as I ran through the next few towns after seeing our RV pass by, thanking me for what I was doing and giving donations. The number of followers on Twitter and Facebook continued to increase as I made my way through more populated areas. It was great to have so many people be a virtual part of my journey. Our message was really starting to get out there. As I made my way into Lawrence, Kansas, I did a few more TV and newspaper interviews, which really helped us on the local level to get the word out. We were still knocking at the door of the national media, but had no luck yet.

The celebration of the 2,000 mile mark was a small one, but one that was good for all of us, as we knew we were well beyond the halfway point, and it was a much needed boost to all of our psyches. Standing out on the road in Silver Lake, Kansas, I took a piece of chalk and drew out the number 2,000, and doing my best to stand up in the crazy wind had Tiff take a picture of a very excited man. Besides the incredible people we met and experiences we had in Kansas, this was one of the other highlights of my time through there. If I never experience the wind in Kansas again, however, I'll be a very happy man.

Minus the wind and heat I had to run through in Kansas, we met some of the kindest people as we passed through. The owner of the Jellystone Campground in Lawrence who put us up for the night and had food delivered to the RV was amazing. The owner of the Blue Heron Grill in Clay Center, who was an Army veteran, left a note on our RV asking us to stop by for a complimentary meal. Lynnelle Kummelehne, who was among those who saw us off in Oregon, grew up in Clay Center and put us up in a hotel room for the night. The UPS driver in Topeka who saw my story on TV and saw me running really encouraged me by stopping alongside the road to say thank you. She told me how proud she was of her niece, who was currently serving in Iraq. As my wife parked in the parking lot of the Cottage Inn in Bellvue, the owner came out and gave us a peach pie (I believe I could have had that every day; it was delicious). Chris and Marilyn, a couple in Kansas City who were members of the local Hash House Harriers, offered us some great hospitality, including some authentic Kansas City barbecue.

I could go on and on because there were so many great people who stepped up to help us out and encourage us along the way. It's just too bad I couldn't have gotten them to form a human barrier in front of me in order to block the Kansas wind while I ran through the state.

## PEOPLE MATTER

I was extremely happy to finally make it into Missouri. Kansas had certainly taken its toll on me both mentally and physically. I was able to adjust to the rolling hills, but the wind really took a lot out of me. *"This is supposed to be getting easier,"* I kept telling myself, when in reality it wasn't. On average, my daily runs increased by almost an hour every day through Kansas, even though I was logging the same mileage. The wind slowed me down that much, and when the wind would subside for a bit, the 95-degree temperatures made sure I didn't receive any relief. At this point in the run, I didn't think much could put a smile on my face.

"I'm sure you'll be fine. We're out of Kansas now," Tiffany kept saying. Little did I know that she had been plotting one of the most encouraging moments for me on the trip with some very good friends.

After a day of running and frustration, I hopped into the shower to cool off both my body and my attitude. I had just finishing shaving when my son knocked on the bathroom door in the RV, asking me to step out because he needed me to help with something. I stepped out into the hallway and my jaw nearly hit the floor.

Sitting on the couch in our motorhome were Aaron and Sandy Yocum, our good friends from back home in West Virginia. I ran at both of them and just held them both for the longest time, shedding tears of joy about their surprise visit. They both had been such an encouragement as I got into ultramarathon running. For this trip across the US, they helped me train, helped us organize and put on the successful silent auction and kept in touch with us the whole way. Now they had driven more than 14 hours to surprise me and join me on part of the run.

They couldn't have shown up at a better time. My spirits were down because of the weather and knee pain, but at that very moment I felt like nothing could stop me from finishing this run. Tiff just kind of shrugged her shoulders and smiled when I asked her how long this had been planned.

"You look like you've lost a little weight the past two months," Sandy commented. "But you're not as skinny as I thought you'd be."

"Tiff has been keeping me well fed," I said with a smile.

After chatting for a while, the Yocums headed to their hotel and took our kids with them so they could swim in the pool. About 30 minutes later, there was another knock on the motorhome door. Brian McClanahan and his wife, Shawnee, along with their two children, Darrian and Brayden, had driven nearly eight hours that day from Dallas, Texas, to meet us in Odessa, Kansas. Shawnee was a part of our "Fun Bunch" in Japan.

One of the greatest things about this run was the opportunity to rekindle old friendships, especially with some former Marines who I hadn't seen in 15 years. That began in Coos Bay at the launch of the run, continued here in Kansas and would also continue later at the end of our journey. It was a bit overwhelming for me that day, but it was super encouraging. Once everyone headed to their overnight accommodations, I just sat down on the edge of the bed in the RV with a huge smile on my face and tears streaming down my cheeks. I couldn't wait to get up the next morning and start running with everyone.

The next morning when we woke up, the temperature was already starting to climb, but thankfully the winds were a bit calmer. I don't think a tornado could have slowed me down, however, because I was so excited to be reunited with such great friends. The first few miles of the day, I was joined by Aaron, Sandy, Shawnee and her 7-year old son, Brayden, leading the way.

"He has been so excited to come run with you," Shawnee told me. Sporting his cool Terminator sunglasses and spiked red hair, Brayden gave a thumbs up and started running. My adrenaline kicked into overdrive, and with the wind almost non-existent, I was running at a pretty good pace.

"You don't slow down at all on the hills do you?" Sandy asked.

My conditioning was the best it had ever been in my life, and I didn't really know any gear other than forward. We knocked those first few miles out, and then Brian joined us for a while.

"When I told my friends we were driving eight hours to come run with you," Brian said, "everyone just looked at me and with the same dumbfounded look on their faces and said the same thing: 'Why?' I told them I believed in your mission. You're doing a good thing, Summerlin. I wouldn't have missed this for the world ... sweat and all."

Shawnee joined us again for another section until we hit 14 miles. We laughed as we ran, recalling stories from long ago in Japan and talking about friends this run had reconnected us with. So many of my fellow Marines encouraged us through email and Facebook and we knew they were with us in spirit on that day. At the end of that section, Shawnee and Brian hopped back into their vehicle and headed back toward Dallas. We spent just a few hours together, but they were hours that I treasured.

When Aaron, Sandy and I headed back out again, it was only 9:30 a.m. but already 85 degrees. They are fellow ultramarathon runners, and have many more years of running experience than I, so they were able to run the 35 miles that day with me, conquering it in just more than six hours, even with a high temperature of 95 that day. As they prepared to drive back to West Virginia, I thanked them so much for their support, encouragement and surprise visit.

"It was only one percent of your journey," Aaron said, "but I was happy to be a part of it."

### MEMORABLE DAY

May 28 was a pretty emotional day for me. The previous day I spent time and ran with some of my best friends in the world, riding an emotional high. The following morning, however, I was on an emotional low. Maybe it was missing our friends who were with us just a short time. Maybe it was realizing I still had more than a month to go before I completed the mission. I think more than anything, however, the realization that it was Memorial Day is what really weighed heavily on my heart. Memorial Day is a day to remember and be thankful for those who lost their lives for the glory and honor of our country. Considering I was doing this run for veterans, the day had even more significance to me this year.

Every Veterans Day, I always called my uncle Butch McPherson, who I was very close to, to thank him for his service. We had the bond of serving this amazing country honorably, and I always enjoyed that conversation. This Memorial Day morning, I called both him and my uncle Roger Clark, who served in the National Guard, to thank them both for their service. I'm sure for the first minute or so when I was talking to Butch, he was wondering what was wrong, because I could barely get the words out I was sobbing so hard. I poured out all of the emotions I had built up and he just listened quietly. When I finally finished talking, Butch paused for a moment and then said some powerful words to me.

"You served as well, and I appreciate you."

My chest swelled with pride as he spoke.

"We just did what was asked of us, and that's all we could do," he continued. "Let's just be thankful we can celebrate our freedom with our families."

I shouldn't have been surprised at his words because fellow veterans have an understanding and appreciation for one another. We are a family, and we understand what serving our country means.

Later that morning I did a radio interview with Jim Stallings of WAJR radio in West Virginia. He was hosting a special Memorial Day show and I relayed to his listeners some of the emotional calls I had already made to my uncles. I also let Jim know how proud I was of his family, knowing that his father had lost his life in Vietnam. I took every opportunity given during this journey to thank veterans and their families, but on Memorial Day it meant just so much more to be able to express my gratitude for those who served and those who gave their lives for our freedom.

## MAKING OTHERS CRY

I have always been an emotional sap, not afraid to show my feelings at any time. My kids have that quality about them as well, and it showed the morning we were headed towards Williamsburg, Missouri.

Tiffany had called the Lazy Days RV Park just outside of Williamsburg, telling them about our journey and asking if they had a spot for us that evening. They stated that not only did they have a spot for us, but the spot was on the house that night. Tiffany learned that the park has a painted wall on the side of the shower house by the pool. In big letters, the wall reads, "I'm Proud to be an American." Also on the wall are signatures and comments from many who stayed there, thanking those who have served our country.

At one of the pit stops, Tiff told me about the wall. I was sitting by Shayna as Tiff was explaining it to me, and I felt this overwhelming desire to sing one of my favorite songs, "God Bless the USA," made popular by Lee Greenwood during my first year in the Marine Corps. I held Shayna tight as I sang each verse and the chorus, doing my best to stay on key. She listened intently as I sang, hanging onto every word as I held her in my arms.

"I'm proud to be an American, where at least I know I'm free. And I won't forget the men who died, who gave that right to me. And I gladly stand up, next to you and defend her still today. 'Cause there ain't no doubt I love this land. God bless the USA."

As I belted out the chorus a final time, Shayna leaned over onto my shoulder and just started crying her eyes out.

"Was my singing that bad?" I asked.

She looked right into my eyes, wiping her tears away. "No daddy," she said.

Later, we talked more about that moment and I asked her why she was moved to tears.

"Because the words of that song reminded me of all the heroes who lost their lives for us."

I cannot begin to explain how proud I was of my 10-year-old girl at that moment. When I was 10, I was focused on playing in the woods and never gave any thought to what our members of the armed forces were going through. Yet here was my daughter being brought to tears thinking about the ultimate sacrifice that so many had made for our country and us. Shayna showed at that moment that even at the tender age of 10, she completely understood why we put our comfortable lives on hold to make this trek across the US.

When we arrived at the RV park and saw what I called "The Wall of Inspiration," it was an absolutely inspiring sight to behold. The wall contained signatures not only from military members and families, but others who expressed their gratitude to those who have served so bravely. I was motivated again later that evening by the opportunity to once again share the story of our heroes when I did a Skype interview with Right This Minute, a news organization with a large national reach.

We were also getting closer to St. Louis, and the entire family was bubbling with anticipation about being able to visit the Gateway Arch and a large city. I took advantage of the cooler temperatures and flat roads over the next few days to pack on a few extra miles each day. I wanted to make our day in St. Louis a shorter running day so we would have as much time as possible to do some sight-seeing.

The day I ran into St. Louis, I only needed to log 26.4 miles. While three years ago that marathon distance would have been intimidating, at this point it was a short, easy run. I wrapped up the run just after noon, and was able to spend the rest of the day touring with the family.

Riding up into the Gateway Arch was something we were happy to experience ... once. We must have been there during the busiest time, because there were people everywhere and we all felt a bit claustrophobic inside. Visiting this monument was something we were looking forward to doing ever since we drove past it three months earlier on our way out to Oregon for the start of the run.

Due to the amount of time I spent running every day, and the amount of recovery time I needed, I rarely had the opportunity to do much other than run, eat and sleep. The afternoon spent touring St. Louis was a great break from that routine. We were also excited to be getting closer to the fourth and final time zone. So after a relaxing afternoon in St. Louis, it was back to running, eating and sleeping.

# 12 | **100 Marathons**

"Jamie Shane Summerlin"

When I heard those words in the late spring of 1990 and began to walk across the platform at my high school graduation, I felt like I was on top of the world. I also felt like I had just conquered the world, having graduated from high school and now ready to tackle adulthood with the force of those football players who used to knock me down on the gridiron. So as I shook my principal's hand and received my diploma, I hoisted it high in the air in celebration of achieving a dream. Looking back, I probably played up the moment a little more dramatically than I should have. Of course as a teenager everything is always a bit more dramatic than reality turns out to be.

I thought that becoming an adult meant that I now enjoyed the freedom to make my own decisions. Seventeen days later, my drill instructors at boot camp proved otherwise. My life was dramatically transformed over the next three months as the Marine Corps molded me into a man.

"Platoon 1094, dismissed!"

As I stepped forward on the edge of the parade deck at Marine Corps Recruit Depot Parris Island, South Carolina, hearing those words was another moment when I thought that I had conquered the world. Even though at that time I was signed to serve my country, I still felt like I could take my life in endless directions and that nothing could slow me down.

"Thank you, Jamie, for what you are doing for our troops."

Graduating from high school or boot camp were wonderful honors to me at those moments in time. But no other words of congratulations could match the words spoken to me time and time again by the countless people who showed their appreciation of my attempt to run across the US to raise awareness and funds for wounded veterans. Each time someone said those words to me, they caused my chest to fill with 10 times the amount of pride I had when I heard the words congratulating me on my graduation from high school or boot camp. I was honored to meet veterans from so many different chapters in our military's history on this trip, from World War II veterans who had stormed the beaches of Normandy, to men and women who were bravely serving today.

"Every step is for my heroes," was all I could muster in response whenever someone showed their gratitude for what I was doing. I just wanted this journey to remain focused on the incredible service members that I was doing this for. I didn't really have the energy to spend focusing on anything else but my mission, and quite honestly, I didn't want to. This was the most rewarding adventure I had ever undertaken, and with every kind word passed along to me, the reward continued to grow.

## PRESSING FORWARD

Realizing that I was getting closer to home, the days started running together quite nicely at this point. I was cruising through Illinois, now my ninth state, and my energy levels continued to increase. The miles seemed to fly by as I headed through fields of freshly cut spring hay, with the aroma overwhelming at times. Strangely, it seemed like my sensitivity to sounds and smells increased during the course of the run. Perhaps it was my isolation out on the roads that allowed me to soak everything in, but I began to notice my surroundings in a way that I never previously had. The rolling hills I encountered in the Midwest were blanketed by grass and trees in varying shades of green and gold. The emergence of late spring and early summer was something I had been longing for since I began the run in March.

As we closed in on Indiana, we often talked about how fortunate we had been on the trip. Except for my shin injury in Oregon and the busted pipe on the RV in Kansas, we knew we were fortunate to have made it this far into the journey with relatively few major incidents. We had fallen into a pretty good routine, which allowed the days to tick off rather quickly to me as I continued to press forward. Tiffany had her routine of taking care of the kids and me down and the children entertained themselves with geocaching expeditions and playing out in the warmer weather when the daily run was over.

Looking back on it, I had it pretty easy, if you consider running 34 miles a day without any rest days easy. I would get a break from everyone (or more likely they would get a break from me) for an hour or so while I was out on the road, interact with them at the next aid stop for a few minutes and then step back out onto the road again. Tiff did her best to put on a smile and keep everyone's spirits high, but the duration of the trip was certainly taking its toll. The kids were most definitely ready to get home, and the thought of sleeping in my own bed sounded inviting.

"I'm going to chain myself in my room when we get home," Nick would say. "You're going to have to drag me out of there." Shayna would always nod in agreement.

While staying overnight in French Lick, Indiana, I did a radio interview with Tony Caridi on Statewide Sportsline in West Virginia, and joked about playing a pickup basketball game with Larry Bird in his hometown.

"You'll be able to play a game in your own backyard soon," Tony said.

That was a great reminder that we were getting closer to home, and while it excited me to know we were almost there, the thought also started weighing heavily on me. I knew that Tiffany and I were both promised by our respective employers that we would have our jobs upon our return, but in the back of my mind I worried occasionally about that, knowing that nobody is irreplaceable. I also wasn't certain how satisfied I would be with returning to my IT job because I was becoming more and more motivated to make assisting and honoring veterans more than just a hobby or fleeting passion.

The realization that this dream I had less than two years ago was nearly over began to sink in around this time. I'm not sure the exact moment it hit me, but I do remember this almost overwhelming feeling of sadness that I had not experienced thus far during the trek.

"It's important to focus on the *now* and your purpose for running to complete and enjoy your journey."

Those words from Chelsea Butters Wooding before we left on this trip popped into my head, but I still could not shake the feeling of sadness that was almost overwhelming me. But I just continued to do the only thing that was natural for me at that point. I slipped my shoes on and ran.

### INTERNAL MOTIVATION

Crossing over into the fourth and final time zone was one of the most special moments of the journey. As I crossed the border from Illinois to Indiana, the clock on my phone kept bouncing back and forth between Central and Eastern time zones. I had been so encouraged to finally make it into the Eastern time zone, only to have the time on my phone bounce back an hour about five minutes later. This left me both confused and a bit agitated.

As I ran through the quaint town of Vincennes, Indiana, I struck up a few brief conversations with people. Finally, I asked one person if he knew what time zone I was in. The man gave me a confused look until I told him I began running that day in Lawrenceville, Illinois, and was heading toward Paoli, Indiana.

"You started running from where today? And you are headed where?"

"It's only another 25 miles to go today," I replied.

"You're nuts!" the man said. But then I explained the purpose of the run and told him as much of the story as I could in a couple of minutes. He listened intently and was intrigued about the purpose of the run, but he still gave me a typical response: "I think it's great what you're doing, but you're out of your mind."

Southern Indiana had quite a few rolling hills, which caused me to think even more about home and how great it was going to be to get back to West Virginia. I was feeling really strong, with no real physical issues to complain about. Mentally, however, I was struggling. Encouragement was flowing from everywhere, and through everyone we met, but I was closing in on almost 80 continuous days of running a marathon plus eight miles each day, without a rest day. I was making great progress and encouraging so many through our efforts, but I just felt a little empty inside.

With the agreement we made prior to the trip, I didn't want to burden Tiffany any more than she already was with everything else she had to deal with, so I took advantage of my time out running to call friends and family, just to hear a familiar voice, trying to rid myself of the void I felt. While those conversations helped at times, the emptiness that was weighing on me just wouldn't subside.

The timing of the visit from our good friends Matt and Maria Brann, along with their two children, Maverick and Makaleigh, could not have been any better. The Branns also live in Morgantown, West Virginia, but had family living in Indiana, so they took the opportunity to visit family and then meet up with us near Paoli, Indiana, which boasts of one of the few ski resorts in the state. Since Matt was helping me write *Freedom Run,* he thought it would be a good opportunity to run with me for a day to gain some firsthand experience about what I was doing.

We met them the next morning, Day 76, at the courthouse square in downtown Paoli and when Matt and I headed out to run it was already approaching 80 degrees and 80 percent humidity. Being southern Indiana, there were some rolling hills on our 33.5-mile route for the day and Matt, being a native Hoosier, made sure to point out that this was not the typical flatlands that Indiana is known for. Matt and Maria had just completed a half marathon the previous weekend, so he was eager to see how much further he could push his body.

We cruised through the first 13 miles, conquering the tallest climb I had run in a while, and spent our time together talking about the journey thus far and making plans for the book. During our aid stops we enjoyed watching our four children play together. I knew it was great for Nick and Shayna to have an opportunity to be around some other kids for a change. Matt commented that he felt much better than he did at the end of his half marathon a week ago. The next leg of the run, however, would be difficult for him, but for me, it was one of the most valuable sections mentally that I had run in weeks.

While the additional mileage and heat was zapping Matt's energy, I was dumping some of my frustrations on him. I let him know that I was starting to feel a little empty for whatever reason. I couldn't pinpoint why, and I wouldn't have traded a single step I had taken on this journey, but I was just feeling a little "blah."

"Have you been keeping track of your own milestones during the run?" Matt asked me.

"Honestly, no I haven't," I replied. "I remember when I surpassed 1,000 and 2,000 miles in the run, which was really cool, but other than that, I haven't focused on what I've accomplished personally. I want this run to be about the people I was doing it for. I don't want people to think I am out here to gain any glory for myself."

"I know you've always said this run isn't about you, but you need to realize that what you're accomplishing is truly amazing. I was reading your blog and based on the mileage you've run, by the end of today you'll have run 2,620 miles."

Sweating profusely, I looked over at him with an empty stare, paused, and said, "OK."

Sensing that I hadn't fully comprehended the significance of the mileage, Matt said, "That works out to 100 marathons that you've run in 76 days!"

I almost stopped dead in my tracks. Matt's words took me right back to the moment that I had accomplished something I never thought I would ever attempt, let alone complete.

"This is a really big deal," I could hear Tiffany telling me as we approached the clock tower at the finish of the Burning River 100 Mile Endurance Run. "You are doing something very few people have ever accomplished, let alone attempted."

It was almost as if Tiff was standing beside me again, helping me see the big picture about what I was accomplishing. It was also the first time in a while that I had really given any thought to the personal portion of my journey.

Matt knocked out the first 19 miles with me that day before he hopped in the RV for a breather. Over the next 11 miles, I thought a lot about what Matt had shared with me. I had worked so hard the past couple of years to keep the focus on the mission, to not allow the focus to be put on me. The story was about the amazing heroes I was taking these steps for, and I wanted it to remain that way. But Matt's words opened my eyes up to the individual accomplishment.

I couldn't just ride the emotion of the mission to make it through. I needed to latch onto every aspect of this journey to help me get through some of the difficult times, especially the way I had been feeling recently. It wasn't that I was getting burnt out on the mission, because that's what caused me to get out of bed every morning, even when it hurt to do so. But remaining so focused on raising awareness for our veterans caused me to almost disregard what got me here in the first place: my love for running. Running my first 50-kilometer race, my first 50-mile race and crossing the finish line at the Burning River 100 miler were all life-changing moments because I understood all of the hard work that went into finishing those races. On this run across America, I needed to take the time to reflect on what I was also accomplishing myself.

Much earlier in this journey I began to contemplate adding mileage onto the end of my run. My goal was to run to Annapolis, Maryland, and finish at the Naval Academy and Chesapeake Bay. I wanted to make a ceremonial finish on Independence Day and march in the July 4 parade in Annapolis. But from there, I mentioned to Tiffany that I had the idea of running 100 miles in 24 hours from Annapolis to Rehoboth Beach, Delaware. Not finishing Burning River in 24 hours still bothered me. But I also didn't want to regret not making this a true coast-to-coast run from the Pacific Ocean to the Atlantic Ocean.

"You're almost there, so why not go all the way" Tiffany said.

Having talked with Matt about acknowledging what I personally had achieved during this journey, it only solidified my desire to make this a true coast-to-coast run. We would use the final 100 miles as a final push at fundraising, but that leg of the run would be for me. I didn't want to look back 20 years from now and think to myself, "I can't believe I ran more than 3,000 miles but didn't go those extra few to the Atlantic Ocean."

Matt joined me for the last three miles of the run that day. I told him of my plans for the big finish, and how our conversation that day just solidified my desire to do it.

"After running that many miles, you want to run 100 more in 24 hours?" he asked, dumbfounded. "You're nuts, but I think it's awesome and I know you can do it."

The Branns treated us that evening to a dinner at Joe Huber's Farm Family Restaurant, which was hosting a huge car show. I took the opportunity to check out the beautiful cars on display, realizing that over the past couple of months I had not taken time very often to get out of the "box" and do something fun and relaxing. Running, eating and sleeping; that's all I knew. And I was about to do plenty of eating. Matt and I both had the Huber's Country Platter Dinner, which was served family style. I honestly could not recall eating that much food in one sitting at any other time during the run.

Having a full belly and a refreshed outlook on my journey, I was excited to see what tomorrow would bring. Matt really helped me look at the big picture that day, and it was something I truly needed.

## EMPTY NEST

When our family first discussed this trip, I don't think our kids fully understood the magnitude of the journey. They were excited about getting out of school and traveling across America in a motorhome and camping out every night, but they probably underestimated the amount of time they'd be spending with their parents and away from their friends. Needless to say, their excitement subsided about 30 days into the trip.

The "box on wheels" was becoming boring, they sorely missed their friends and Tiffany wasn't letting them slide by on their schoolwork. They were great helpers for Tiffany and me, and we were building incredible memories during the trip, but it was definitely a struggle for them. Nick and Shayna were both at the age that they were carving out their identity, emotionally and physically, so that just added to the stress that everyone felt.

I have to admit, it was a bit unfair to Tiff, who had to deal with not only making sure the run was a success, but also meeting the needs of the children. I was able to escape throughout the day as I was out running, and did my best to support her and the kids when my day ended, but there were many times that I was thankful to exit the RV and hit the road again. We did have some incredible times during the run together, and we built memories that will stay with us forever. I also understood, however, that it was wearing on all of us, and a change needed to be made soon.

My parents planned on picking the kids up when we came into Huntington, West Virginia, and taking them back home for a few days to relax before rejoining us for the final leg of the run. Using our map and daily calendar, the kids had been counting down the days until they arrived. Unbeknownst to the kids, my parents had been planning to arrive a week early, meeting us in Frankfort, Kentucky. Tiffany and I began to overemphasize the countdown with the kids for the few days leading up to June 11, so we were surprised the kids didn't pick up on it.

A number of exciting things happened on our way into Frankfort that day, none of which was more surprising than finally running in the pouring rain. I had a couple of nights while running where we woke up to rain in the middle of the night, but it had been 60 days since I last ran in the rain. The rolling, green hills that I witnessed when entering the Midwest had now turned into patches of brown, dry land as a drought was sweeping its way across the region.

It was a very gray and dreary day all the way into Frankfort, but the rain felt better than a massage as it beat down on the back of my suntanned neck. I have always enjoyed running in the rain, and I really missed it while doing this run, especially on the extremely hot days through the Midwest. Despite the wet weather, several people in the area who had seen my story the previous night on their local newscast came out to meet me during my run, lifting me up by providing drinks and words of encouragement. I was so happy that the purpose of this run continued to spread and that so many were being reminded of our brave men and women we were doing this for.

When we arrived at the Elkhorn Campground in Frankfort, my parents had already set up a spot for us and were waiting. The rain was really coming down when we pulled in, and we saw their truck parked off to the side. After Tiff went in to get the parking pass, we pulled around to the camping spot for the night and asked the kids to sit down for a few minutes before they got settled for the night. I stepped outside, pretending to get the RV connected and waved my parents over.

"Surprise!" my mom yelled as she stepped inside.

"Mawmaw!" Shayna yelled as she jumped up to greet her, while Nicholas sat there, unable to move, with a shocked look on his face.

It was a great reunion for everyone. The kids were excited to see their grandparents, as were we, and they were especially excited because they knew they were headed home. We knew it was something the kids really needed, but it was a bittersweet moment for all of us. After we returned from dinner, my parents packed up all the kids' things and Tiff and I smothered Nick and Shayna with enough hugs and kisses to last for a few days.

It was one of the saddest moments I had on the trip because we—especially Tiffany—had pretty much been with the kids 24/7 over the past three months. My children had been so encouraging and helpful during the trip, and we were going to miss them terribly, but we knew the break was necessary. We would be back together in a week, but it really pulled at our heartstrings to watch them drive away.

Months later, as I reflected back on how difficult it was for us to see our kids leave, I began to think about the sacrifices *families* of veterans make. We knew we were only going to be separated from our kids for a week before we were reunited. Families of service members don't know when, or if, they'll be reunited. Sons, daughters, fathers, mothers, husbands and wives are often called to serve overseas without knowing exactly how long they will be gone. When they return, with a moment's notice they could be called back abroad again. It can be an emotional tornado for family members back home, as uncertainty and worry swirls around in their minds.

Sadly, there are too many times when families are never reunited. In those instances, I believe the people of our country do their best to offer comfort, love and support. Yet in instances when a loved one is stationed overseas, it seems like we often neglect to recognize the emotional toll that daily uncertainty takes on families back home.

The mission of my run was to demonstrate an appreciation for the daily sacrifices our veterans make. But it's also important to acknowledge the sacrifices by family members back home.

### DITCH DIVING

The day after our children left, the cool rain was gone and the sun returned, continuing to bake both the land and me. Additionally, the road I was running on just north of Lexington, Kentucky, was not pedestrian friendly. Twice on this day I had someone drive by me yelling at me to get off the road, and counting this day it only happened a total of three times the entire trip.

There really was no shoulder for me to run on along Route 460, so I tried to run along the white line on the edge of the road. I actually ran on the white lines of roads often during hot days. The white lines were a little cooler on my feet than running on the dark blacktop. On Route 460, though, just on the other side of the line, where the pavement ended, there was about a one-foot drop down into a ditch, sandwiched on my left by a hand-stacked, waist-high stone wall. As vehicles would drive toward me, very few of them got over to give me room, even when there was no oncoming traffic. As a result, I had to do a lot of ditch diving the entire day. That prevented me from getting into a good rhythm. I was stressed over the kids being gone, mad at the inconsiderate motorists and the heat was blasting me.

One of the local Lexington Lunatics Hash House Harriers members, Heather Auman, came out to ride her bike some with me that day, and helped block traffic for me for a few miles. The Hash House Harriers (H3) is an informal, non-competitive and social group of runners with local chapters throughout the world. During a hash run, which typically occurs weekly, one runner goes out ahead and marks a path for the rest of the group to attempt to follow. At the designated meeting place at the end of the run, the group gathers at a local establishment to socialize. My first experience with H3 was on the narrow streets of Japan 17 years earlier.

When Heather joined me, I was 20 miles into the run that day, and she just laughed as I said I only had another 16 miles to go. As I ran along the narrow, two-lane road, she continued to ride in a way that kept vehicles away from us as they approached. She knew, however, that I was worried about her getting hit, so after a few miles she turned back after offering my wife and me her house for the night, as well as a home-cooked meal. She had heard about my run through some of the other hash kennels (each local hash group is called a kennel) along my journey across the US, and was excited to help out any way she could. And after not finding any places to park the RV for the night, we were happy to take her up on the offer.

The last 10 miles of the run that day were literally a blur. The heat made it difficult for me to eat, and the thought of the kids being gone had been weighing on my mind all day. I was so used to them greeting me at the RV when I ran up and saying, "Hi daddy, how are you feeling?" We also developed our own way of saying goodbye when I would leave for the next leg of my run. Before I would step out of the RV, we would always fist bump on the way out the door, and now I had a missing component to my routine.

With all of the stress and heat taking its toll, I simply wasn't refueling like I needed. Thirty miles into the run, Tiff informed me that I had only consumed one gallon of Gatorade the entire day, which was a full gallon behind my normal intake for that distance on a day with normal temperature. I also realized at that point that I did not even remember Tiff driving past me prior to that aid stop. Every time she passed me in the RV, she would ring a cowbell and I would give her a wave. While driving through Oregon we discovered the need for the cowbell because there were so many passers-by that honked. The cowbell set Tiff apart so that I didn't have to turn my head at every random and well-meaning horn-blower. She told me I did wave, but I couldn't recall it. Blocks of time were empty for me that day and we were both concerned for my well-being. I forced myself to drink cup after cup of Gatorade before I took off for the last leg that day, trying to get my electrolytes back up where they needed to be. By the end of the run, I was completely exhausted, physically and mentally. Day 79 could not have ended soon enough.

The timing of staying at Heather's house that night could not have been better. A nice, cool house, a wonderfully home-cooked meal of pasta and bread and Tiffany being able to do some laundry were big blessings. I slept better that night than I had in a long time, while Tiff took the time to chat with Heather through the evening.

The following morning I awoke feeling completely refreshed. I ended up adding three miles to the original route for a total of 38 miles that day, but felt like I could have run even farther. I also achieved another milestone, as I surpassed 2,750 miles in the run. In 2011, with all of the races and long training runs I had done, my total mileage for the year was 2,750 miles. It was amazing to think that 80 days into my run I had surpassed my total mileage from 365 days the previous year.

## WHO LET THE DOGS OUT?

One of my concerns on the trip was what kind of wild animals I would encounter. Of course, my biggest fear was of snakes, but for runners, dogs are often the most dangerous animals to encounter. Many runners even carry protective devices such as mace specifically to keep aggressive dogs away. I was very fortunate to not have any incidents with dogs—until Day 81.

The morning air was a refreshing 50 degrees when I headed out for the run, and the predicted high for the day was only 81. The route for the day had me running mostly on back roads, including one that took me over a mountain that had nearly 2,000 feet of elevation change in the short eight-mile section. There was a route that went around the mountain that would have added about 90 minutes to the run but saved my legs from some heavy climbing, and for a brief moment I considered that option since I just traversed the flat plains of the Midwest and had gotten out of the routine of conquering climbs. But since I hate to add unnecessary mileage, I took off for the narrow, single-lane road over the mountain.

As I ran past one of the first homes I passed heading down that road, I noticed a young man in cutoff blue jean shorts mowing his yard. I always made it a point to wave to people and say hello when I ran by, because I never knew what good could come from the encounter, but I didn't wave to this man because he had his back to me when I ran past.

As I ran a little farther down the road, I heard the rumble of the lawn-mower engine shut off, but that didn't strike me as being odd. About a minute later, I heard a car coming up from behind, and since it was a single-lane road I moved over to the far left-hand side. But as the car approached me, it slowed down and I felt like it was driving right on my heels.

I looked back and saw that it was the young man I had passed earlier mowing his yard who was creeping up behind me in a 1980s white Dodge Aries K with more rust than paint near the bumpers. Strangely, he wasn't driving fast enough to pass me. He crept up slowly until he was right beside me and he stared at me from behind the steering wheel with a glazed look in his eyes. I quickly looked to make sure both of his hands were on the wheel and that no weapons were visible, because I wasn't sure what to expect. He continued to drive alongside me for about 50 feet or so. He didn't say a word, but the entire time I felt him peering out the window at me. I decided to pick up my pace, and he matched it. I was getting nervous because my cell phone was out of range for service and the only thing I had to defend myself with was the bottles of Gatorade in my FuelBelt. I certainly didn't think dousing him with orange Gatorade would fend him off for very long.

Fortunately, a large truck then drove up from behind, so he sped off. A couple of minutes later, however, he was now driving back towards me. Thankfully, a couple of cars were behind him, so he drove on by without slowing down. For the next five minutes, every car that came up behind me caused my heart to beat a little faster. Tiffany finally drove by in the RV, which eased my nerves a little, but I was also now concerned about her being in the RV by herself. When I made my aid stop, I explained what happened and we decided to have her pull over every mile until we made it back to the main road. Fortunately, we didn't encounter the man again.

Before I made my way back onto the main road, however, I ran around what looked to be an abandoned home, with overgrown brush and trees surrounding the area. I heard a couple of dogs barking from somewhere to my left in the overgrown brush, but could not see where they were. I ran by a very small camper trailer just past the rundown home when all of a sudden the dogs came running out from behind the trailer.

I was already on edge after the lawnmower man was seemingly stalking me in his car, so seeing these dogs charging toward me heightened my nervousness. Quickly I formulated a plan to kick the smallest dog in the group, if necessary, in hopes that would scare off the larger one.

"Get back!" I growled as the dogs got closer. But they didn't obey my command. All of a sudden a voice resonated from the small camper in one of the most Southern drawl accents I have ever heard.

"Kick the piss outta both of 'em!" yelled the voice.

The dogs reacted to his voice just as I was preparing to kick my leg, and they turned and ran back towards their home behind the camper. The situation was frightening initially but turned out to be humorous. I think I laughed all the way to the end of the road where Tiffany was parked.

"What's so funny?" she asked me when I stepped inside the RV.

"Do I have a story for you," I said.

"Is it a salacious story of someone naked?" she asked in jest.

I laughed and then relayed the story of the invisible Southern savior from the camper.

"A good naked story would have been icing on the cake," I said, "but I had enough of naked guys out in Oregon, thank you very much!"

With a rather intriguing day wrapped up, we camped at Carter Caves State Park, where my cousin Darren had made arrangements and the owners gave us a complimentary spot. Tiff and I talked to the kids on the phone for a while that night, then both of us headed for bed a bit earlier than usual. Without the support of the kids, Tiff was now taking care of everything for the trip, and although she had the routine nailed, I knew she needed just as much rest as I did.

"Now, how about another good naked story?" I said with a sly grin as I lay down beside her.

All I heard was snoring.

# 13 | Take Me Home

One of the most surreal moments of my entire journey was when I crossed the state line into West Virginia. It was difficult to fathom that just 90 days earlier we had driven out of the state, heading toward Oregon and unsure of what this trip had in store for us. Now, 83 days into my run, I was returning to my home state on foot with more memories in tow than miles logged.

Running into West Virginia was something that I had anticipated for a long time, largely because I was eager to be reunited with friends and family. I remember returning home after being stationed overseas while I was in the military. The homecoming was sweet.

At the same time, I felt a little guilty. I had only been gone for three months, and my immediate family had been by my side most of the way. I recalled many conversations I had with family members of current military members during my run, and many of them shared stories of their loved ones serving multiple tours overseas, sometimes lasting as long as 16 months at a time. The stories broke my heart. I could hear the pain in their voices as they talked about how much they missed their loved ones, but that pain was also balanced with the pride they had in their spouse, child or parent that was serving.

The support of family and friends means so much to active members of the military when they are away, and the US military wouldn't be as successful as it is without that support system in place. Families, friends and communities play such a pivotal role in helping military members feel supported and get through some tough times, whether they are stationed at home in the US or abroad.

After I ran across the bridge into Kenova, West Virginia, I posed for photos next to a "Welcome to West Virginia" sign and belted out the chorus to "Country Roads" by the late John Denver. Just then a woman pulled up behind the RV and walked up to greet us. She introduced herself as Monica and explained that she had heard my interview on the radio the day before and had hoped to time her drive to work that morning so that she could meet up with us. Monica told us about fitness challenges she was organizing locally and that she was planning to use my run across America as motivation for those in her exercise group to see that anything is possible. It made me feel great to know that what started out as a singularly focused run to assist wounded veterans was having a wider impact than we ever imagined.

### STUMBLING INTO HUNTINGTON

I was constantly thankful that throughout this journey across America we had been relatively free from mishaps. Except for the shin injury in Oregon and much later a slight pain in the IT band of my right knee, I had been injury free–I never even developed a blister on my feet. Except for a few mechanical problems with the RV, which were quickly fixed courtesy of several generous individuals, the motorhome had performed very well. When a road I was running on came to an abrupt end, we were always able to find another way to get back on course. These minor issues, including when some of our laundry was stolen, were really only hiccups on the trip.

As I made my way into Huntington, even though I had been in that city several times prior, I wasn't very familiar with the roads. I had to pay close attention to the maps on my phone and remain in constant communication with Tiffany to make sure she was taking the same route. One of the things Tiffany always reminded me when I was heading out the door of the RV was to not look at my phone while I was running. Since my arrival in West Virginia, however, I was constantly receiving texts, tweets and Facebook posts from family and friends. As a result, I found my eyes drifting toward my phone more often. I'd usually glance around to make sure Tiff wasn't nearby, then text away. It was amazing I hadn't been hit by any of the drivers that I encountered on the road who had their faces buried in their phones while behind the wheel. I'd just shake my head whenever I saw someone texting while driving. Then my phone would buzz and I'd do the same thing.

Heading through a residential section of Huntington, I knew a turn was approaching soon, so I pulled my phone out to check the map while jogging along the sidewalk. All of a sudden, I found myself heading face first towards the pavement. I had caught my right toe on a section of the sidewalk that was in desperate need of repair. Acting on my instincts, I put my hands out to brace my fall, forgetting that my smartphone was cradled in my right hand. The next sound I heard was the cracking of the display on my phone, followed by the thud as I landed flat on my stomach, briefly knocking the wind of out me.

I immediately turned my phone over and saw where the shiny display was now a spiderweb of splintered glass. It was still functional, but I had to press down really hard on some of the keyboard letters to get them to work. I called Tiff, very upset with myself and the situation, and asked her to come meet me as soon as possible. When she arrived she could tell I was very upset, so she did her best to get me to shrug it off and keep pressing forward.

"It could have been worse," she said. "It's just a phone. It could have been your ribs that cracked."

I was still upset that I allowed myself lose the focus that had been so sharp the past three months. I was also mad that I had cracked a fairly expensive phone. There was nothing I could do about it at that point, however. I was thankful that at least it still worked so that I would continue to have communication capabilities with Tiffany.

As I stepped out of the RV to run again, Tiffany gave me a kiss and said, "Don't let it get you down. Just keep moving forward."

After running about 20 miles through Huntington, Tiffany picked me up so that we could drive back to Pullman Plaza, which was hosting the West Virginia State VFW conference. There was a haircut fundraiser for wounded veterans that I was invited to attend. My cousin Darren, along with his wife, Lisa, and daughter, Sophie, met us at the plaza. He and I had talked a lot while I was out on the road, especially when I was dealing with a rough stretch. It was great catching up with them, and I was so happy to see family again.

We were introduced to a number of the conference attendees at the fundraiser and were presented with a $200 check from the event. We thanked everyone and then headed back to the point where Tiff had picked me up so that I could run the final 11 miles of the day. The day seemed to last forever because of my fall and the interruption in my run. It had been a long time since we had to backtrack during my run to attend an event. But I wrapped up the last of the miles and we arrived at FoxFire KOA campgrounds, which donated a camping spot to us. What began as a bad day ended up being pretty good after all.

## A CAPITOL CLIMB

The Tallman Track Club in Charleston had been tracking my run for a while and the members contacted me a few days prior to my arrival in West Virginia to make arrangements for several runners to run with me into Charleston, the state capital. I was really looking forward to the following day not only because I would be joined by the Tallman Track Club, but also because it was Father's Day and I would be reunited with Nick and Shayna. A number of events were scheduled for the afternoon, so I needed to get an early start.

We drove to the starting point for the day, arriving around 5:20 a.m. and immersed in quiet darkness. I hoped I had given the track club proper directions to our meeting point but at 5:35 and with nobody in sight, I decided to head out. Tiffany drove on ahead and a few minutes later she texted me to tell me that several runners were at an intersection up ahead waiting on me. I was excited to have runners join me, so I picked the pace up to meet up with everyone. As I approached the RV I could make out the shadows of five or six runners standing there talking to Tiffany.

The next 30 miles were some of the most enjoyable and easiest miles I ran during the entire trip. Everyone had questions for me, and I had all kinds of answers. "Can you tell us the story of the naked guy in Oregon?" one runner asked. I shared stories that made them laugh, stories that got me choked up and statistics about the run that just blew everyone away. I loved hearing about how several of the runners had been tracking my progress and used what I was doing as motivation to push them to run greater distances.

About eight miles into the run, we met up with a second wave of runners that joined me. The sun had finally burnt off the morning fog and it was starting to warm up quite a bit. We were preparing for a couple of heavy climbs up and over a mountain as we headed out of Teays Valley.

"Have him tell you the naked guy story," one of the first wave runners said to the second group. "Make sure he's running uphill when he tells it. He doesn't stop talking or run out of breath!"

My conditioning was the best it had ever been by this point. I could talk and run all day long, which was a dramatic shift from the beginning days of training for this journey, when I preferred to run alone because I didn't feel like I was capable of carrying on a conversation while running. As we climbed the mountain, I told the story again, laughing the whole way. I also didn't realize just how quickly we were moving. Some of the slower runners in the group didn't want to slow me down, so they encouraged us to keep going at my pace and said they'd catch up with us when we made my next aid station stop. A couple of us plowed up to the peak of the mountain on County Route 46, then headed back down the other side where the RV was waiting. We waited for the rest of the second group to get to the RV and shortly into the next leg of the run we picked up the third wave of runners that would accompany me to the West Virginia State Capitol building.

Prior to departing with the third wave, members of the track club invited me to return to the area in September and speak at the runner's clinic for the 40th Annual Charleston Distance Run, which is a 15-mile race. I was honored to accept the invitation because it is one of the state's most prestigious distance races.

The final leg of the run flew by, as we made our way across the Kanawha River and headed into downtown Charleston toward the capitol. A reporter from a local TV station was there to capture video of our group running into town. One of the runners who joined us, Joni Adams, told me how she had used my run in her classroom over the past few months, taking the opportunity to teach her students not only about the geography and science behind the run, but other aspects of it as well.

"You're doing something incredible for other people, and that is something I want my students to emulate," she said. I loved hearing stories about how people used the run to benefit others in ways other than my initial intention. Stories like Joni's proved that we were making a difference much greater than I ever imagined.

As we approached the capitol I could see the golden dome of the building glistening in the sun, which was beginning to fade behind some dark clouds. When the sun illuminates the gold-leaf rotunda dome of the State Capitol, it's a beautiful sight, making it quite possibly one of the most magnificent state capitol buildings in the nation. A number of people were out to greet us as we approached the steps of the capitol, including Jim Sweezy of West Virginia Radio Corporation. Jim had coordinated regular radio interviews with WCHS as I made my way across America, and he also helped arrange many of the upcoming events of the weekend.

We ran up the steps of the capitol, humming the tune from *Rocky* when he climbed the steps of the Philadelphia Museum of Art. We stood at the top of the steps, jumping up and down with our arms raised in the air, emulating the Italian Stallion in the scene from Rocky. I'm sure we looked foolish, but it didn't matter to us. I had just crushed 32 miles in a total running time of 5 hours and 20 minutes, earning the right to celebrate any way I saw fit. The joy of the day, however, was only just beginning.

Kelly Rippin, a reporter from WBOY-TV in Morgantown, did an interview with me. While I was on the road, she checked in with me weekly to report on my progress. After a brief interview, we quickly headed to Appalachian Power Park, home to the West Virginia Power, a minor league baseball team. I was honored to be chosen to throw out the ceremonial first pitch before the game. When we arrived at the front gate in the RV, our kids and my parents were there waiting for us. I squeezed the children tight and shed some tears of joy because I missed them so much during the time we were apart.

After a quick shower and change of clothes in the RV, we headed into the stadium, where we were greeted by Charleston mayor Danny Jones. He was also a former Marine, so it was even more of an honor to have him express his gratitude for what we were doing for veterans. We walked out to the pitcher's mound, where the mayor presented me with a key to the city and then handed me a microphone to address the crowd.

"If you are a veteran of the United States military, please stand up," I said. "Would everyone please give them a round of applause? These are the men and women I am doing this for, and they are the ones who deserve the applause, not me."

I then climbed to the top of the pitcher's mound for the ceremonial pitch, hoping not to embarrass myself in front of my wife and kids. I did my best to keep the catcher in his crouched position, making sure I threw the baseball hard enough to get it across the plate. He stood up quickly to catch it, but at least it didn't bounce across the plate. I raised my arm like I had just struck out the final batter to win the World Series and then jogged off the field. What a great Father's Day experience that was.

After watching part of the game we said goodbye to our kids, knowing they would rejoin us in a couple of days when we made our way into Burnsville. Tiffany and I then received massages from Kristin Pauley, a licensed massage therapist in Charleston who is friends with Jim Sweezy. I hadn't had a complete massage since I started the run, and she worked me over, laughing about how tense I was. We then enjoyed a great meal at the Bridge Road Bistro, although I was in a complete fog during dinner because the massage had completely relaxed me. We both slept better that night than we had in a long time.

## RUNNING WITH HEROES

The following morning I got moving early, but instead of heading out to begin my run I dropped by a West Virginia Radio Corporation studio to conduct interviews with some of the stations that had so loyally given me publicity and support during the journey. Without their continued support, we wouldn't have reached nearly as many people to inform them about our mission.

Mike Agnello and Rick Johnson with WCHS-AM faithfully did interviews with me a couple of times a week during the run. It was great to finally sit down with them that morning to share more stories about the journey and to personally thank them for all of their support. Brian Egan from WKWS-FM not only interviewed me, but said that after his morning shift wrapped up he would come out to run a few miles with me.

We left the station around 6:45 a.m. and headed over to the capitol, our finishing point from the previous day. Fellow West Virginia Mountain Trail Runners members Greg and Paula Smith, motorcycle riders from the American Legion and numerous media and police vehicles escorted us out of town. The biggest highlight for me, though, was having members of the 130th Air National Guard running alongside me.

The rain was pouring down, but it didn't bother me. I cherished the opportunity to chat with the guardsmen for the next five miles about their service and how much I appreciated their company on the run. Without realizing it initially, I discovered that we ran those first few miles at a seven-minute pace, which was a good three minutes faster per mile than I had been running. But since my adrenaline was flowing, I just decided to ride the wave of excitement. Having some of my heroes running by my side was one of the most enjoyable moments of the trip.

At my first aid stop the rain began to let up and I said goodbye to the soldiers and others who had escorted me that morning. When I began running on Route 119 I had a huge smile on my face thinking about the awesome experience of running with the soldiers. As I continued to make my way down the road, Joni Adams from the Tallman Track Club met up with me again.

"I just didn't get enough miles in with you yesterday," she told me, "so I wanted to run with you some more today."

As we ran she began sharing with me her experiences running ultramarathons and other races she had completed over the years. I quickly realized I was running with a very seasoned runner, although she was very humble about her accomplishments. Instead, she preferred to focus on the effect my run was having on many of her students.

We continued north on Route 119, and had a lot of residents along the path standing outside waving and cheering us on. The story of the run had reached so many in the area, and they all just wanted to come out to encourage me. At one point, a gentleman ran out to the end of his driveway and presented me with an American flag that he had plucked from his flagpole in his front yard.

"I want you to have this and carry it with pride," he said.

Joni, noticing the man approaching, slowed down so that she was off in the distance in order to allow the man to have some personal time to talk with me. Tiffany had just driven past in the RV and she stopped when she noticed the encounter. With tears streaming down my face, I thanked the man and began running again, spreading the flag out behind my head. Tiffany was right there to capture the moment and it was one of my favorite photographs of our entire journey.

It was such an honor to do this run, and having a stranger hand me his American flag meant so much to me. It took me a few minutes to compose myself, and when I did I slowed down so that Joni could rejoin me. I appreciated her falling back to allow me to reflect on that special moment.

"Feels good, doesn't it?" she stated. "A lot of people are very proud of you for what you are doing, and you're inspiring a huge number of people."

About 15 miles into the run, the rain began to let up and Joni left to head back home. I did an interview with Chris Lawrence from West Virginia MetroNews, who had been following and filming me since I left on the run that morning. When I was about nine miles outside of Clendenin, David Brinckman, the town's chief of police, met me. It was his day off, but he said he wanted to provide me with a police escort to my finish point for the day. He followed behind me, keeping the cars that approached us from behind a safe distance away. With so many blind spots on this road, I was thankful for his escort.

As we got within a couple of miles of town, I noticed a number of kids standing alongside the road. When I got up to them, they said they were members of the local middle school cross country team and asked if they could join me for the last couple of miles of my run.

"Of course you can!" I said. I was happy to have the company, especially of young runners. After we got moving I asked if any of them had any questions for me about my run.

"How much do you eat?" asked one of the kids.

"Do you sleep?" asked another.

The time passed quickly as I answered their flurry of questions. It was great to see so many kids in this small community out being active. I encouraged them to continue to train hard for the cross country team and thanked them for being a part of my journey. When we arrived in Clendenin, the parents of all of the kids were there to cheer us on to the finish. I was also pleasantly surprised to see my good friend Rusty Walker there cheering with everyone else. I talked to him numerous times on the run, especially when I needed someone to listen to some of the trials I was enduring that I didn't want to burden Tiffany with. Rusty joked that after all I had been through, he was happy to see that I was still alive.

I finished up the 30-mile run just north of Clendenin, with Chief Brinckman blocking traffic from the rear and Brian Egan from WKWS-FM joining me for a run again to wrap up my day. For the first time in my life, I rode in the front seat of a police cruiser when Chief Brinckman drove me back into town, where Tiff was waiting for me at Dairy Queen. A large hot fudge sundae was calling my name.

"Don't even think of paying us for that," said the store manager. "You've earned it."

The Brinckmans offered us their home for the night, and after cleaning up there we headed back to Charleston to attend an event at the Quarrier Diner, which was organized by the owners and Jim Sweezy. The owners of the diner, David and Anna Pollitt, were the parents of a good friend of mine, Tim Pollitt, who had tragically passed away a year earlier. His parents talked about how proud Tim would be of me and how honored they were to host a room full of friends, veterans and community members. I addressed the crowd, thanking them for coming out to support us and our veterans. The encouragement we received that night and the stories we heard from those who had served our country, dating all the way back to Vietnam, was something I'll never forget. It was another reminder about why we were doing this, and how much of a difference we were truly making.

## RUNNING WITH A PURPOSE

As I made my way toward the border of Braxton County, where I grew up, on June 20 (which coincidentally is West Virginia Day) I noticed a sign hanging on the end of a guardrail just below the county sign. I couldn't make it out until I got about 20 feet from it, and when I was able to read it, a huge smile came across my face.

"Braxton County Welcomes <u>YOU</u> Jamie!"

For the next five miles, I saw similar signs posted all along the roadway, some of which I could tell were made by young children.

One that was made using purple glitter read: "Running for Wounded Warriors."

"Thanks Jamie!" read another.

One sign in particular literally stopped me in my tracks. In bright purple glitter it read: "Running for Purple Heart Veterans" with the shape of a heart in place of the word. It was a very touching sign because it was about the wounded veterans for which I had specifically begun this run.

The rest of the way into the small town of Gassaway, I was continually greeted by friends I hadn't seen since I was in school. During one stretch I was joined by the daughters of Lauri Spencer, who was one of my former classmates. Kate and Anne were on the high school cross country team and ran with me for a few miles until we came to a large crowd gathered to greet me. Among the people in the crowd was a World War II veteran who I was honored to speak with briefly. The encouragement I received from the people in the area really meant a lot to me.

When we wrapped up the day early that afternoon the temperature and humidity were both in the 90s. Tiffany told me that earlier she received a phone call from Riki Hall, who had been looking after our cats in our home in Morgantown. When Riki walked into our house earlier in the day she was blasted by the warm air, a result of our air conditioning unit failing. She had already contacted a local heating and cooling company to repair the unit. We were so thankful we had many friends like that who were always there to help out in a time of need.

We checked into the Flatwoods Days Inn a little early and were waiting for our room to be prepared when the owner, John Skidmore, met Tiffany in the hall. Noticing her Running for Wounded Warriors shirt, he politely asked, "Are you with the runner guy?"

"Yes," she said. "He's outside getting more of our things for the night."

Posing with members of the American Legion, who gave me a motorcycle escort out of Charleston • It was emotional to be back home in Braxton County, West Virginia • Shaking the strong hand of World War II veteran Thurman Ratliff

Meeting the Braxton Belles, a group that included some Rosie Riveters • With the National Guard Color Guard in Burnsville, West Virginia • Speaking to the crowd at the Wounded Warrior 5K in Burnsville

Getting an escort through Fairmont, West Virginia, flanked by Aaron and Sandy Yocum to my right and Mayor Bill Burdick to my left • Receiving a Marine Corps League donation from Gunnery Sgt. Thomas Hellyer in Morgantown, West Virginia • Enjoying the view at Coopers Rock State Forest with The Daily crew

Climbing up Sideling
Hill, Maryland •
Dodging downed tree
limbs on the C&O
Canal Trail after the
derecho

Running with the Two Rivers Treads crew, Harpers Ferry, West Virginia • Proud to stand in front of the Marine Corps War Memorial in Arlington, Virginia • An emotional surprise visit from Bart Ingleston and his son Liam

Tiffany and I at the Navy-Marine Corps Memorial Stadium in Annapolis, Maryland • Standing with Navy personnel that welcomed me at the U.S. Naval Academy in Annapolis • Nick and I sharing a high five after jumping into the Chesapeake Bay • I couldn't have arrived at the finish without the help of my family

An interview with Fox News Channel on July 4 • I watched the corn grow from buds to all the way over my head as I ran across America • 50 miles down, 50 more to go • Exhausted but in my 16th and final state

Taking a break on my 100-mile run to eat some of my favorite food to refuel—watermelon • Racing to the finish in just less than 24 hours • The tired feet and legs that brought me to the finish • Celebrating the finish in the Atlantic Ocean in Rehoboth Beach, Delaware

"I've got a different room for you guys tonight," he said. I met them in the lobby, and we were quickly escorted to the Governor's suite.

"You guys deserve a good night's rest," John said.

"I don't know what to say," I said humbly as I thanked him.

"Don't say anything. Just enjoy the downtime. Maybe we'll get a chance to run together soon."

"I'd like that, but I think I'm done for the night," I laughed.

The Braxton County Rotary Club was holding its meeting at the hotel and the group invited us to attend the dinner and share the story of our journey. Joined by our kids and my parents, we enjoyed the opportunity to thank the community for being so supportive of us. I told them I wanted to not only make West Virginia proud of our efforts, but especially the people of Braxton County and my hometown of Burnsville.

"You've done more than you'll ever know!" one of the attendees told me.

## ROSIE THE RIVETER

The next morning I headed off from Gassaway toward the WDBS-FM radio station, where my former classmate Palmer Stephens worked and had been doing regular interviews with me throughout the run. There we were met by Lauri Spencer and her second grade class from Frametown Elementary. Lauri had been using my run as a geography lesson, allowing the students to track my progress across America. They also had spent the past couple of months raising money for our cause. At the radio station, the class presented me with their donation. I was so excited to meet all of the students and I let them know the money they had raised would go toward helping those who served in the military.

With the interview and presentation from the second grade class complete, Tiffany and I backtracked in the RV to the Braxton County Senior Center, where my mom had arranged for me to speak at 9 a.m. I hopped out of the RV and ran across a bridge that led to the center. Many of the residents were lined up along the bridge, cheering me on as I ran.

When I approached the entrance to the facility, I saw some of the most beautifully dressed women I had ever seen. They were a group of ladies at least 70 years old that call themselves the Braxton Belles. The oldest member was 93. They were dressed in Victorian-style dresses, right down to the frilly hats and gloves. Each one had on a different color: bright yellow, red, aqua and green.

"You didn't have to get all dressed up for me!" I joked as I approached them.

"It only took us a couple of hours to get all this on," answered one of the ladies, standing there with a beautiful smile on her face.

I addressed the crowd, thanking them all for coming out to be a part of this amazing journey and asked if any in attendance had served in the military. A number of the men and women raised their hands, as did a couple of the Belles.

"I was a Rosie the Riveter," said one of the Belles. "I volunteered and was happy to do it. I worked on aircrafts, doing my best to ensure our boys returned home safely. It was hard work, but I'd do it again if I could."

As a veteran, I had heard the term *Rosie the Riveter* before, but I didn't know the full history and meaning of the term or the sacrifices made by those women. I later took some time to research the term, which was coined during World War II and referred to women who took factory jobs to replace men who were called off to fight in the war. Many of those women worked at factories where parts were made for aircrafts or other equipment that was used by the US military in World War II. While opportunities for women to serve in the military have expanded since the 1940s, women who served our country as a Rosie the Riveter played a pivotal role in the war.

It was a true honor for me to spend time with those women. I thought about them and their contributions to our country several times throughout the remainder of my run that day. After leaving the senior center, I was joined by a few runners and a motorcycle and EMS ambulance, which escorted me into Burnsville, where many of my family and friends were waiting for my arrival.

## BURNSVILLE'S TOUGH

For the past 82 days my focus was on honoring veterans with each step that I took. But now, with each step that I took I looked forward to being reunited with family and friends from my hometown who had been so encouraging and supportive of this journey.

The temperature was climbing rapidly, approaching the mid-90s before it was even noon. Dustin Smyth, one of the runners that joined me that day, peeled off in the little town of Heaters (what an appropriate name considering the temperature) about eight miles from Burnsville in order to allow me to run the last several miles into my hometown on my own. I was also set to cross the 3,000-mile mark on the run just as I was entering town.

I had driven this stretch of road hundreds of times over the years, and probably could have run it blindfolded. Instead, I was being escorted into town by the RV and a motorcycle, with the Burnsville chief of police following close behind me. As my shoes slapped the hot pavement beneath my feet, bringing me closer to Burnsville, I became so anxious that I disregarded the effects of the heat. Tiffany pulled the RV over four miles before we got into town and forced me to drink more Gatorade. I was so excited that my pace had increased considerably, although I felt like I was floating during this eight-mile stretch. My mom actually called and asked me to slow down because she was tracking me and was worried that something she had planned wouldn't be ready for my arrival.

Passing the trailer park that I called home for a few years as a kid and crossing over the last climb into town, I flashed back to the days as a kid when I would ride my bike up this hill, remembering the first time I was ever able to ride the whole way without stopping. Here I was, 30 years later, conquering this hill on foot. Mount Everest could have been in front of me at this point and it wouldn't have slowed me down. As I reached the crest of the hill, looking down into the little town I grew up in, it was difficult to believe how far I had come, literally and metaphorically, since my childhood. I had obviously grown tremendously as a person in the past 30 years, but much of that growth had occurred in the past three months.

Making my way toward town, I could see a crowd of about 75 people gathered there, waving signs and flags and cheering me on as I approached. A large American flag caught my eye and I noticed that an honor guard had been assembled from the local VFW. With the honor guard leading the way, the crowd walked the final 500 yards with me to the finish for the day.

When I finished, among a large group of family and friends, there stood my grandmother. She had the biggest smile on her face. As I approached to give her a big hug, tears streaming down my face, the cheers became muffled and I became completely unaware that anyone else was around except the two of us. Mamaw, as I called her, was about to celebrate her 87th birthday, and I was so happy to see her. My biggest concern throughout our trip was that something would happen to her while we were gone. I knew that was one of the only things that would take me off schedule. To have her there hugging me and telling me how proud she was of me was a moment I will never forget.

Sadly, about seven months later, she passed away, leaving a tremendous legacy and spirit behind that touched so many people. Knowing that she was there to see my accomplishment and that she was able to create some great memories with all of her many children, grandchildren and great grandchildren really helped ease the pain of our loss. A few of my friends from the military have passed away over the years, and I remember them fondly not only for their friendship, but also for their love of country and service. I think the best way we can honor those who have passed on before us is to take the qualities and values we learned from them and pass them on to our family and friends.

My uncle Butch McPherson addressed the crowd, we said the Pledge of Allegiance and a prayer was offered. I then took the time to thank everyone for being there. A few of my friends yelled out, "Burnsville's Tough!" a saying we said since we were kids. I was happy to add a little to the legacy and significance of that phrase, which really was an accurate description of the hard-working people from the community.

We capped the celebration with a chocolate cake with chocolate icing, my favorite, courtesy of my mom. Written on the cake in white icing was "Welcome Home Jamie 3000", celebrating not only my return to Burnsville but also surpassing the 3,000-mile mark. As I celebrated with friends and family, I ate several pieces of cake. Having run 3,000 miles in the past three months, I wasn't really worried about the calories.

# 14 | **The Longest Days**

**M**y mom had been feverishly working on the Wounded Warrior 5K in Burnsville, starting with the planning and arrangements a few months before we left for Oregon. I ran into Burnsville on a Thursday and the race, to be successful, was scheduled for that Saturday. So on Friday I would run the 29 miles north to Jane Lew and then return to Burnsville to be there for the race the following morning. Saturday, after taking part in the race and festivities, we had to drive back up to Jane Lew for a noon presentation at the Jane Lew Veterans Memorial. From there, I'd run about 20 miles north to Clarksburg, where I was scheduled to visit a VA hospital. Following that, I'd have another seven miles to get to the stopping point. I knew Saturday was going to be a long but fulfilling day.

Burnsville was blanketed by a dense fog when I left for my run early Friday morning. I was so glad to be able to run on familiar roads. I ran right past the home I lived in as a very young kid, down roads that brought back fond memories of riding my bike and swimming in the creeks. The trees were a deep green, and birds provided a constant song for me as I climbed up and over the beautiful rolling hills.

As I made my way through Weston with a police escort behind me, I was greeted by staff at the courthouse and community members who came outside to cheer me on. I was worried about slowing up traffic, but the policeman told me to move at my own pace. After the escort peeled off, I picked up the pace considerably and we made our way to Jane Lew by about 1:30 p.m. I was invited to the Jackson's Mill State 4-H Camp that afternoon to speak to a group of young leaders. Tiffany worked hard the previous couple of days to put together a slide show of photos she had taken so far on the trip, and we were excited to share our journey with them.

I was in their shoes at one time, participating in 4-H as a kid. I learned a lot about the local community and working together by participating in 4-H. As the slideshow played behind me, I shared stories of the amazing people we met, how I overcame trials during the run and what I hoped to accomplish after the run. It was also a chance to share a valuable message that I learned while I was running across America.. I told the group that if they woke up every morning and set out to inspire someone that day, as night fell, they would be able to look back on their day knowing they lived a fulfilling and meaningful day.

A number of the campers came up to me afterward, some of them very emotional, talking about their fathers who were serving overseas at that time, and how proud they were of them.

"Make sure you tell them that I appreciate their service," I said, "and let them know how proud you are of them every chance you get."

We left Jackson's Mill and headed to the Weston Military Museum, where members of the Patriot Guard motorcycle club and VFW were waiting for us. While on our way out to Oregon, I received a phone call from a couple of veterans from Weston who assured us we would have a welcome like no other when we ran through their town. Mike and Ron didn't disappoint. They helped coordinate our visit to the museum and American Legion, and media and local community leaders that were there welcomed us like we were royalty.

An honor guard made up of Patriot Guard and local VFW members flanked both sides of the walkway toward the entrance and they raised the flags and saluted me as I walked past. I did not want to disrespect them by asking them to not salute me, so I saluted back and thanked them for being there. We toured the museum, which displayed the rich history of local servicemen and women. We wrapped up the visit with a stop by the American Legion Post #4, and headed back to Burnsville to get some much-needed rest.

## WOUNDED WARRIOR 5K

The 5K run Saturday morning turned out to be so much more than just a fundraiser in support of our run across America. We had 157 participants driving in from Kentucky, Pennsylvania and Virginia as well as from all over the state of West Virginia. The turnout helped me realize that our run wasn't just benefiting veterans. The run was affecting so many more people in so many different ways.

My mom had been telling me about the meetings she had been attending with the planning committee leading up to the 5K. She said the weeks leading up to the race created a scene driving though Burnsville like she had never seen before. Every evening in town, she saw groups of people out walking or jogging together to train for the 5K. There were many competitive runners from the region who ran in the race, but what moved me was the number of men, women, boys and girls who were participating in their first-ever race. Several of them told me they had never previously run or walked anything close to the 3.1-mile distance of the event.

That was also the case with many of my former high school classmates who participated in the run. It was almost like a class reunion with 12 members of my graduating class there, and many of them started running after they saw the transformations I had made in my own life after picking up the sport. Seeing the lifestyle changes in people as they realized the benefits of running, or even walking, was a side benefit I never expected with the run, but was excited to witness.

After taking the stage to thank everyone for coming out, it was time to run. Knowing that I had another marathon distance to run later that day, my original plan was to take it easy and enjoy the run. My pace had obviously slowed while running across the country, averaging around 10-minute miles. I also hadn't raced in months and had put down 3,000 miles in the past 89 days. My friends Aaron and Sandy Yocum, who ran with me in Missouri, drove down from Morgantown for the race. Aaron told me he would roll with whatever pace I wanted to keep. We made it about 200 yards after the bell sounded before the competitor in me came out.

"Let's do this," I said as I picked up the pace.

"Let's go," Aaron responded, and off we went.

My adrenaline was higher than I had experienced in a while, and I felt really good as we picked up the pace. Aaron and I began to pick off quite a few runners during the first half of the race. At the halfway turn, Sandy was about 100 feet ahead of us, doubling back toward the finish. We caught up to her, and as we went by, Sandy yelled, "I thought you weren't going to race!"

"Well, it is a race!" I yelled back as I picked up the pace even more.

I did take the time to give high fives and pass along words of encouragement as we passed runners and walkers headed out to the turnaround. I wanted each of them to know that I appreciated them all for participating. I couldn't have done this without their support, and our men and women needed each of them to continue to find ways to support and encourage our veterans each and every day. It was also great to see a group of Marine veterans who were wearing shirts with their squadron logos on them from when they served carrying the American flag and Marine Corps flag during the entire run.

As we approached the last couple of turns before the finish line, I saw Tiffany at an intersection taking photos of the runners. She took so many beautiful photos along the run, and we wanted to make sure everyone had memories of this day. As we ran up, she had a surprised look on her face and I just threw my hands in the air.

"Well, it *is* a race!" I said, with a smirk on my face.

Aaron and I had set our sights on a couple of runners we wanted to catch, and of course he wasn't going to let me slow down once I decided to go, so we pushed the pace even harder at the finish. Passing the last couple of runners, we threw our hands in the air as we crossed the finish line. The clock read 22 minutes, 44 seconds, meaning I had just knocked out the 5K with a 7:19 pace, which was good enough for second place in my age group. It was not my fastest 5K, but considering the circumstances, I wasn't going to be upset with myself.

"Nice run," Aaron said as we made our way back to the finish line to greet the incoming runners.

"I couldn't help myself," I said, smiling back at him. It felt so good to get out and push it for once. I felt so alive at the end, and it helped break up the monotony of what I had been doing the past 90 days.

I was proud of everyone who crossed the finish line and was honored to be able to hand out the awards and thank the crowd once again for participating in a great event and fundraiser. It's a race I certainly want to build upon each year, and I am looking forward to making it an annual event for my hometown. Burnsville mayor Paul Bragg then presented me with a key to the city before we had to head out with the kids to drive up to Jane Lew to start my real run for the day.

## GIVING THANKS

We pulled into Jane Lew right at noon, where a group of community members had gathered at the Jane Lew Veterans Memorial, my starting point for the day. I spoke briefly to them about my mission and how things had gone so far, and expressed my thanks to all of the veterans in attendance.

The temperature was starting to really soar and having run so hard during the 5K, I was feeling a bit out of sorts when I began my run at 12:30 p.m. It was also difficult mentally because usually by this time I was finished running for the day, and here I was just getting started. After logging about 10 miles, I had to stop on the side of the road and drink all four of my 8-ounce bottles of Gatorade. My head was pounding from the heat and the effort I had put out earlier in the day. Tiff drove by and I waved her down so I could refuel my body and mind. When I headed back out, I received some much-needed encouragement when a number of people driving past cheered me on or said how proud the state of West Virginia was of me. Good things like that always happened when I needed it most.

Three hours after heading down the road we arrived at the Clarksburg VA Medical Center, where we had one of the most incredible experiences of the trip. When we set off on the journey, my wife and I knew the types of people we would encounter and we had a personal appreciation for the sacrifices they made. Our children, however, hadn't seen first-hand what so many of these men and women endure when they return home from serving in the military. We made every effort to involve our kids in Veterans Day parades and local events that honor our military, instilling in them the importance of patriotism. But being 12 and 10, they didn't fully grasp the sacrifices and circumstances these people went through on a daily basis. We wanted them to experience this part with us so that they could develop a greater appreciation for the men and women who serve this country.

As we made our way from room to room, introducing ourselves to each patient, laughter and tears were shed not only by the veterans we encountered, but by my family as well. Hearing the stories of their service, their struggles and of the things they deal with now made this whole adventure really sink in for all of us. Some had no family to go home to. Others couldn't wait to get home to loved ones. Our kids said, "Thank you for your service" to each person we met, and listened intently to the stories they shared.

We were all tired, but could have listened all day to their tales. It was definitely 90 minutes well spent and gave me the energy I needed to finish the final 11 miles of the day. We arrived in Charles Point around 7 p.m. as the sun was dropping below the horizon, bringing to a close one of the longest but most rewarding days of our trip.

## MOUNTAINEER PRIDE

Day 91 started off foggy, both in and out of my head. The previous day had been one of the longest running days since the first week when I walked due to the shin injury. It had all been worth it, but I was tired. I had hoped other runners would join me that day to help clear my head and keep me moving.

Arriving at the starting point at 7 a.m., I took off with five other runners. Each of the runners had followed me across America on my website and couldn't wait to join me for a small portion of my run. I told them I needed them more than they needed me. Because most of them were accomplished runners, I immediately apologized for the slowness of the pace I would run, but they all told me to not worry about it. As usual, though, I picked up the pace when others were with me.

We picked up a police escort about six miles in, and knocked the first 9.5 miles out in around 90 minutes, when the second wave of runners joined me. Aaron and Sandy joined me, as did the mayor of Fairmont, Bill Burdick, who presented me with a certificate proclaiming it to be "Jamie Summerlin Appreciation Day." He then joined us to run through Fairmont, escorted again by the city police. Pulling into the McDonald's parking lot to refuel in the RV, we were greeted by members of the local VFW who came out to show their support.

Saying goodbye to the mayor and VFW members, Aaron and Sandy continued on with me toward Morgantown. We had another 14 miles to go, all of it on the state's famous rolling hills. A couple of miles in, we picked up a Monongalia County Sheriff escort, which took us the rest of the way into Morgantown. As Aaron and Sandy ran with me toward Morgantown, they shared with me how much it meant to them to be a small part of this journey, dating all the way back to when Tiffany and I invited them over to dinner two years earlier to get their thoughts on this idea.

"I remember how crazy we thought you were at the time," Sandy said. "Even though we told you we'd do everything we could to help you out, in the back of our minds we wondered if the run would really ever happen. I guess we didn't know you that well then!"

I thanked Aaron and Sandy for supporting me from the beginning, even if they initially had their doubts. They provided such valuable guidance for me since they were both more experienced runners, and it meant a great deal to me that they were a part of the run not only now but also when they surprised me in Missouri.

"After we ran those 35 miles with you in Missouri, all I could think about at the end of the day was that I was so happy I didn't have to do that again tomorrow," Sandy recalled. "It was amazing to think that you had also run that distance the day before and were going to run it again the next day and the day after that!"

Months after the completion of the run, Aaron and Sandy shared some special words with me.

"Many times you meet dreamers in your life and very few actually make their dreams come true," they told me. "Jamie, you did just that and to us that sets you apart from the rest. It's an honor to call you our close friend."

The Mountaineer Triathlon was being held in Morgantown that day, and our route covered a section of the bike course. We made our way down to the Waterfront district in Morgantown, our stopping point for the day and also the finish point for the triathlon. When the race director saw our RV, he told Tiffany he wanted me to run through the finish line. They even presented me with a finisher's medal afterwards. That planted a seed in my mind, and since my journey has been complete I began training for my first triathlon, a half Ironman followed, hopefully, by a full Ironman later.

Aly Goodwin-Gregg, my PR representative, arranged a welcome ceremony at the Waterfront Memorial Park in Morgantown and since we didn't have much time to get cleaned up, we decided to wait until after the event to head to our home. Our kids had previously threatened to chain themselves to their beds when we got home, so we didn't want to take the chance.

"Besides," I told Nick, "when we make our way up to the ceremony, we'll be running with Miss West Virginia Spenser Wempe and all of the Miss West Virginia pageant girls."

"I'll stay," he said.

When I spoke at the welcome home ceremony, I used the same message I had shared at the 4-H camp earlier that week. I encouraged everyone to find a way to inspire someone each day. It was a message that grew with me as I made my way across America, something that fit into my mission. What I was doing was the most difficult thing I had ever done in my life, but putting a smile on a veteran's face was worth every step. Letting them know that we cared and wanted to support them pushed me to get out of bed each morning, lace up my shoes and head out on the road. I hoped to inspire others to think about how they could be selfless and serve others, too.

Jim Manilla, the mayor of Morgantown, presented me with a key to the city, and various local organizations presented generous donations, including the Marine Corps League, which I am proud to say I am a new member of. Former POW Jessica Lynch spoke at the event, talking about how veterans who deal with traumatic issues every day and live with the physical and mental scars of war rely on some of the charitable organizations that we were supporting with the run. The Daily, a news organization from New York, sent a crew down to film the event and spend a couple of days with me, giving the run even more exposure.

We stopped by the Hazel Ruby McQuain Amphitheater before we headed home because the West Virginia Bass Federation was in town for a tournament. They "passed the hat" around over the weekend, and presented us with a $500 donation. A number of veterans were in the crowd, giving me another opportunity to say thank you.

We were all excited as we pulled into our driveway, seeing the house for the first time in 102 days. We had eight more days to get to Annapolis, Maryland, but right then I just wanted to plop down on my own bed. Riki Hall, who was watching our cats and trying to get our air conditioning fixed, thankfully installed two portable air conditioner units in our home while a part was being ordered for our unit. Even with the portable units, there wasn't much relief because it was so hot and humid outside. Even in a muggy house, I was still looking forward to crawling into my own bed.

"Now, about getting naked," I said as slipped under the sheets with my wife. It was good to be home!

## HOW I LOVE THOSE WEST VIRGINIA HILLS

When Tiffany mapped out the daily routes before we left on this trek, she intentionally made Day 92 the shortest run (about 13 miles) of the entire trip. We wanted to enjoy a few extra hours at home and also get in front of the local media as much as possible. I didn't begin my run until 10 a.m., after doing several interviews with radio and TV stations.

During the interviews, I talked about how happy I was to be home and almost finished. The radio hosts commented on my suntan and the fact that I was skinnier than when I left Morgantown. I also made the official announcement that I would continue the run on from Annapolis, wrapping up with a 100-mile, 24-hour run to Rehoboth Beach, Delaware, in order to make this a true coast-to-coast run. I told Jim Stallings with WAJR-AM that it was his fault I was running an extra 100 miles because he was the one who initially gave me grief for finishing at the Chesapeake Bay and not making it all the way to the Atlantic Ocean. I invited him to run the 100 miles with me, but he politely declined. The Daily crew joined us at the radio stations and filmed every step of the run that day.

When we gathered at the Waterfront district to begin the run, I knew there were going to be other local runners joining me. I was pleasantly surprised to see a couple of local police officers ready to run with me. Just like those in the military, law enforcement officials put on a uniform every day to serve their local communities and I let them know I appreciated their service and company on the run. With a county sheriff's officer leading the way, we made our way through downtown and headed out toward the scenic Coopers

Rock State Forest. A few employees at downtown businesses stepped out to wish me luck, as did the staff and children at a child care facility.

We also received some great news from the sheriff's department. We hoped to run across the old Iron Bridge crossing Cheat Lake to head up to Coopers Rock. Unfortunately, the Department of Highways shut down the bridge due to safety concerns while it simultaneously worked to build a replacement bridge just adjacent to the old one. The only other way across the lake was either running across Cheat Lake on Interstate 68 or running an extra 12 miles around the lake.

Tiffany had many discussions with the local sheriff's department prior to our arrival into Morgantown about whether I could run on the interstate, which is against the law in the state, or cross over a bridge that had been shut down for months. Before I began the run that morning, the sheriff's department told us we would be able to run across Iron Bridge and we would be one of the last few people to do so since it was going to be disassembled soon.

With the police motorcycle leading the way, and Tiffany behind us in the RV, I headed out with a group of runners. We picked up more runners along the way, including a couple of veterans wearing Army and Navy shirts. Triple S Harley Davidson, one of my key sponsors for the run, had scheduled a welcome home stop for me as we ran past their facility that morning. They presented me with a shirt signed by their entire staff and asked me to autograph an article about the run that had been published in the newspaper, which they placed on their Wall of Heroes, a wall dedicated to those who serve this great country.

We left Triple S and began the trek out Route 857 toward the Iron Bridge, now with the Triple S truck behind us blocking traffic. Tiff drove the RV across the interstate bridge to meet us on the other side of Cheat Lake since vehicles were prohibited from crossing Iron Bridge. As we were running down Route 857, I noticed a few signs had been placed along the road with "Run Jamie Run" and "Running for Wounded Warriors." A vehicle approached, blowing its horn at us, and I couldn't help but smile when I saw

Sandy Yocum accompanied by Michael Yura, another very good friend of mine, waving and cheering us on as they drove by. They had made the signs that morning and wanted to show their support.

Following the police officer on his motorcycle, we made our way across the old bridge to hook back up with the RV. A group of construction workers who were working on the new bridge were standing there cheering us on and presented me with an envelope full of cash that had been collected by their crew that morning to donate to the cause. I continued to be blown away by the level of sacrifice and support we received from so many different groups of people.

## CAUGHT ON FILM

The police escort headed back toward Morgantown as we made a left onto Quarry Run Road. Even though I have lived in Morgantown for many years, I had never previously been on this road, so I had no idea what we were about to approach. When we left the bridge a couple of miles back, Emma Barker from The Daily hooked me up with a wireless microphone. She wanted to run a few miles with me, with the video crew in the lead filming us as we ran. But we were in for a surprise once we turned onto Quarry Run Road.

About a quarter of a mile straight up Quarry Run Road, I realized that this was one of the steepest roads I had run on the entire journey. There was literally no break in the climb as we continued to run straight up the mountain. Emma dropped back to get into the RV with Tiff while the film crew in the truck stayed in front of us, capturing every step we took. A bit of pride crept in, and I told John Snodgrass and Robert Klenk that with The Daily filming us, we were going to run the entire way up this mountain. Making the climb even more challenging, the videographer in the back of the truck kept firing questions at me, and I was trying to answer them without huffing and puffing too much.

"What do you want your kids to get out of your run?" the interviewer asked.

"I just want them to be proud of their daddy," I said, getting a little choked up. "I want them to know that even though life is tough, and we all make mistakes or get dealt a bad hand at different times, never look at a hurdle in life as something that can't be overcome. I want to set a good example for them, and I hope this journey is doing just that."

At the top of the climb, I wasn't sure whether to go left or right at the split. I also wasn't thinking too clearly after running all the way up that steep hill, but a quick check of the map had us turn right and head straight down a dirt road that was washed out and pretty beat up.

"Will your wife be able to bring the RV down the hill?" asked one of the runners.

"After the past 3,100 miles," I responded, "I have no doubt she can handle this road."

With the treacherous washboard road behind us, we continued along the frontage road toward Coopers Rock before meeting up with the RV.

"Wow!" Tiff said, eyes still wide. Emma was sitting in the passenger seat of the RV, still a bit frazzled from the trip down the dirt road. "That was fun!" Tiff exclaimed. "Nothing fell out of the cabinets in the RV, so it couldn't have been too bad."

We refueled and rested for about 15 minutes, catching our breath and grabbing another plateful of watermelon. I also made the rare suggestion of running a few miles out of my way, knowing that The Daily crew had never been in West Virginia before.

"We only have a few miles to get to the finish point for the day, but there is no way I am getting this close to the Coopers Rock overlook and not running out there," I said. "It'll add three miles to our run for the day and take us off our route, but believe me, it'll be worth it."

As far as I'm concerned, there's no better beauty than the wonderful hills we were running through, and Coopers Rock provides one of the most gorgeous views in the area.

The film crew continued to ask questions and get video of all of us running down the sun-speckled road through the Monongahela State Forest. As we approached the overlook, The Daily crew wanted to get video of me running out to the overlook, but I asked them to do me a favor.

"When you get to the bridge that crosses over to the overlook, please let me go out there first," I said. "I want to see your eyes as you take in the view for the first time."

The last time I had run out in this area, the trails and roads were covered in snow, with very few tracks other than my own in the snow. Today, it was well over 90 degrees, and everything was a beautiful green. I couldn't help but smile as I stepped out where I could see for miles, with the Cheat River a thousand feet below me, and the rolling hills with a haze of humidity sitting on top of them. Looking to the west, I could see Morgantown, and the roads we had just run a few hours earlier. There was something surreal about looking to the end of the horizon and knowing that my feet had carried me from there and beyond.

I turned around just in time to see Emma and her crew step up to the overlook.

"Wow! What an incredible view," Emma said. "And to have this in your back yard? This is amazing."

"This is my playground," I said. "West, by God, Virginia."

"You've made us feel like we were family the past couple of days," Emma said. "We can't wait to come back. Now I understand how easy it is for you to do what you're doing. Some of the most caring people we've ever met were here in West Virginia."

"It's who we are," I said. "We are a proud state, and with the highest number per capita of men and women in the armed forces, it's very personal to us. We either served, have family members who served or know someone who has served. And we're very proud of every single one of them."

We departed the overlook to head back to Morgantown, but later in the day, we were reminded that not everything in life happens as you think it should.

## BROKEN PROMISES

When we began this journey, one of the things I wanted to get across to everyone we encountered was that every community could support their local veterans. We may need to sacrifice some things we would want for ourselves, but the veterans, who oftentimes sacrifice everything for the good of the country, far too often find the tools and resources that have been established for them don't always meet their needs.

Tiffany is a service disabled veteran, so we have a personal understanding of the obstacles that may occur when attempting to get the care and help from a VA hospital or other organizations that have become so big that, at times, they lose sight of their original mission. The men and women who have worn the uniform, especially those who have service-related physical or mental disabilities, should never have a need that isn't met by these organizations. Unfortunately, red tape and bureaucracy far too often get in the way, and a lot of veterans just give up fighting what at times can seem to be a never-ending battle. They feel let down, and the fight for the care they have been promised sometimes seems to be more of a burden than it's worth.

It was very encouraging for us to find that more often than not, communities across the country wanted to help our veterans. We just found that a lot of times they didn't know exactly what to do. That revelation gave me a lot of things to think about while I was out running. I wanted to discover how we could better support the veterans at a local community level. I also wanted all of the effort that we had put into this journey to pay off in more ways than just serving as a short-term fundraising effort.

My family made a lot of sacrifices to make the run a possibility. We had to work with the school systems to get approval and support to take our kids out of their classrooms. We were excited that they not only gave us their blessing, but also provided us with the materials and curriculum to make sure our children didn't fall behind academically while they were gone. The schools even used the run as an educational tool for their classes.

Tiffany and I were also asking our respective employers to be equally as supportive of the run since it would require about a four-month absence from our jobs. I accepted a new position at CityNet shortly before we left for the run. Jim Martin, the CEO, hired me knowing that I would soon be gone for an extended period of time. He supported the mission 100 percent and said that my position with the company would still be there when I returned. Not only did he follow through on that promise, but CityNet also provided support and encouragement throughout the run. CityNet was another example of a local company doing what it could to support my mission and, as a result, our nation's veterans.

Tiffany was eligible for assistance through the Vocational Rehabilitation and Employment Program after she was discharged from the military, and used it to pursue a bachelor's degree in dental hygiene. She enrolled at West Virginia University (WVU) as a freshman at the age of 29. WVU has one of the top baccalaureate dental hygiene programs in the country, and Tiffany worked hard her four years in school to do the best she could. She was recognized as not only the top graduate in her class, but also as a WVU Foundation Scholar, one of only 50 students to receive the prestigious award in the 2008 graduating class. As a non-traditional student, married with two young children, it was difficult at times for her to balance everything, but we did our best to support her in her education, and it all paid off.

The unfortunate part about living in a college town is that in her career field, a lot of the graduates end up remaining in the area to work. The job market gets saturated, and when someone finds a great place to work, they don't leave. The job hunt was initially difficult for Tiffany, but she finally settled into an office working part time for a wonderful dentist. He was very supportive of the military–he had family who served–and was 100 percent behind us and our mission. Ownership changed in her office, however, and the new dentist inherited the decision to grant Tiffany a leave of absence. He assured Tiffany that her position would be there when she returned, and wished us well on the run.

But much like veterans who have to deal with broken promises from some organizations set up to assist them, we, too, received what at the time was devastating news.

"My services are no longer needed," Tiffany told me when I walked into our home after running some errands in Morgantown following our return from Coopers Rock.

"What are you talking about?" I asked, completely shocked.

"I just got a phone call from my boss, who told me things have changed and that my hours would not be there for me when I was supposed to come back to work."

Her words were more devastating than the Kansas winds or the hill I had just run up Quarry Run Road. Our job security was one of the few things I often thought about while running across the country. Now one of my biggest fears had come true. I took it personally since I was the one responsible for taking her away from her job in the first place. She was the manager, caregiver, physical therapist, nutritionist and incredible mother and wife during this whole trip. And I was the reason she was out of work.

"Don't worry about it right now," she told me. "It'll all work out. Everything happens for a reason."

I could tell in her voice, though, that she was very let down. I just couldn't believe that we had come all this way, and eight days before we finish she gets hit with this news. If we had left for a vacation or extended time away for selfish reasons, I could understand being told that a job wouldn't be available on our return from the beginning. But this trip wasn't about us, it was for men and women who truly needed and deserved our support. We knew we were putting our employers in a difficult situation by being away for four months, but we left under the impression that our jobs were secure.

What also hit Tiffany so hard was that we had received so much support from her patients and she was really looking forward to getting back to work, thanking them for their encouragement and sharing some of the amazing stories of our trip. Now she didn't have that opportunity.

I stewed about it for a couple of days, keeping my thoughts to myself, but my emotions got the best of me and I posted a short version of what happened to her on my blog. The response from our supporters and followers was overwhelming. We received countless phone calls, texts, Facebook posts, tweets and comments on the blog in support of Tiffany. People were just as irritated as I was, but Tiffany wanted to allow it to all blow over. While we appreciated everyone's efforts to do what they could to help us through the situation, she didn't want to cause any trouble. That is just not who she is. Professionalism and integrity to her profession came before personal feelings.

"Life is strange sometimes," she said, remaining confident that everything would work out for the best. I was amazed at her strength and resolve. She also didn't want me to stress out about her job situation, especially since we were so close to our goal. So I did my best to follow her lead and put it out of my mind until we returned home.

Tiffany was right. In just the few short months since the completion of the run, she has enjoyed some amazing and rewarding work experiences, which she never would have done if her old job would have been there waiting for her. What started out as a stumbling block turned into a launching pad to a more fulfilling career. Her new job opportunities take her all over the state of West Virginia and she feels very satisfied, knowing that she is doing good things for many people.

We learned that yes, indeed, everything happens for a reason.

# 15 | Freedom Run

Knowing we were leaving our house again for another 10 days was tough. Our kids certainly didn't want to go, and to be quite honest, I didn't want to leave either. But we had a mission to complete. The weather over the next week looked to be the hottest temperatures I would deal with, and of course, it would hit right when I would be in the toughest climbs of the journey.

We left Coopers Rock, joined by Bob Henderson, a Morgantown resident who happened to be out for a run that morning. His excursion had been sidetracked by an encounter with some bears, so as he doubled back down the road, he ran into us getting ready to leave. As fate would have it, he was a Marine Corps veteran as well, having served during the Vietnam era. He told me that he had been following my journey and couldn't begin to express how proud he was of us. While he ran a few miles with me, he marveled at how I was able to hold up physically.

"I assume you'll run on your hands or crawl from here if you have to," he said with a laugh. I didn't argue.

After a few miles, I made my way into Brandonville, West Virginia's smallest incorporated town. One of Tiffany's former professors in her dental hygiene program at WVU, Carol Spear, was standing alongside the road waving at me as I ran up to her. After a brief hug, she told me that she had surgery on her knees a few months ago, but wanted to take a few steps with me. Carol has a special place in my heart because of the way that she motivated Tiffany in class and clinic, and she served as a great example for Tiffany.

"We are all so proud of you and Tiffany, and think what you're doing is a wonderful thing for some wonderful people," she said. "There are some people up here that want to say thank you."

A few members of the local VFW, including a World War II veteran, stood at attention as I ran up to greet them. They presented me with a check to pass along to the Wounded Warrior Project from their unit, as well as food and drinks for myself and my crew. Tiffany was excited to see Carol, and I was elated to have another opportunity to shake the hand of a World War II veteran.

"You gave us a great foundation to work with," I told him. "If it wasn't for your efforts during World War II, things could have been a lot different in this country, and I respect each and every one of you who served so much."

With a handful of American flags given to us by the crowd there, we took off and headed toward my 13th state. But just before I reached the Pennsylvania border, we came upon a couple of very cute ladies in a golf cart. The driver of the cart, who happened to be the mother of the lady with her, was a spry 92 years old but didn't look a day over 60. I ran up to the cart as the mom turned to me with a huge smile.

"You look *rugged!*" she said with a twinkle in her eye.

I think that was the only time I blushed the entire trip.

Our time spent in Pennsylvania was very brief, lasting only one day. A former coworker of Tiff's, Kim Fine, and her husband, Larry, put us up for the night, and showed my kids a whole lot of fun. After the kids each got a ride on the back of an ATV, Kim and Larry took them out for a ride on their boat on the Youghiogheny River Lake. Meanwhile, I stayed back to rest and catch up on some blogging for my website. The run that day really wore out my legs.

Everyone I spoke to prior to the trip who had done similar trips, whether it was biking or running across all or part of the country, told me that running through the Appalachian Mountains would be my toughest challenge. When I conquered the mountains in the Rockies, each climb and descent were all fairly gradual in nature. It was either a steady climb up for a few miles or a long stretch of gradual downhill running. But those were easy days compared to running through West Virginia, Pennsylvania and Maryland toward Washington DC.

I felt really strong heading into this section, mentally prepared for whatever the roads would bring. But as I made my way away from Coopers Rock toward southeastern Pennsylvania, the rolling hills seemed to get steeper and steeper with each step I took. Seeing a 9 percent grade sign posted along the side of a road didn't really intimidate me because I conquered some of those earlier in the trip. But in the Appalachians, a climb up a 9 percent grade was often immediately followed by an 11-13 percent grade heading back down the mountain. That pattern would continue to repeat. I would get to the top of a climb, head back down and without relief would have to start climbing again. The non-stop rolling hills were unforgiving, and put more demand on my legs than I had experienced at any other time during the trip.

### RESPECT

After a solid night of rest at the Fine's house, we drove up to our start point in Addison, Pennsylvania. The climb from the lakeside up to Addison was no joke, but I wisely ran the last climb at the end of the previous day so I wouldn't have to face it first thing in the morning. We took a few minutes before I left to check out some of the historical monuments in Addison, which included Tollhouse #1 on the old Cumberland Road. Running along these roads, I was fortunate to see many historical markers from years gone by, which included memorials to veterans. Now that I was plowing through the eastern part of the country, the markers continued to date further back, signifying battles and roadways from as far back as the Civil War.

Tollhouse #1 in Addison provided a great history lesson. We read the details of its operation, how it came to be and all got a good laugh at the cost shown on the tollhouse of the tolls paid by travelers on the old Cumberland Highway.

Horse and Rider – 4 cents

Sled Drawn by Horse – 3 cents

Oxen (Pair) – 3 cents

Chariot, Coach, Coaches, Stage Phaeton or Chaise with 2 Horses and 4 Wheels-12 cents

Refusal to Pay Toll - $3.00 FINE

As I began my run that morning, which would bring me into Maryland within the first hour, the elevation, as well as the temperature, continued to climb. I had to slow down my pace as I approached a 3,000-foot elevation mark. Just a couple of days prior, I was down to 900 feet in Morgantown, but I knew I only had another two days of serious climbs before it was all downhill from there.

All the climbing was also making me extremely hungry. I devoured all the food Tiffany provided at the first aid stop as if I hadn't eaten in a week. The kids were excited for me to hit the road again because there was a fast food restaurant across the street and they didn't want to eat their breakfast from the restaurant in front of me. Of course, I could still smell it when I climbed into the RV at the next stop, but I appreciated their consideration. It smelled so good, but I didn't want to introduce anything into my system to disrupt the flow, so to speak.

During this second stop I made a couple of phone calls to Morgantown because Tiffany's job situation became a hot topic on one of the radio stations. We just wanted to reiterate that we didn't want to cause any trouble, but I also didn't regret sharing my personal feelings about the situation on my blog that week.

At the next aid stop, as I continued down Route 40 through Grantsville, Maryland, an older gentleman came up to the RV to introduce himself. Mitch told us briefly about his service to our country during Vietnam, and wanted to know what we were doing. I explained to him that my trip started out as a way to honor wounded veterans, but it had morphed into an opportunity to say thank you to all veterans. I didn't want to exclude anyone, and I wanted all servicemen and women to know that we appreciated each of them for their service.

With a tear in his eye, he explained to us the horrible reception that he and his fellow military members encountered when they returned home from Vietnam. He was so thankful that our men and women returning from Afghanistan and Iraq were being treated better.

"Things like what you are doing help me feel a little more respected than I once did," he said. "I know it means a lot to those coming home now, but it also touches older veterans like me. We don't want to see anyone go through what we had to when we came back from war."

"You have my utmost respect sir," I responded. "We are all very thankful for your service."

"Here's my last few dollars I have in my wallet," he said as he pulled out eight $1 bills and handed them to me. "It's all I have, but I want to do what I can to help these men feel welcomed when they return."

It made me sad to hear his story about how those returning home from Vietnam were treated so poorly by so many Americans. They experienced nightmares and had emotional and physical scars from their time fighting the war. Current service members share those same experiences. But as Mitch shared, the veterans from his generation weren't welcomed back home with open arms–they were often cursed at, called terrible names and treated poorly even though the veterans were just carrying out their orders. I held my head a little higher knowing that in some small way my run had made a Vietnam veteran feel better about his service.

The next several miles flew by with those thoughts swirling through my mind until I got into an uphill/downhill footrace with a horse and buggy being driven by a young Amish boy. I laughed with our kids as I told them the story of their dad briefly outrunning a horse that day while running uphill. Then I would hear the clippity-clop clippity-clop of the hooves of the horse as it rolled past me heading downhill. The jockeying back and forth was fun but I was also a bit concerned that the horse would literally run me down. That's all I needed–for next day's headline to read, *"Man running across America trampled by Amish horse and buggy with five days to go."*

## THE CLIMB BEFORE THE STORM

I had two big climbs over Town Hill and Sideling Hill and 33.2 miles to conquer on Day 96, and the forecast was calling for near-record temperatures. I woke up around 4:30 a.m. and, after downing a 32-ounce cup of Gatorade and my daily breakfast staple of two chocolate fudge Pop-Tarts, I began running 30 minutes later, hoping to complete my mileage before the temperatures peaked. It was already 85 degrees when I took my first step that morning.

The first four miles were more of a fast-paced walk. I did my best to maintain a solid pace up the side of the mountain to Town Hill, but the incline combined with the humidity kept me from moving too fast. Once I reached the peak, I was joined by the family and we took some time to stare out at the vastness below. I pointed to Sideling Hill, an area known for a 340-foot cut into the mountain ridge we had driven through hundreds of times before, knowing what a difficult drive it was to get over that mountain. I looked at my mom and said, "That's the big one for the day."

"You've got to climb that one, too?" she questioned emphatically.

"That's the last mountain of the journey, mom. Just stick with me."

"You've got this, dad!" my daughter yelled out. And with a fist bump for both of my kids, I dashed down the mountain.

Trying to stay in the shade as much as possible, I hugged the edge of the road running with traffic, trying to stay out of the rising sun. I was getting very little relief running due east into the path of the sun, and I knew it wasn't going to get any easier that day. The stops were more frequent, but the RV didn't provide any relief because Tiff didn't want to waste the gas using the generator to have the AC running. Stepping into 90-degree temps in the RV didn't help me cool off, but Tiff would wrap a cold washcloth around my head and neck and throw my running cap into the freezer to cool it off, which felt great for the first 30 seconds or so after I put it back on.

As I approached Sideling Hill, one of my good friends Rick Rohn, who lives in Martinsburg, West Virginia, texted me to say he was watching me approach the hill using the MyAthlete Live tracker and he was thinking about me as I drew closer to the finish. I took one last break at the base of the mountain, then began the last serious climb.

"Are you on a bike or something?" Rick texted about 30 minutes later. "You're *flying* up that mountain!"

I sent him back a quick text. "I'm feeling great. I think I just got my 10th wind."

By the time I hit the top of the mountain, the heat had topped 100 degrees, and I was completely drenched. My socks were making a sloshing sound as the sweat was pooling inside my shoes. When Tiff caught up to me on the other side, my Gatorade bottles were completely dry and I was in serious need of fluids and food. Tiff handed me a plateful of oranges, strawberries, watermelon and a peanut butter sandwich with the crust cut off, and had me wash it down with an ice cold 32-ounce Gatorade. The ice packs we kept in the freezer were lying on my neck and groin, as Tiff was doing her best to get my core body temperature down. I still had another seven miles to go, and we wanted to make sure I didn't break down just before the finish.

Although I was excited to wrap up those last few miles that day, I certainly wasn't out to break any speed records. The heat wasn't letting up, and the air was extremely thick. I did my best to stay focused on the road, making sure I was alert as vehicles approached me.

I couldn't wait to get to the Falling Water Campground that evening so we could crank up the AC and relax. My good friend Clayton Myers from Martinsburg, West Virginia, promised us a hearty meal that evening, and I was excited to see him. He arrived with enough food to feed a small army, and over an excellent meal I shared stories about the run. We also talked about the upcoming college football and basketball seasons, which was a good diversion for me. I love college sports, yet I hadn't given it a single thought over the past few months on the run.

Although the food was amazing, the blazing heat won out, causing us to wrap up our visit a little early. The wind was starting to pick up, so we pulled the awning back in on the RV as a precaution and escaped the heat as the AC did its best to keep us cool. We were awoken later that night by one of the most horrendous rainstorms I have ever heard in my life, but we didn't realize the extent of the damage until the following morning when I headed out to run.

A derecho, which is a strong and sustained straight-line windstorm along with heavy rain, barreled through the area, causing massive damage in several states. We were right in the path of it, and we would see first-hand the damage caused during the next few days. As I rolled into Martinsburg, we saw trees and power lines down in the roads, devastating destruction to homes, windows knocked out of storefronts and brick facades crumbled on the sidewalks. Tiffany had to take a few detours to get around downed power lines and trees in the road. Several roads were either closed or blocked due to the incredible damage from the storm.

Many people sent us messages on social media checking to see if we were OK, but we couldn't call or text because the cell towers in the area weren't working. Tiff was able to post a message online to let people know we were OK and that the tracker would come back online as soon as cell service was restored. As I made my way to Harpers Ferry, every little neighborhood and town I passed through had a widespread loss of power and damage to homes and businesses.

"I'm glad we pulled the awning in last night," Tiff said. It was just one of the many tangible times that we knew God was protecting us and sheltering us from harm.

## FREEDOM RUN

Having no athletic sponsors on board meant that all costs for my clothing, shoes, and nutrients would be out of my own pocket. I figured I would need 10 pairs of shoes to make it across the country, and the cost of those alone was around $1,000. A mutual friend introduced me to Dr. Mark Cucuzzella, a Lieutenant Colonel in the U.S. Air Force Reserves who owns a shoe store in Shepherdstown, West Virginia, called Two Rivers Treads. Mark promised that if I wasn't able to get my shoes donated from the manufacturer, he would take care of me. Mark is a huge advocate of minimalist and barefoot running and did his best to convert me, but I told him that my current shoe had worked for me for the past 2 1/2 years and I wasn't going to change things up just before the run. A few days before we left for Oregon, a FedEx truck pulled up to our house and delivered 10 pairs of my preferred running shoes compliments of Mark and Two Rivers Treads. Having made the trip without any blisters or black toenails, I considered his contribution a major factor in the success of my run.

When I arrived in Harpers Ferry, a few members of his staff scheduled a group run for us that evening, giving me the opportunity to share a bit of my journey. We parked behind Mark's office, where the power was out in that neighborhood. We later learned that nearly five million customers lost power due to the derecho. It was great to finally meet Mark in person when he stopped by the RV and dropped off a box full of Power Bars and a technical running shirt from the Freedom's Run Marathon that he directs every year. He took us to downtown Harpers Ferry, where they had electricity, for some pizza and ice cream, then dropped us back off at the RV so I could get changed and ready to go run with the group that evening.

Paul Koczera, the assistant manager at Two Rivers Treads, picked Tiffany and me up, while mom and the kids remained in the RV, to take us to Private Quinn's Pub, where we met the group for a short run over the Potomac River and back. We were also joined by a young veteran who had been following my run and wanted to come along. He didn't have time to change his clothes after work, showing up in jeans and a T-shirt. He shared a little bit about the things he had been dealing with since being medically discharged from the Army. As we ran, he described the pain in his back that he dealt with every day, but he didn't let that keep him from coming out to be a part of this journey in support of fellow veterans who were injured even worse. It was a very humbling moment to see him brushing his back pain aside in order to honor fellow veterans.

Based on the storm damage that we had seen that day, and knowing I would be running about 20 miles on the historic Chesapeake & Ohio (C&O) Canal trail the following day, I anticipated a long, slow day of running. Little did I know what was ahead.

## BRANCHES OF GOVERNMENT

*"Forty-eight hours from now, I will be completing my initial mission, on target and on time."* That was the first thought that entered my mind when I woke up the following morning. It had been 2,352 hours since I pulled my wet feet from the Pacific Ocean and slipped my running shoes on. I had no clue what obstacles awaited me, but I knew I was ready for any challenges that were thrown my way. Running into our nation's capital seemed like only a dream a few months ago, but now I was less than 100 miles away.

Learning that power was out for millions of customers and hearing news reports of so much widespread damage, we felt very fortunate to have escaped any real damage ourselves. The wrap advertising our run on the RV had a few long scratches from broken tree branches hanging low along the road. But because of the derecho, the run from Harpers Ferry to just west of Germantown, Maryland, proved to be more like one of my trail runs during my training than anything I had experienced during the entire journey.

I started down the C&O Canal trail with Paul and Doug, two runners from the night before at Private Quinn's Pub. When we met at 6:30 a.m. the heat was already scorching, but we knew the first 18 miles would have plenty of shade as we ran on the trail. The trail was beautiful and I really enjoyed talking with fellow distance runners about the nuances of the sport because I always gained more knowledge and tips. I learned about the vast array of diets and nutritional aids that people swear by, the types of running gear they prefer and the other sports they participate in to stay in shape. I always told people who asked me what my secret was that I had no secret. I was still a baby at this running thing. I just enjoyed absorbing as much knowledge as possible in order to be the best runner I could be.

We were about two miles down the trail when we came to a sudden stop. A massive tree was lying directly in our path and it wasn't just a trunk that we could hop over and continue on our way. So one after another we crawled through the web of tree branches, being careful to avoid any poison ivy that was wrapped around them. Our pace picked up again, but once again it literally slowed to a crawl just a few thousand feet away when we came upon more trees blocking the trail. This time we met other runners coming through the trees from the other side.

"I've been running these trails for many years," said one of the ladies, "and I have never seen it this bad."

We encountered more runners along the way, and each time we would swap warnings about what obstacles were ahead. We even came across a few bicyclists who were carrying their bikes through the trees. It almost felt like an obstacle course at boot camp as we figured out the best way to get under, around and sometimes up and over the downed trees. What should have been a leisurely jog turned into a physically exhausting and frustrating off-road hike.

I was glad to have Paul and Doug join me on the trail. It was interesting to learn that we had participated in a few of the same races in the past. After we had run about 13 miles and sharpened our tree-climbing skills, we parted ways but knew we would probably cross paths again during an upcoming race. I am very grateful for the friendships I developed during this trip and look forward to continuing to build those relationships in the future.

When I met up with the family for an aid stop, the RV was trapped. Tiffany had parked in an area that was separated from the road by a railroad crossing. As luck would have it, the train that came through the area was stopped on the tracks, preventing the RV from getting back on the road. Our friends Scott and Margie Payne and their children, as well as Loren and Bridget Jordan and their kids, were on the other side of the tracks, blocked from entering the parking lot. I hung around for about 15 minutes but didn't want to sit idly in the heat very long, so I headed on down the trail. Tiff texted me 30 minutes later to let me know they were finally able to cross the railroad tracks and get on the road again. When we met up a bit farther along, I was crossing over the Monocacy Aqueduct. Looking downstream from the crossing, I could see where the Monocacy River merged with the Potomac, thinking about how nice it would be to jump in the river at that very moment.

The rest of the day I was off the trails and back on the pavement with no shade to protect me from the 100-degree temperature. I convinced myself that I only had a few more days of running, so I would stop worrying about the weather. *"One foot in front of the other, positive forward motion,"* I kept saying to myself. I also went back to my old trick of saying my ABCs to myself, which I hadn't done since Oregon. As long as I could get through all 26 letters without a hiccup, I felt like mentally I was still OK.

As I headed toward the finish of my run that day, I saw a car driving toward me slowly, and as it approached me, they blew their horn and yelled, "Go Jamie, go!" I had no idea who it was, but it turned out to be a couple that lived in the DC area who had been following my journey since the beginning. They were graduates of WVU and had spent many years in Morgantown, and just wanted to congratulate me on a successful run. As they were talking, the RV and Scott and Margie pulled up, with their children and ours packed into their vehicle, which was much cooler than the RV.

"We have no power or air conditioning at my mom's house," Margie said, "but we will have lots of food for you to eat tonight."

"You had me at food," I responded. "Just don't make me climb any more trees to get to it."

Margie's mom, Peggy, fixed us a wonderful meal that night, loading me up with all kinds of carbs and protein. One thing about this trip was that I was never malnourished at any point. I literally could recall three times during the whole trip when my stomach growled due to hunger, and that was my own fault when it happened. Tiff made sure I always had plenty of food during my runs, and we had so many great people provide many meals for our family.

The next couple of days would be draining, not only physically, but also emotionally. I was looking forward to standing in front of the Marine Corps Memorial in less than 24 hours. I was also looking forward to more family joining me, Tiff, the kids and my mom. Tiff's mom and stepdad were driving from Oregon with our dog, Emmie, to Morgantown to drop her off at her doggie daycare and then continue on to Washington DC to meet us. My stepdad was also preparing to join us, especially since he lived where they lost power (meaning there was no more salvageable food to eat in the refrigerator) and it was going to be a few more days until the area had power restored.

## SEMPER FI

Ever since our original plans for the finish changed from Baltimore to Annapolis, I was very excited for Day 99. In my mind, running into Washington DC and finishing at the U.S. Marine Corps War Memorial, staring at the five Marines and one Navy corpsman raising that flag over Iwo Jima, could not have been a more fitting ending to the day. It is easily the most recognizable statue to Marines and it symbolizes the true brotherhood and support we have for one another.

Tiffany and I knew we would have to communicate via phone much more often this day than any other time on the road. Not only was driving a 31-foot RV through the streets of Washington DC while trying to track me down going to be challenging, but there were still road closures and detours due to the storm damage. With all of the downed tree limbs and power lines, it made for a dangerous run and drive. At least twice I stepped over a downed limb, only to find a power line lying beside of it as well. Out west I had to worry about snakes slithering under my feet; now I had to be careful not to step on any power lines.

As I was making my way toward downtown, my original route was supposed to have me turn off of Route 190 onto Persimmon Tree Road, taking me toward the Potomac River so I could enjoy the beautiful view the trail provides. As I approached the intersection, I realized the Department of Highways had beaten me to the scene.

ROAD CLOSED TO ALL BUT LOCAL TRAFFIC

I called Tiff to let her know that we would have to change plans. I continued running down Route 190 while plugging the new route into my map, and was pleasantly surprised. Instead of having 12.9 miles to go, I was left with 12.5 miles. Even though I would miss running along the Potomac and would instead be running through congested traffic, I wasn't going to complain about the shorter distance.

The next 10 miles into DC flew by. Much later when I looked back at the online street view of the path I ran, I can remember passing many of the buildings along the route, but in that moment, everything was a blur. I was so excited to get to the Iwo Jima Memorial that I didn't pay much attention to the eclectic buildings and old-town charm that make the DC area so unique. I did see some devastating storm damage to some beautiful homes as I ran through several neighborhoods, but reaching the finish that day was really all that was on my mind.

As I ran down the cobblestone of 35th Street toward the Francis Scott Key Memorial, I could see the Potomac River in front of me. I thought my heart was going to pound through my chest, not because of exertion but because of excitement. I had just one more mile to go until I stood before one of the most significant milestones of the run.

Playing Frogger as I crossed M Street onto the Key Bridge, I was singing the Marine Corps hymn in my mind, and probably garnered a few strange looks from people I passed on the bridge as I'm sure those verses escaped my lips a few times.

*"From the Halls of Montezuma,*
*To the shores of Tripoli;*
*We fight our country's battles,*
*In the air, on land, and sea..."*

Making my way up the last hill of the day on N Lynn Street, I passed a news reporter getting into his vehicle with a video camera.

"Are you looking for a story?" I asked. "I'm finishing up Day 99 of my run across America to honor our veterans. I'll be down at the Marine Corps Memorial in two minutes."

He smiled at me as he got in his truck. I never saw him again.

The RV was in the parking lot facing the U.S. Marine Corps War Memorial, with the Washington Monument and Capitol building off in the distance. The view could not have been more perfect that day. As I approached the RV, I did so slowly, taking in every step toward that beautiful sight. Everyone was standing outside of the RV cheering as I walked up, tears already in all of our eyes. Tiff asked me to come inside to get a drink first. She knew that because of the heat, I wasn't thinking clearly at that point. Once I cooled off a bit, we headed down to the Memorial, and as I approached, as I did with every flag I have ever run past, I threw a sharp salute and stood at full attention for a few seconds. As I was standing at the base, with tears of joy flowing, a small boy, maybe 4 years old, ran up in front of me smiling and yelled, "Hi!"

"Hello young man," I said, taken back a bit.

Then I saw someone walking up toward me from the left out of the corner of my eye, and I stood there in complete disbelief at the sight of Bart Ingleston. We spent a few years stationed together at Marine Corps Air Station Beaufort in South Carolina, and he arrived in Iwakuni, Japan, about three weeks after I did to serve his final year in the Marine Corps. We had always been very close friends, and while we had stayed in touch over the years, it had been almost 13 years since I had seen him. We hugged like brothers who hadn't seen each other in years, and neither one of us could hold back the emotion of the moment. His son Liam was the young boy who had run up to me, but, of course, I had no clue who he was.

I was brought to tears again a few moments later after I met David Moust, who had been following my progress online and wanted to meet me. I cried and hung onto every syllable as David shared the heartbreaking story of his cousin, who recently served in the Middle East. While inspecting a building, David's cousin and his cousin's platoon sergeant were sent flying over the roof of the building when an improvised explosive device (IED) went off. The platoon sergeant died in the explosion and David's cousin lost three limbs.

"I am so glad you are doing this for them," David said. "You may not ever meet my cousin, but you are making a difference in his life. What you are doing is very important to a lot of people, and they appreciate the respect you are helping to bring to them. You're doing a good thing, Jamie. Keep moving forward."

"I intend to do just that," I said, choking up. "We're not done yet."

### WHATEVER IT TAKES

Back in Indiana, Tiffany and I talked about how we wanted to be well-rested for the final day of the run as well as the next two days since we would be marching in the Fourth of July parade in Annapolis and then I would be heading out for my big 100-mile, 24-hour run to the Atlantic. She made a few phone calls then to nail down our stay in the DC area. With both sets of our parents joining us, we needed to make sure the rooms were nice and comfortable, so after an extensive search online, she called the Doubletree by Hilton Hotel in Annapolis. She spoke to the manager, who became very excited about what we were doing. He had only two questions for Tiffany: "How long are you staying and how many rooms do you need?"

"We'll need two rooms for the first night and three rooms for the next two nights, if possible," she replied.

"No problem," he responded. "By the way, because of what your husband is doing, your stay is on us."

"All three rooms?" Tiff asked, having learned that she needed to confirm every organizational detail.

"All three rooms," he assured her. "We're happy to do it."

After the emotional time at the U.S. Marine Corps War Memorial, we traveled to the hotel to clean up and spend some time with Bart, his wife, Hannah, and Liam. As we headed back to our room after a good dinner at Gordon Biersch Brewery I feared I would have difficulty sleeping. I was experiencing the same butterflies in my stomach that I typically experience the night before a big race. But I think the exhaustion and emotions of the day really wiped me out and I ended up sleeping great.

I was refreshed and ready when we pulled out of the parking lot at 4:52 a.m. on July 3 to start Day 100. Daylight was starting to break as we pulled into the parking lot at the Marine Corps War Memorial. Bart rode with us in the RV from the hotel and we were joined at the Memorial by Army Captain Dave Rodriguez, who was an old friend of mine from West Virginia. He was one of the first people I called when I came up with the idea of running across America and it was a true honor to have him there with us to start off the final day. Dave had knee surgery a couple of years earlier and since then he hadn't attempted to run any considerable distance, but he was going to give it a go.

"I wouldn't miss this for the world, my friend," he said. "I'm just honored to be here."

"Dave," I responded, "the honor is all mine. Thanks so much for being here, representing your unit and the soldiers you serve with. And don't worry, I'll take it slow for you," I said with a sly grin.

We left at 6:05 a.m., heading south past the Arlington Cemetery. As we ran past, all three of us offered a crisp salute in reverence to those who had lost their lives. The only thing breaking the silence was the pitter patter of our feet slapping the pavement as we ran in unison. We were all experiencing similar feelings, and it was good to be in step with one another on so many levels.

When we were crossing the Arlington Memorial Bridge and headed toward the Lincoln Memorial, Bart said, "I've never been to Washington DC until this trip."

"What?" Dave and I responded at the same time.

"This is a first for me," Bart continued. "I'm going to take as much of this in as I can. My family and I will come down here later today, so we don't have to spend much time checking everything out, but I'd like to take in as much as possible."

"We'll gladly be your tour guides for the next few miles," I said.

We stopped at the Three Soldiers Statue, then made our way to the Vietnam Veterans Memorial. We took our time here, each brushing our hand against the wall as we walked by. Besides the Marine Corps War Memorial, I don't think there is a monument in the area that moves me as much as the Vietnam wall. During my trek across the country, I saw so many small veterans memorials honoring the names of those who served in those local communities. Now to see all of those names and many more all in one location really made me aware of how many lives were tragically lost in that war.

Unfortunately, the reflecting pool at the National Mall was empty due to construction.

"Forrest Gump gave a speech here once," Dave said, cracking up at his own sharp wit.

"You're the first person to mention his name to me during this run," I said sarcastically. In reality, I heard the comparison and the shouts of, "run, Forrest, run!" just about every day, but it was funny now standing in the scene from the movie.

As we made our way to the World War II Memorial, I talked about how I had met a number of World War II vets during the run, including some Rosie Riveters. I couldn't help but reflect on all of the amazing people I had encountered on this journey, and how each of their stories made a lifelong impact on me. We were a better country because of so many of their sacrifices and service.

Tiffany was waiting for us as we ran up to the Washington Monument. By the time we got there, we were all soaked with sweat, and neither Dave nor Bart could believe we had run through the area of monuments. Besides making a few stops for photos and to pay our respects, we had put down a pretty good pace but everyone still felt really good. I told them our next scheduled stop was at Lincoln Park, and verified that they wanted to continue with me.

"Let's keep moving," they both responded.

We made our way up to the Capitol building and then ran to Lincoln Park, seemingly catching every green light for pedestrian traffic along the way, which helped us maintain a steady pace. The time and miles flew that morning, and it was great catching up with two good friends. Bart was going to take the Subway back from Lincoln Park to meet up with his wife, and Dave was going to ride out the whole day with us. I knew I'd miss not having Bart with me the rest of the day, but I was excited that he was going to be able to tour the nation's capital with his family for the first time. It truly is a remarkable city and offers a never-ending supply of our country's rich heritage.

With the final day being a 36-mile finish to the Chesapeake Bay, and knowing I needed to be at the U.S. Naval Academy around 3:30 p.m., once Bart left and Dave hopped into the RV to ride with the family, I picked up the pace. I could have spent all day taking photos and running around DC, but I knew I had to stay on schedule. I would love to go back sometime and take a "running tour" of the city.

One of the coolest parts of the trip for my family was the people they had a chance to meet. Tiffany and the crew had many experiences in which people would stop by and share stories, and that day was no exception. Dave thought it was the coolest thing to have people approach them in the RV and ask questions, even donating money at times.

"It happens all the time," my kids told him. "Daddy's famous. And crazy."

Since it was once again another hot day and I had picked up the pace, Tiffany made sure I was consuming plenty of fluids during the aid stops. As I headed out of town and north toward Annapolis, there were no pedestrian paths so I was running on four- and six-lane roads. I was just waiting for a cop to pull over and ask what I was doing. I did my best to make smart decisions on the roads, not wanting to take any risks and die on the last day of the run!

Around 11 a.m. Tiff texted me to let me know I would be joined shortly by some Air Force personnel from Fort Meade. At my next stop, four men and a woman were in their blue and white Air Force PT gear, hanging out by the RV ready to run. They presented me with an Air Force coin and blue and gold towels that read, "Whatever it Takes."

"Truer words were never spoken," I said to them as they gave the items to me. "I'm stubborn as a mule, and I'm willing to do whatever it takes to finish this. Let's roll."

We logged a few miles together and even though the heat was oppressive, we stuck together. When one or two started to tire and fall back, we all slowed up a little so that we could continue to run as a team. It meant the world to me to have them out there, and it again was an opportunity to just say thank you.

Turning left on Riva Road, I had the chance to enjoy some beautiful scenery as I approached Annapolis. As I crossed the South River Bridge, I had an immediate flashback to the first day of my run as I ran across the Cape Arago Highway Bridge in Charleston, Oregon. The makeup of the bridge and scenery looked like it had almost been duplicated here. Having that flashback caused me to reflect on how far I had come in 100 days, not only distance-wise, but mentally as well. I was truly a different person, and it felt good.

## A SPECIAL DETOUR

Mike Brown and Ned Hazlett, two retired officers from the Air Force and Navy, respectively, had organized my arrival at the Naval Academy a few weeks prior to our arrival. They were WVU grads who followed my journey and wanted to make sure our welcoming party was a good one. Mike also set up a little detour for me near the end of my run that day.

I ran up to the entrance of the Doubletree Hotel, where Tiff had parked the RV and was waiting for me to arrive. Her mom and stepdad had arrived, and my cousin Barbara Pyle met us there with her kids. Dave stepped out of the RV and said he was going to run the rest of the way with me, so we made our way down West Street towards the Academy. Mike asked me to take a slight detour on Route 435 before we got to the Academy. We ran up to the front of the Navy-Marine Corps Memorial Stadium, where he was waiting with a bag full of Marine Corps gear for me.

"Let's go for a little run," he said.

With the RV parked near the entrance of the football stadium, Mike led me, Dave and Nick through the gates and allowed us to take a victory loop around the football field. It was incredible having the privilege of not only being there, but running on the field with my son by my side.

Nick wanted to join me for the last leg of my run to the Academy, and there was no way I was going to tell him no.

"Thank you for being a part of this journey with me, son," I said as we ran stride for stride through the intense heat.

"I think it's awesome that you did this, dad," he replied. It was one of the proudest moments of my life.

We arrived at the entrance to the Academy, where Ned was waiting for us. Tiff and the rest of the family had already been given access to the docks, so Ned just needed to get us through the gate so we could run to the finish.

*"I've done it. I've really done it,"* I kept repeating to myself as we entered the Academy. We turned the corner on King George Street and headed to the finish line on Turner Joy Road. A crowd of Naval cadets, sailors and Marines

were gathered on both sides of the road, forming a gauntlet of encouragement and creating a path for me to run through as they cheered for Nick and me. We ran down the cement stairs to the water's edge, where one of the men standing there looked at me and said, "Are you going to jump in?"

SPLASH!

SPLASH!

Nick jumped in right behind me. We gave each other a high five, celebrating the accomplishment. As I climbed out of the bay, I could hardly believe I was standing there, wet from head to toe, in front of so many servicemen and women at the finish line. It was then that the raw emotion of everything we had just accomplished came out.

"I did this for each one of you," I told the crowd. "My hope and prayer is that none of you ever have to walk through the doors of any of the organizations that we are supporting on this journey, but if you do, just know that their door will always be open."

I took the time to shake hands and pose for photos with each and every person there, thanking them for being there and for serving our country. I reminded them all that this run was not about me; it was for each one of them. What started out as a journey to honor and support our wounded veterans grew into something so much more. I wanted all service members, whether a veteran or an active member, to know that they were appreciated.

After spending some time there with everyone, and drying off, we hopped back into the RV. It was exhilarating to think about what we just completed, yet I was even more excited about what lay ahead. I still had a "little" run to go on July 5. And as I told everyone at the Naval Academy, our mission didn't end when my son and I jumped into the Chesapeake Bay. I couldn't wait to build upon what we had just accomplished.

# 16 | What's 100 More?

For the first time in more than three months, I didn't have to wake up before sunrise and head out to run 35 miles when I climbed out of bed on the morning of July 4, 2012. But instead of waking with a smile and a sense of euphoria about completing my initial mission, I was cranky and remained in a foul mood the entire morning. Even though we were celebrating Independence Day and my trans-American run, I was in no mood to party. The feelings I told myself I wouldn't experience at the end of the run surfaced anyway, hitting me like a runaway train. I was depressed, confused and as strange as it may seem, I had a strong urge to run.

I knew we had a full day of events planned and I had the 100-mile run to look forward to the following day, but I still was left asking myself, "Now what?" Being out of the routine that I had stuck to so rigorously for the past three-plus months just made me feel very uncomfortable. I didn't realize it at the time, but it was just a preview of the emotions I would become overwhelmed by when I returned home.

I knew, however, that I needed to get my mind right because the day would provide me with an awesome opportunity to spread the news about the mission of my run. Fox News Channel called us the previous day to schedule a live interview with me on their midday "Happening Now" program with Arthel Neville. After all of the pre-run efforts and attempts during the past

100 days to catch the national media's attention, we finally had our opportunity. I knew I couldn't blow that chance, so I had to snap out of my funk.

Fox News sent a car to our hotel at 10 a.m. to drive Tiffany and me to their
studio in Washington, DC. The driver did a great job of making me feel comfortable by not only giving me tips for the interview, but also cracking jokes
to lighten the mood. When we arrived, we were escorted to the green room,
where a handful of other on-air guests were also waiting. Among them were
columnist Mary Katharine Ham, journalist Juan Williams and retired U.S.
Army Major General Bob Scales, who were all regular guests on Fox News.

After having the shine removed from my forehead, we were taken to a
small interview room that contained only a remote-operated camera, small
TV monitor to my left showing the live feed, flatscreen TV as a backdrop
and a chair off to my right for Tiffany. It was a bit odd to talk to a camera
instead of directly to a person standing in the room, but at this point I had
done so many interviews with local radio, TV and newspaper reporters that
I was comfortable and the responses I gave to questions were things I had
repeated countless times. Overall, I was happy with how the interview went,
although I neglected to give the URL for my website where people could
donate because I thought it would appear in a graphic along with my name
during the interview.

After returning to our hotel, we met the rest of the family for lunch in
the hotel restaurant. I was sipping on a Sierra Mist and nibbling on my food
when Tiffany looked over at me and said, "You don't look good."

"I don't feel well," I said. "I think I just need to go back to the room and
lie down."

I suspect it was being out of the routine of not only running but eating
every hour that had left me in this funk. Whatever it was, when I woke up
from my nap I was refreshed and had a new outlook on the remainder of the
day. It was only the second nap I had taken since we began our journey.

Mike Brown had invited us all over to his home that afternoon, where
we enjoyed a great meal. He had recorded my interview on Fox News, so we

were able to watch it and enjoy my three minutes of fame. He also said he would allow us to use his driveway to wash our RV before the parade. As we stepped outside to wash the RV, I walked around the corner and was greeted by two very familiar faces. Rusty Walker and Jim Wilson, my good friends from back home that I had spoken to often on this journey by phone, were standing there with the biggest grins I have ever seen.

"We came to help you wash the RV," they said. They had made the trek over from Martinsburg, West Virginia, just to let me know how proud they were of me and to wish me well on the final leg of my run.

"Would you guys mind washing my feet too?" I asked.

"Not after you just ran across America, man, sorry."

### FREEDOM PARADE

My mom and kids walked along with me during the 90-minute parade while Tiffany drove the RV. The crowd was absolutely phenomenal. The parade snaked through the historic downtown roads, and every time we turned a corner we'd see a mass of people lined up 10 deep on both sides of the road. I saw several familiar faces in the crowd and it was a rush of adrenaline to have so many people cheer for us. I got a good laugh several times when people would ask me, "When are you starting your run?"

"I just finished yesterday," I'd respond, "and tomorrow I'm doing a 100-mile, 24-hour run to Rehoboth Beach."

The parade went well, but the generator quit working in the RV, which meant there was no air conditioning other than up front in the driver's cabin. We suspected it overheated because Tiff had to drive so slowly in the parade, but we were in store for more trouble with the generator later.

We also had trouble trying to maneuver out of traffic after the parade. Tiffany had to drive around Church Circle in historic Annapolis and with cars parked on both sides of the circle, we literally had about one inch between each side of our RV and the parked cars. I walked in front, guiding Tiffany, a man who rode in the motorcycle stunt group in the parade walked behind the RV and the rest of the family in the RV was as quiet as a church mouse as Tiffany, frustrated and hot, slowly but masterfully squeezed the RV through the street.

It was getting late in the evening and I knew I had to get as much rest as possible for the final 100 miles early the next morning. As my mind turned from the Independence Day activities to the 100-mile run, I got more and more excited and energized. It may seem strange that I was anxious to run those 100 miles, but no ultramarathon runner goes into a 100-mile run dreading it. They go into it thinking, "This is going to be awesome!"

I was also getting myself in a different frame of mind because this final 100 miles was for me. While my focus the previous 3,352 miles had been on others, running these 100 miles to the Atlantic Ocean, and doing it in less than 24 hours, was all personal. I didn't want to look back 20 years from now and regret being so close but not going all the way to the coast. I wanted to be on the prestigious list of true coast-to-coast runners.

## 100 MILES, 100 DEGREES

When I woke up early on July 5, my energy level was as high as it had been during the entire journey. Part of that is because I finally enjoyed a rest day, but I know I was also riding a wave of adrenaline. I went about my customary routine of applying lotion and eating two chocolate fudge Pop-Tarts and then grabbed my No. 3 pair of running shoes. The last few weeks of the run I paid particularly close attention to which pair of shoes felt the most comfortable. Even though they had become worn at the same rate, pair No. 3 just felt better, so those are the ones I slipped onto my feet, which is where they remained for the next 100 miles.

We left the hotel at 5:13 a.m. and by 5:32 a.m. I was off and running. And it was already 82 degrees! I actually could have made it from Annapolis to Rehoboth Beach, Delaware, in 76 miles, but I wanted to stick with the '100' theme of 100 days and now running 100 miles, so our route would take me a bit south and then I would run north along the coast of the Atlantic Ocean to get to the finish.

I had a 4.5-mile route to get from the U.S. Naval Academy to the edge of Sandy Pointe State Park on the west side of the Chesapeake Bay. It cost us $16 for Tiffany to be able to drive the RV into the park to pick me up. From there I hopped into the RV to drive across the Chesapeake Bay Bridge. Pedestrians are not allowed on that road, and even if it wasn't against the law it wouldn't be safe because there's no shoulder for pedestrians and cars and wind would be whipping past me at 70 miles per hour. We tried to get clearance or an escort from the Annapolis police to run across the bridge, but it didn't work out. But considering I was running 24 more miles than if I would have taken the most direct route to the Atlantic Ocean, I knew that would more than make up for the four miles on the bridge.

After driving across, I hopped back out, went to the edge of the bay waters on the east side and started heading toward Rehoboth Beach once again. Another online follower of the run who lived in the area, Dave Zeitlin, joined me for the first five miles on the east side of the bay as we ran past some beautiful (and expensive) boats and homes along the shore in Stevensville, Maryland. After drifting away from the water, the road began to open up and I had about 12 miles of open road ahead. I was flanked by corn fields on either side, and I noticed that the stalks were now taller than me. It was interesting to reflect back to when I first noticed tiny green buds sprouting out of the dirt early in my run across America. Now the corn stalks were more than six feet tall. It was an introspective moment as I compared the growth of the corn to my own growth during the past three months.

Since there were no trees along this stretch, the heat was really beating down on me and it would only get worse. It actually ended up being the hottest day of the entire journey, with the temperature exceeding 100 degrees. I consumed salt tablets more often and sucked down as much Gatorade as possible, going through nine gallons during this run, more than triple the amount of fluids I drank on a typical day.

I was glad that, aside from walking in the parade, I was off my feet most of the previous day. Since I had no recovery days built into my run for the previous 100 days, my body had adapted to having a short recovery time. So extending that recovery period by not running July 4 really gave me some fresh legs.

When I ran from Coos Bay, Oregon, to Annapolis, Maryland, I was focused on getting from point A to point B but was never really concerned with how quickly I got there. But this was different. I had a burning desire to complete this 100-mile run in less than 24 hours since I missed that benchmark at Burning River. Throughout my journey, and even during my training runs in the two years leading up to this, I never really looked at a watch when I ran. But during this last leg, I found myself constantly checking the time on my phone and trying to calculate when I would finish.

I did a couple of radio interviews during this portion of the run with radio stations that had been following me throughout the journey. Usually I would slow down and walk as I gave an interview over the phone, but I knew every minute was precious and I couldn't afford to slow down, so I talked as I ran. I'm sure my answers were shorter than normal and listeners could hear heavy breathing.

## A STICKY SITUATION

Around 2 p.m. I came to a freshly paved asphalt road. I was already hot and sweaty and was now literally in a sticky situation. My shoes were sticking to tar as I ran, reminding me of Burning River, when my shoes also stuck to the tar on the road. With each step I took, I could hear the Velcro-like sound of my shoes peeling away from the blacktop. The smell of the warm blacktop was almost overwhelming, and the heat radiating from the road just zapped my energy. I tried to run along the white line on the side of the road as much as possible, but even that little trick wasn't doing much to cool my feet. At 3 p.m. I checked the weather and wasn't shocked to see that it was 99 degrees.

When I crossed into Delaware a half hour later, it was my 16th and final state on this journey. But running into a new state didn't seem to have as much significance to me as it typically did because my motivation was 100 miles and 24 hours, not another state.

My mileage from 3-6 p.m. wasn't piling up very fast. I slowed down considerably, much of that intentionally to try to keep from overheating. I took more frequent (every three miles for a while) and longer (20 minutes a couple of times) aid stops. I knew this was cutting into my pace but I hoped the longer periods of rest would pay off the final 30 miles.

At the 52-mile mark it was 5:30 p.m. I stopped and changed my shorts and shirt. I had lost so much salt through my sweat that there were patches of white salt stains on my dark blue running shorts. I also iced my left groin during this aid stop. A couple of weeks earlier I had developed the start of a sports hernia in the groin area of my left leg. During those couple of weeks it would be painful the first mile of each day's run but would then subside. This 100-mile run, however, was causing it to flare up even more.

I was eager for the sun to set, hoping that would provide some relief from the oppressive heat. But I wasn't the only one suffering from the heat. Around 7 p.m., with temperatures still in the upper-90s, the RV's generator stopped providing power to the air conditioner. Tiffany took the RV to a gas station to troubleshoot the problem and finally determined that it was a failure somewhere between the generator and the power distribution box. When we plugged the RV into external power, everything worked like it was supposed to. It was getting late and they had me to chase down, so we all resigned to just be hot and miserable. In order to gain some relief, my mom and stepdad, who joined Tiffany for this 100-mile journey, would occasionally cram into the cabin, turn on the AC full blast and pull shut the curtain that we installed to divide the cabin from the rest of the motorhome. This helped to trap some cool air in the cabin, but even that didn't help much.

The equipment failure not only made life miserable for the family, but it also meant I wasn't able to get any relief from the heat during my aid stops.

In a way, that was a good thing, I guess, because I figured if I was going to be hot in the RV I may as well just get back on the road.

## LIGHTNING STRIKES

During one stretch when Tiffany was still trying to troubleshoot the problem, I told her to drive ahead and try to figure things out. It was dusk and I realized I wasn't wearing my headlamp or any reflective gear, but I thought I would catch up to the RV before it got too dark. Once the sun started to go down, however, it dropped like an anchor. Suddenly I found myself out on the road with nothing to light my path and I was unable to see the ground in front of me. I pulled out my phone and used it to provide a faint glimmer of light so I could make sure I had proper footing on the road. Because it was dark, I missed a turn I was supposed to make, which really frustrated me. Fortunately, I was able to go a bit further down the road and turn, eventually hooking back up with the original route.

About this same time, some wicked streaks of lightning were flashing in the sky. The previous few nights, lightning was pretty common following the derecho. At this moment, however, I was thankful for the lightning because each bolt that spider-webbed across the sky provided a split second of light.

Running with lightning in the area didn't concern me, but my mother was definitely expressing her concern for my safety. "Can't you just stop and finish this 100 miles over the next day or two?" she asked. I understood her having those motherly instincts because she had never seen me run an ultramarathon and was not used to seeing me push myself to my limits physically and mentally. But obviously the answer to her question was an emphatic, "No."

I was actually hoping the skies would open up and it would start raining so that I could get some relief from the heat. At 8 p.m., it was still 94 degrees. It did sprinkle a few times here and there, but never enough to cool me off. In fact, it probably had the opposite effect since it just made the air even more humid and muggy.

After I caught back up to the RV at a gas station, I put on my headlamp and some reflective gear and headed back out. Shortly after that, I came to Georgetown, Delaware, where I would turn off Route 404 and head south on Route 113. I saw a sign near this intersection that read: "Rehoboth Beach, 20 miles" with an arrow pointing straight ahead. I checked my map and saw that since I was heading south I still had more than 35 miles before I would get to Rehoboth Beach. I thought to myself, *"Why don't I just keep going straight so I can get there quicker and not have to run the extra miles."* But, of course, I stayed on course for the 100-mile run.

Running through the night, the temperatures began to cool slightly, giving me just a bit of relief from the heat. At 1 a.m., it was down to 81 degrees. Not only was I getting weary, but my crew was also growing tired. I was thankful that my mom and stepdad, Alan, accompanied Tiffany on the trip. It allowed her to get a couple of short naps in during the overnight hours, although Alan stayed awake the entire time and offered me some encouraging words a few times during this time.

During the next stretch my mind became fatigued and started playing tricks on me. I had run for nearly an hour without an aid stop and hadn't seen the RV drive up past me yet. I checked my phone frequently as I waited for them to approach from behind. It had been an hour and 10 minutes and still no sign of them. Five more minutes passed and still no RV. I began to get worried, discouraged and angry. *"Where are they? Are they OK? They've left me out here for more than an hour without checking on me. They don't even care about my well-being anymore."*

Finally, at about 2:30 a.m., the RV approached and I was able to get a brief rest. But during this stop, as I was calculating my pace and time remaining, I realized I was now in jeopardy of not finishing in less than 24 hours. I had run 87 miles, and since I began this run at 5:32 a.m. the previous morning, I had three hours to run the final 13 miles. At Burning River, I had run 85 miles at the 21-hour mark, so I was two miles ahead of that pace. But in the back of my mind I was thinking about how I crashed at the 89-mile mark at Burning River and, as a result, it took me nearly four hours to run the final 15 miles.

## SPRINT TO THE FINISH

Because of the time crunch, I knew I had to stretch out the distance between my aid stops and shorten the time I spent refueling. Each of my next couple of aid stops were only three or four minutes long. I only took enough time to refill my fluid bottles and head back out on the road.

I was entering the Fresh Pond area of Delaware Seashore State Park and would be running on a sandy walking trail. The RV obviously couldn't be on this path, so Tiffany had to drive around and meet me on the north side of the park before I could rejoin them and get on Coastal Highway, which would take me north toward Rehoboth Beach and was flanked on the right side by the enticing roar of the Atlantic Ocean. When I entered the park I felt like I was running inside a dark box. It was pitch black outside, except for my headlamp, and the trail path was narrow and absorbed the light from my lamp. My senses were heightened and with every shadow I saw or noise I heard, I glanced all around, preparing myself for any animal (or human) that may run out from the trees toward me.

I was glad to exit the park area and get back out on the road. But then I became frustrated because I was now right along the coast of the Atlantic, meaning I was literally a few steps away from completing a true coast-to-coast run. But because we scheduled the route for 100 miles, I still had about 10 miles of running to go.

At this point I was joined by my cousin's husband, Ben Pyle. They had a house in the area and he wanted to run the last several miles with me. I was happy to have company and encouragement during these last several miles. Ben has the build of a tight end in football as opposed to a long-distance runner, so he said he would push me as best he could but for me not to wait around for him. When we headed out I looked at the time on my phone: **3:40 a.m.** *"I've got 112 minutes to run 9.7 miles,"* I told myself. I quickly did a rough calculation and, factoring in another aid stop, estimated I would have to run quicker than 11 minutes per mile to break the 24-hour benchmark.

We pushed forward for the next four miles until we caught up with the RV for a quick aid stop. I looked at my phone again: **4:23 a.m.** I knew time was dwindling, so I refueled and we were back on the road by 4:27 a.m. *"I've got 65 minutes to run 5.7 miles,"* I told myself in somewhat of a panic. My leg muscles were cramping, my energy was zapped but my determination remained strong.

We labored another few miles, finally crossing over a bridge that brought Rehoboth Beach into view in the distance. I looked at the map on my phone and saw I had one mile to go. The time: **5:20 a.m.** *"I've got less than 12 minutes to run this last mile,"* I shouted in my head. I feared that my body would shut down at any moment, but I knew I had to push hard. I looked over at Ben and said, "I've got to go!"

"That's fine," he said. "Go for it!"

In that last mile, not only did I draw from every ounce of strength in my body, but I also drew motivation from several different sources: my desire to prove to people that I was good enough, which was cultivated by my rocky relationship with my stepdad; my failure to meet the 24-hour benchmark one year earlier at Burning River; my family, friends and followers who expected me to finish in less than 24 hours; but most importantly, all of the incredible veterans I met prior to and during this journey whose stories of heroism were what this entire run was really all about.

That inspiration carried me those final 5,280 feet. I ran past the boardwalk, where the RV was parked and my family was gathered to cheer me on, and onto the sandy shore of Rehoboth Beach. I continued down to the water, meeting the morning tide of the Atlantic Ocean, and looked at my phone: **5:29 a.m.** Tears streamed down my face and I was overcome with emotion, realizing I had completed the 100-mile run in 23 hours, 57 minutes!

I tugged my shoes and socks off and allowed my pale, white feet to be consumed by the frothy waters of the ocean, ending this journey the same way it began. In between soaking my feet in the Pacific and Atlantic, I had covered 16 states and the District of Columbia, 3,452 miles and approximately six million steps. But much more important than those numerical milestones were the generous people I met, the veterans who inspired me and the opportunities I had to say thank you to America's heroes.

Off in the distance, the orange glow of the sun was beginning to peek over the horizon of the Atlantic Ocean and into the pinks, purples and blues that formed the eastern sky. The sunrise signaled the beginning of a new day. While I had just completed an incredible journey, I knew the completion of the mission also signaled the beginning of a new chapter in my lifelong pursuit to honor and assist America's veterans.

# Epilogue

The last step of my run across America was really just the first step in my quest to honor our country's veterans. Although I always held a tremendous respect for those who served in the military, what my journey did was allow me to sharpen and intensify that appreciation. After the run, everything that I did and planned to do in my life, I wanted it to raise awareness of the sacrifices veterans have made.

Before I even departed on the run, I expressed concern about how I would adjust once the run was completed. I also often contemplated throughout the trek about how satisfied I would be in returning to my IT job after having experienced something so life-altering. I really didn't feel like I was capable of being satisfied by slipping on a shirt and tie and returning to the traditional workforce. Don't get me wrong; I was grateful that my employer allowed me to take the time off from work yet still return to my previous post, especially after Tiffany lost her job during our trip. But I knew that I would be cheating my employer if I wasn't fully immersed in the job.

A couple of months after my return, I made the decision to commit myself personally and professionally to serving veterans. As a result, I left my IT job to pursue work that would enable me to become more fulfilled. I am now the President of the Board of Directors of Operation Welcome Home, a non-profit organization "for veterans by veterans" in north-central West

Virginia that strives to alleviate common barriers to services and employment that veterans face.

Operation Welcome Home is a parent organization to CamoToCap, a program that was formed largely due to a need I saw during my run across America. The majority of people in our country have a desire to assist veterans, but many of them simply don't know where to start. One question that was commonly posed to me while on the run was, "How can we help the veterans in our local community?" CamoToCap was started to be one of the answers to that question. It was created to allow local communities to ease the transition of veterans returning to civilian life who desire to pick up or even begin their pursuit of a college education. On a state level, Wal-Mart has partnered with local communities to place collection bins in their stores where supplies can be donated to veterans for the CamoToCap program, which has been adopted by a few colleges in West Virginia and is something we hope to launch nationwide soon.

In addition to pursuing new career paths and launching new initiatives, I have continued to raise funds to benefit veterans through the non-profit that was set up before my journey across the US. Two weeks after completing the run, I received a phone call from a man who committed long ago to donate a dollar per mile for the run. He told me he was inspired by my story and achievement and he was rounding his donation to an even $3,500.

Later in the summer of 2012, I was given the opportunity by Cliff Sutherland, owner of Triple S Harley Davidson, which gave me some financial support during the run, to get on stage at the MountainFest Bike Rally before a concert by country singer Trace Adkins to briefly share my story. The money raised from that event surpassed $5,000. Opportunities such as that continued to present themselves and allow me to broadcast the story of the run and my continuing mission to honor and assist veterans. I have been invited to speak at veterans' gatherings, business meetings, academic events, Labor Day festivities and running races. I was also fortunate to be able to partner with Subway restaurants in the state of West Virginia in November 2012 as the chain used the month to honor veterans and raise funds for the Wounded Warrior Project.

Later in the year, I was extremely humbled to be chosen the grand marshal of the Morgantown Jaycees 2012 Christmas Parade. Thirty years earlier, I was riding my bike with my friends down the streets of Burnsville as if I was the grand marshal of a parade. Seven months earlier, I was participating in an impromptu parade through Imperial, Nebraska, on Mother's Day. Five months earlier, I was a participant in the July 4 parade in Annapolis, Maryland. Now here I was serving as the grand marshal of the biggest parade in the area, with its theme being "honoring our heroes." It was truly a neat experience and capped a whirlwind five months since the end of my run.

People often asked me when I completed the run if I was ever going to lace up a pair of running shoes again. I'll be honest, the first couple of weeks after the journey was complete, I had no desire to go running. I knew that I needed to allow my body to rejuvenate and recover from the pounding of running nearly 3,500 miles.

It was interesting, too, to see how my body responded to not being on the routine I strictly followed the previous 100 days. The first few days at home my body was all out of sorts. My metabolism was still through the roof, so even though I wasn't running, my body was basically acting as a furnace consuming itself, burning through calories faster than I could consume them. During the run, I knew I had to increase my caloric intake to keep from getting weak. I only lost 17 pounds during the run, and five of those were extra pounds I intentionally packed on prior to the run so my body would have extra fat to burn through in the beginning of the run. Yet after five days back home, because my caloric intake had returned to normal, I lost five more pounds, getting down to 158 pounds after starting the run at 180. I doubt any diet pill on the market could have worked as well at increasing my metabolism as running across the country did.

I had a friend tell me to get some rest and get back to a normal routine, but I couldn't figure out what "normal" was. When we left for Oregon, we left behind a "comfortable" life. When we returned, I wasn't certain that was the type of life I wanted back. Much like a veteran returning home and attempting to enter the civilian world, I found it somewhat difficult to conform to my previous way of life. There was something unnerving about having a house to wander about when we were used to being confined to a small and efficient space.

My run across America changed my perspective on life, increased my passion for honoring and assisting veterans and fortunately provided me with the platform and opportunities to live out my desire. The primary reason I wanted to write a book about this journey and share the story in greater detail was because it is my hope that it will inspire others to dream big and accomplish something for a greater good. As someone who had never run more than 12 miles at a time less than three years earlier, I never thought I'd be able to run 3,452 miles across America in 100 days. But I dreamt big and accomplished my goal.

I'm dreaming even bigger now, and I can't wait to see what can be accomplished down the road.

# About the Authors

**Jamie Summerlin** is a Gulf War era veteran, having served in the United States Marine Corps for six years. Currently, he serves as the president of the board of directors of Operation Welcome Home in Morgantown, West Virginia, and is involved in other veteran-focused programs, such as CamoToCap. He is also an inspirational speaker for business and professional organizations, schools, veteran groups and the running community.

Matthew L. Brann and Jamie Summerlin

Summerlin's passion for running began in 2009 while training for his first marathon. He has been hooked on ultramarathon running ever since. Though he has completed many challenging runs and races, one of his prides is a finisher's medal from the Burning River 100 Mile Endurance Run that he completed in July of 2011 in a time of 24 hours, 53 minutes. His love for pushing himself to great distances, as well as witnessing the phenomenal things that Operation Welcome Home and other veteran-focused organizations have done for veterans, inspired him to come up with the idea of running across America in order to raise funds and awareness for such organizations.

Summerlin's "Freedom Run," a 3,452-mile, 100-day endeavor that he completed in 2012, began in Coos Bay, Oregon, and ended in Rehoboth

Beach, Delaware, and covered a total of 16 states and the District of Columbia, with the final 100 miles being completed in just less than 24 hours. He became the 48th person ever to complete a true coast-to-coast transcontinental run across America. His journey not only raised money for national and local organizations whose mission is to assist veterans, but it inspired communities and veterans alike to dream big and find ways to support the United States military and veterans.

His wife, Tiffany, a Marine Corps veteran herself, met Summerlin in Iwakuni, Japan, while stationed there together in 1995. They reside in Morgantown, West Virginia, with their two children, Nicholas and Shayna.

To learn about the latest progress of Summerlin's mission to honor veterans or explore in even greater depth his "Freedom Run," visit www.FreedomRunUSA.com.

**Matthew L. Brann** is the director of Fitness Information Technology (FiT) and the International Center for Performance Excellence in the College of Physical Activity and Sport Sciences at West Virginia University. Prior to his appointment as director, he served as the senior editor of FiT for eight years. A graduate of Purdue University with a degree in communication, he began his career as a sports journalist, working for daily newspapers in Illinois and Indiana. He later worked for a weekly sports magazine, covering Purdue athletics, and during that time was also a syndicated columnist for various newspapers in Indiana and a weekly guest on a local CBS affiliate's weekend sports show. Brann has also served as a contributing writer for various regional and national magazines and websites.

After vowing to never run a marathon again upon completion of his first in Baltimore in 2004, Brann was inspired by Jamie Summerlin's run across America and, along with his wife, Maria, ran the Indianapolis Monumental Marathon in 2012. He and his wife reside in Morgantown, West Virginia, with their two children, Maverick and Makaleigh.